DOSTOEVSKY
Essays and Perspectives

DOSTOEVSKY

Essays and Perspectives

———

ROBERT LORD

1970

UNIVERSITY OF CALIFORNIA PRESS

BERKELEY AND LOS ANGELES

Published by
University of California Press
Berkeley and Los Angeles

SBN 520-01639-4

LC NO. 70-100018

Printed in Great Britain

CONTENTS

ACKNOWLEDGEMENTS

IT is with the greatest of pleasure and gratitude that I acknowledge my indebtedness to numerous authors and scholars, many of them long since dead; especially to Konstantin Mochulsky, Leonid Grossman, M. M. Bakhtin, and Helen Muchnic, on all of whose labours I have patently drawn on more than one occasion. I would also like to thank my various friends and colleagues, and also Helen Rapp and Professor Hunter, for the encouragement and constructive criticism they were able to offer when it was most needed. My thanks also to Irene Wells who was such a great help during the time I was preparing the manuscript, and to Ates Orga who made numerous last-minute corrections.

Thanks are due to David Magarshack for permission to quote from his translation of *A Gentle Creature and Other Stories* by Dostoevsky.

R. L.

AN INTRODUCTION

*'The truth is not that we need the critics in
order to enjoy the authors, but that we need
the authors in order to enjoy the critics'*
(*C. S. Lewis*: An Experiment in Criticism)

THERE is hardly a paragraph in Dostoevsky which does not
contain some paradox. He is a maze of paradoxes. And even
the most trivial of them needs no very powerful microscope to
grow into bewildering proportions. The only way to enjoy the
novels *as novels*, one supposes, is to let one's curiosity flag deliberately, to read on regardless, and above all to shun every
critic and commentator. The main drawback however with
such an attitude is that, even if *you* succeed, others will very
soon come along and undermine your complacency. There is
no doubt at all that Dostoevsky's novels are great literature
as literature, but there is always the lurking suspicion that
they reach over and beyond what they seem to be, not unlike
the vague recollections of some disturbing dream. If only one
could reach a little deeper, then one might bring up something truly worthwhile. This explains why the reader of
Dostoevsky, even, or rather, especially after the impact of
the first novel, is usually a trifle overenthusiastic, his higher
faculties inebriated.

It was not out of affectation that Dostoevsky exercised his
flair for paradox, but through sheer force of circumstances.
The greater part of his work was composed in a state of mind
compounded variously of harassment, anguish, bewilderment, nervous and physical strain, and plain worry. Any
suspicion that his novels were *consciously* planned may be
promptly dispelled by a glance at the notebooks containing the
rough drafts. They are more like log-books recording some
interior exploration than serious plans. And yet, as we are
all well aware, the finished products maintain a constant
high watermark of literary achievement. Which brings us to

the central paradox: Great art, unbelievably intricate, un-rivalled in virtuosity and architecture as well as insight, arises in Dostoevsky's case out of a literally personal turmoil, out of mental and physical disarray, chaos. Work on his later novels was constantly and for long periods interrupted by severe attacks of epilepsy which would have disabled many a lesser man. Dostoevsky was no 'giant', certainly no Beethoven, Tolstoy or G. B. S. Frail physically, in many ways a typical 'weak character', hypochondriacal, given to bouts of self-pity, spite and on occasion obsequiousness, Dostoevsky, except in his last few years, managed to lead a life of anxiety, in-security and physical hardship, a few months of which would be sufficient for any normal lifetime.

Perhaps this explains why there are still a number of important stretches of Dostoevsky which defy analysis. The situation has been worsened by those who could not resist the temptation to look for the real Dostoevsky in his characters, in their utterances, in their words. And how difficult it is to resist this temptation. For in what other writer do the characters make such astonishing, profound and intriguing statements for such a great proportion of the time? Even Dostoevsky himself was never completely certain of his own convictions, suspecting that all the while he might be actually or at least on the verge of humbugging himself as well as his readers. He is rather like his own creation, the Man from Underground in his *Notes from Underground*, who warns his indecently inquisitive readers: 'It would be better if I myself believed in anything I had just written. I assure you most solemnly, gentlemen, there is not a word I've just written that I believe in! What I mean is that perhaps I do believe, but at the same time I cannot help feeling and suspecting for some unknown reason that I'm telling a pack of lies . . .' This had better be an added warning to Dostoevsky's readers to be on their guard against taking any statements at their face value. Along with a number of his major characters, Dostoevsky was sometimes a joker, a highly serious joker.

The 'no nonsense' approach to Dostoevsky is hazardous too. Originating among the Russian critics of the twenties, and so warmly applauded by Mirsky in his introduction to E. H. Carr's critical biography,[1] its main value was that it came as a much-needed antidote to the multiplicity of tendentious, often vapid, usually misleading interpretations of Dostoevsky. For it seems that Dostoevsky really starts from the precise point where logic, scientific objectivity and commonsense encounter their limits. The final essay in the present collection, 'Stylistics and Personality', is an attempt to explore this aspect. The hey-day of Dostoevsky criticism in Russia, besides bringing together masterly editions of almost the entire manuscripts, correspondence and fragments, was well on the way towards a fruitful 'structural' approach when, lamentably, it was cut short by political developments that were soon to culminate in Stalinism. But the 'objective' criticism of those early days produced little, and even the most ingenious of these critics, M. M. Bakhtin,[2] was forced to admit that the relationship between Dostoevsky and his characters was a highly peculiar one, as though they were on the same footing. Dostoevsky's voice is not even *primus inter pares*. He gets lost somewhere in the interstices between his characters. One is reluctantly compelled to turn to the so-called mystical interpreters for ultimate guidance. The outlandish interpretations of a writer such as for instance the Russian symbolist poet Vyacheslav Ivanov are in the final reckoning of more help to the reader of Dostoevsky than any of the 'scientific' studies.

The by now numerous critical biographies of Dostoevsky include some that are excellent: Troyat, Carr, Mochulsky, to mention only a few. There would be little point in trying to better these, and the aim of the present work is to avoid as far as possible duplication of what already exists. With what justification then the present miscellany, one might well ask, when the main task has already been completed?

The scope of the present work is both modest and ambitious. In the first place, there are more than enough obscure corners in Dostoevsky badly needing investigation. To devote entire studies to them would have seemed unduly perverse. It is partly for this reason the term 'perspective' is employed.

'Hole filling' if you like, but several items in the present collection are intended to do just this, although *not* merely this. The further aim was to throw light at the same time on the genesis of Dostoevsky's works.

'Charades' contains a sketch of Dostoevsky's connection with the politically suspect Petrashevsky circle, which led to his arrest and deportation to Siberia in 1849. Although this affair has been well documented, a few of the actual historical facts and their importance in Dostoevsky's life have in the past sometimes been lost sight of. The importance of epilepsy, not only in the novels, but also for Dostoevsky himself, is tentatively explored in 'An Epileptic Mode of Being'. The character Prince Myshkin in *The Idiot* is taken to be Dostoevsky's own attempt to fathom the nature of epileptic experience. Two figures who cast a spell over Dostoevsky in his later years were the young philosopher and mystic Vladimir Soloviev and the cranky 'scientific resurrectionist' N. F. Fyodorov. The essay 'Transmuted Dialectic' aims amongst other things to trace the powerful cross-current set up between Soloviev and Dostoevsky; the ironic disparity between the intellectual pitfalls Dostoevsky could see were in store for this heady and precocious philosopher, and the resolution of the Karamazov situation implicit in Soloviev's theory, which had so far eluded Dostoevsky's grasp. Fyodorov deserves an important place in any work on Dostoevsky, if only because of his paltry treatment so far. Fyodorov's influence upon the scheme of *The Brothers Karamazov* is more considerable than has been realised. Besides this, he represents an attitude which has always found an important place in Russian life.

Next and much more important: Dostoevsky, more than almost any other writer, is one of those whose work except in minor details does not date. His novels provide something new and hitherto undiscovered for each new generation. As our outlook changes, constant reinterpretation and re-examination of almost everything is called for, even of fundamentals. The views of many of Dostoevsky's earlier critics, valid in their own time, have quickly receded into the past, leaving Dostoevsky behind in the present, demanding new and ever more compelling reinterpretation. It is only since Kafka and Nietzsche, since depth psychology, since the philosophical analyses offered by phenomenologists and existentialists that Dostoevsky can be at all properly understood. Dostoevsky was certainly well in advance of his own time. It will be interesting to see how far he is ahead of our own.

The majority of the essays in the present collection attempt to approach Dostoevsky from the present day. 'Roots' is a title so familiar in our own day as to be almost a cliché. Dostoevsky's approach to the problem, starting from a late slavophile movement of his own day, becomes in his hands startlingly modern. The short essay 'The Temptation of Philosophy' is a sketch of the parallel treatment of freedom in the work of Kierkegaard and Dostoevsky in the context of present-day existentialist philosophies. More fundamentally it points the dilemma of the reader's participation in any interpretation of Dostoevsky's underlying meaning. Again, 'An Epileptic Mode of Being' approaches his novel *The Idiot* phenomenologically. (The reader may be reminded of the recent phenomenological approach to psychological medicine which one finds outlined in Laing's *The Divided Self* or in his *The Self and Others*.) By contrast 'An English point of View' is a historical sketch of English attitudes to Dostoevsky since his 'discovery' in the 1880s. 'Stylistics and Personality' is placed at the end, partly because it takes in the longest perspective of all, spanning Dostoevsky's literary career in its entirety; but mainly because the present writer considers that if there is any culmination to his 'essays and perspectives' this is it. No originality is claimed for the original idea, put forward by the Russian critic Bakhtin in the twenties (although still unfamiliar in this country). But it is especially since Joyce and Sartre, and much more recently McLuhan, that Bakhtin's approach to Dostoevsky can be extended well beyond mere prose technique.

Finally, a word of justification for including a biographical sketch 'Dostoevsky at Close Quarters'. It contains no original material and is intended as a kind of interlude. It attempts to condense an atmosphere of the kind of life Dostoevsky and his second wife lived in the early years of their marriage. More significantly it provides a backcloth for the novel *The Idiot* whose composition is contemporaneous with the events described in Anna Grigoryevna's diary.

It happens, as if by a quirk of history, that Dostoevsky can be said to belong to a tradition of prose-writing which had scarcely become established in Russia at the time when he inherited and developed it. Its roots can be traced to the Gothic novelists, certainly to Balzac, and in a number of important respects to the very beginnings of the European novel, to Richardson. The model for all the Russians was Pushkin. Like Dostoevsky, Pushkin was both a great virtuoso and something of a sphinx. Pushkin developed the art of exploring the world in terms of the experience and mental outlook of his own creations. Belkin is not just a fictitious person who is supposed to have related the *Tales of Belkin*; he emerges live from Pushkin's hands and tells his *own* stories not Pushkin's. With a master stroke of ironic cunning and high fun, Pushkin then laughs his Belkin off the stage. The technique is not new and we find a similar device used in Chaucer's *Canterbury Tales*. In Pushkin's novel *The Captain's Daughter* the narrator, who is at the same time the hero, begins the story as the very caricature of the eighteenth-century *ingénu* and gradually grows in stature till he reaches apotheosis. The whole novel, in so much as its events and people are seen through Grinyov's eyes, distinctly reflects this gradual development of his character. Unlike the early nineteenth-century European novel, Pushkin's characters do not emerge out of a backcloth, a situation; they create their *own* situation. This is not sufficiently realised even now. For Pushkin, the universe is simply not something given, it has to be created. His characters each proceed to spin their own universe. Dostoevsky is in direct line with Pushkin in this respect. One is tempted to apply the term 'monadic' to Dostoevsky's own technique. His characters carry around with them their own worlds, and it is the conjunction of 'monads' which produces the unique phenomenon: a Dostoevsky novel. Like Leibniz's monads they are windowless. Dostoevsky's characters do not peer into each other's lives, but seem to clash blindly. We find kindred features in later writers such as Chekhov and Pasternak.

The meaning of any one of Dostovesky's works lies inextricably bound up within its *form*. Any attempt to establish an objective world-view based on the works themselves is certain to end in failure. Even the now popular comparative method has produced negligible results. It is little wonder then that a number of the more intuitive, 'subjective' critics have more to offer (Ivanov, Rozanov, etc.) by way of elucidation. Why is this so? Perhaps the answer is that Dostoevsky's own grasp was only slightly greater than that of some of his readers. Dostoevsky, one should add, was more than once the bewildered onlooker of what was taking shape beneath his pen. It is tempting to regard the novels as epiphanic, with their ultimate depths still unsounded. It is not surprising then that each generation of critics comes up with its new interpretations. Dostoevsky one finds successively compared with Nietzsche, Kafka, Beckett.

An ostensibly scientific approach, it has already been suggested, will not take one very far with Dostoevsky. E. H. Carr, to take only one example, concludes that Dostoevsky is favourably disposed towards Ivan Karamazov's philosophy owing to the fact that 'Ivan Karamazov's denunciation of God remains more powerful and more cogent than the defence which is put into the mouths of Alyosha and Zosima'. It was Lossky who found it necessary to point out that the answer to Ivan's argument cannot be formulated in terms of 'reasoning theses', if only because Ivan is the quintessence of rationality, having (to his eventual misfortune) woven his entire existence into a tissue of rational critique. Neither Alyosha Karamazov nor Zosima is capable of attacking Ivan on his own ground. The structure of *The Brothers Karamazov* contains the separate worlds of Ivan and Alyosha; and one can see that there is indeed an answer to Ivan's thesis, but an answer of an entirely different kind. Much Dostoevsky criticism of the 'scientific' kind has fallen short of success for the very reason that it has not been able to rise above the level of Dostoevsky's own characters. At the very point of coming to grips, the critics lose themselves in the same dilemmas as the characters.[3]

An exclusively 'structural' approach will not do either. Despite the unrewarding nature of much of the biographical material relating to Dostoevsky, especially the correspondence, it is dangerous to keep Dostoevsky and his work in two separate compartments. Yet the converse is equally dangerous; too much significance can be ascribed to biographical events. An effective balance has been achieved in Konstantin Mochulsky's critical biography. This work has managed chronologically to juxtapose biography and commentary. Alternation of the two aspects enables the reader to draw his own conclusions as to the extent of the inter-relationship. Mochulsky's only serious drawback is that he overemphasises what he takes to be Dostoevsky's brand of Christianity, and this has produced a number of superfluous and even misleading conclusions. His study nevertheless remains unmatched in its interweaving of biographical material with genetic studies of Dostoevsky's works.

The psychoanalysts wasted no time in landing what seemed to them a particularly handsome catch. For the first of these we have to go back to the 1880s.[4] They reach their culmination in Freud's *Dostoevsky and Parricide*, where Dostoevsky's alleged flair for the criminal and the abnormal is explained away as masochism, and his reconciliation to punishment at the hands of an autocratic Tsar is dismissed as a substitute for what he unconsciously felt were his deserts for desiring the death of his own father as a child. A. L. Bem[5] ably disposed of Freud's tendentious conclusions. Freud was behaving like Procrustes, and not facing up to the universally profound roots of Dostoevsky's creative impulse. It is true that Freud's conclusions are not without interest, but they add nothing to our understanding of Dostoevsky. They are of value only to those concerning themselves with the vicissitudes of psychoanalysis since Freud's day.

The sternest deterrent to those undertaking a study of Dostoevsky is the knowledge that scrutiny of this author is like peering into a queer kind of mirror, the suspicion that after protracted labour nothing more will emerge than one's own distorted image. Berdyaev and Lossky have found only a highly profound kind of Christianity in Dostoevsky. Others have come up with very different interpretations. Shestov has compared him with Nietzsche, and became convinced that both Nietzsche and Dostoevsky had abandoned humanity in favour of cruelty. Any thesis one may care to put forward can be refuted by arguments based on exactly those points which appeared to support one's own.

In this respect, Dostoevsky is among the most daunting of all writers. His literary technique, especially from *The Devils* onwards, embodies the principle of unqualified freedom. *The Brothers Karamazov*, from the point of view of its central theme, its structure and its technique of composition, is a vast illustration of this principle. From every angle, the reader is faced with a *choice*. And the choice will be the measure of the reader. The critic who is bold enough to extract metaphysical, ethical or other systems from Dostoevsky finds an abundant source upon which to draw, but in so doing falls into a trap. He becomes enslaved in precisely the same way as the 'under-devils' (Kirillov, Verkhovensky, Shatov) allowed themselves to be chained to Stavrogin's leash, and in the same way as Ivan Karamazov found himself ensnared in his own hallucinations.

It is no use trying to find for Dostoevsky a niche in the history of ideas. As a philosopher he is unpromisingly small fry. It is not ideas that Dostoevsky is about, but that central unknown factor–existence. Raskolnikov, when he reaches the threshold of freedom, finds himself confronted with a void, a nothingness which he cannot bear, and before which he collapses totally.

The temptation to decipher messages in Dostoevsky has produced a curious and recurrent phenomenon. Traditions of interpretation have sprung up which perpetuate themselves regardless of their source. One of the toughest and most tenacious of these is the one that runs the length and breadth of Europe and which is without difficulty retraceable to De Vogüé, whose sensational *The Russian Novel*, originally written in French, was an immediate and universal success. It is almost impossible for the modern reader to come for the first time uninitiated to Dostoevsky, for he somehow picks up this tradition, either before or after reading a particular novel, a kind of invisible screen which distorts his view. Readers find an understandable need for frames of reference, and it is for this reason that relatively easy interpretations, such as those offered by De Vogüé and Merezhkovsky, satisfy this need.

Finally, while his great Russian contemporaries, Tolstoy and Turgenev, recede with the gradual passage of time into the past to which they firmly belong, Dostoevsky remains timeless except in minor details. Yet despite this, the prejudice that Tolstoy and Dostoevsky are of the same blood is hard to uproot. 'Tolstoyevskyism' is still going strong. To the present writer these two writers seem as far apart as Alexander Pope and Wagner. Although one of Dostoevsky's characters, the Man from Underground, purported to be presenting a diagnosis of the nineteenth century, he was in effect raising problems only beginning to emerge in our own day. Audiences familiar with Beckett and Ionesco stand a better chance of comprehending Dostoevsky than the contemporaries of Tolstoy did. There are good grounds for supposing that Dostoevsky will continue to astonish his readers for many decades to come.

A collection of essays can seldom be anything but miscellaneous. But some miscellanies are less miscellaneous than others. It may well be that the reader, although familiar with some of Dostoevsky's work, is not at all familiar with his life. For this reason, the 'essays and perspectives' are placed, except for the first and the last, roughly in chronological order, despite the unavoidable and considerable chronological overlap. They need not however be read in this order. All the important periods of his life and creative activity are touched upon, and none of his major works and only a handful of his minor works escape attention.

A translation of Stavrogin's Confession is included for a number of reasons. Firstly, it does not appear in any of the translations of *The Devils* (*The Possessed*) with which it is associated. It has been published separately in several editions but is long out of print. Secondly, the final essay 'Stylistics and Personality' will fall especially flat if the reader is not acquainted with this controversial document. Thirdly, and perhaps most important, the Confession represents a watershed in Dostoevsky's creative life, after which time there is a marked change when his work begins to pursue more 'positive' paths, culminating in *The Brothers Karamazov*.

AN ENGLISH POINT OF VIEW

V IRGINIA W OOLF began her famous essay[1] on the Russians with these words: 'Doubtful as we frequently are whether either the French or the Americans, who have so much in common with us, can yet understand English literature, we must admit graver doubts whether, for all their enthusiasm, the English can understand Russian literature.' These remarks came at a time when the Dostoevsky cult was barely past its peak (1925). The novels were still a novelty for all but the widest read. Enthusiasm ran high. Just as now, people wanted to understand. They went wrong, of course, for lack of guidance. They are still going wrong, but again, not always in the way they suspect they might be going wrong.

A single example will do to point the hazard. Virginia Woolf had divined that a major obstacle to the English reader was the Russian word 'soul', which sprinkled the pages of Russian literature, as she put it. 'Indeed, it is the soul that is the chief character in Russian fiction. . . . Perhaps that is why it needs so great an effort on the part of the English reader to read *The Brothers Karamazov* or *The Devils* a second time. The "soul" is alien to him. It is even antipathetic.'[2] Now Mrs. Woolf was only partly right. For, although the conventional translation of the Russian word *dusha* is admittedly 'soul', a better and more accurate translation is very often 'heart'. And it cannot at all be said that 'heart' is foreign to the English sensibility. The Elizabethan poets and all the significant novelists of the last century have relied heavily upon it.

'Soul' then is often a mistranslation. No wonder that the concept seems to her, as to practically everyone else, 'formless . . . confused, diffuse, tumultuous, incapable, it seems, of submitting to the control of logic or the discipline of poetry'. How indeed could matters be otherwise? But, let us admit that Mrs. Woolf was partly correct as well. It would not be simply a question of substituting for 'soul' another noun or even a different turn of phrase, but of a complete reshaping of the style, the manner of putting things. Even the more recent translators, learning from their forbears' mistakes, have not succeeded in rendering Dostoevsky less perplexing and intoxicating to the average reader. Whatever it is that tumbles out of the pages goes on being 'hot, scalding, mixed, marvellous, terrible and oppressive'.

Reactions to Dostoevsky among the English literary public have ranged from ecstatic revelation (J. Middleton Murry) to outright condemnation (D. H. Lawrence). The majority of his critics – and not only the English ones – have, however, only seldom risen above biographical chit-chat. This is not to deny the achievement of those who have excelled themselves in this genre. Among the more recent, David Magarshack's *Dostoevsky* (1962) is at once a reliable and most readable biographical study. Perhaps even more significant is Marc Slonim's *The Three Loves of Dostoevsky* which appeared just over ten years ago. The demand for the biographical approach among the reading public remains insatiable. It would be interesting to compare the success of the paperback translations of Berdyaev's 'study' with, say, Magarshack's.

The impression remaining from a cursory reading of the English critics is one of lack of imagination coupled with a readiness to fall in with traditional interpretations. The 'traditions' die hard, and yet how curiously un-English they are when analysed – a concoction of smoke-raisers like Merezhkovsky and the sensational and discredited De Vogüé. The toughest myth of all – 'Tolstoyevskyism' – is still finding converts,[3] and seems to be set fair for at least another decade.

It is only when we leave behind the biographers and turn to the critics proper, the 'metabiographers', that we discover the English point of view as such. The latter fall into two distinctly opposed groups; those very much pro Dostoevsky and those very much contra.

To take his supporters first. The line begins, surprisingly enough, with Robert Louis Stevenson. The first noteworthy British writer to react at all to Dostoevsky; and at the same time one of the most perspicacious judges. At that time, as long ago as the 1880s, *Crime and Punishment* was the only one of Dostoevsky's novels in translation, and not a particularly good translation at that. It appears, however, that Stevenson was familiar with the French translations which were at that time more numerous. The plot of his short story *Markheim* bears more than a superficial similarity to *Crime and Punishment*, and it would be surprising if *Dr. Jekyll and Mr. Hyde* was not the least bit influenced by Dostoevsky's earlier story *The Double*. Stevenson's first reaction to Dostoevsky was this: 'Raskolnikov is easily the greatest book I have read in ten years. . . . Many find it dull; Henry James could not finish it: all I can say is, it nearly finished me. It was like having an illness.'[4] Stevenson claims to have responded sympathetically to Dostoevsky's already notorious reactionary affiliations: 'to something of that side the balance leans with me also in view of the incoherency and incapacity of all'.

The 'ecstatic tone', which soon became the fashion, was none of Stevenson's making. It was entirely due to the English translation of De Vogüé's *Le Roman Russe* which appeared very shortly after the publication of the original in 1885, the only full-length book on Dostoevsky for years to come; so much the more disastrous its effect. Dostoevsky crawled out of De Vogüé's pages a creature from another planet, 'an abnormal and mighty monster', a colossus, the embodiment of dark primitive Russia, a 'true Scythian'. It was De Vogüé too who cast the spell of 'mystical realism', that quasi-profound psychological insight with all its late-nineteenth century Blavatskyist overtones. The phrase 'the religion of suffering'–probably coined by De Vogüé–has left an indelible mark on several generations and is only now on the way out. Even the best of Dostoevsky's critics have sometimes echoed De Vogüé without even being aware of the fact.

Reinforcement came from the 'psychological' approach to literature, which had become fashionable by the turn of the century. Abnormal psychology was soon to be popularised. An important contributor was Lombroso. In his study of genius[5] (translated into English in 1891) he spoke of Dostoevsky in the same breath as Socrates, Rembrandt and Darwin. The characteristic they were supposed to have shared was a cretinous physiognomy. Dostoevsky was also supposed to have resembled Whitman and Rousseau in his awareness of his malady and in his inclination to proclaim it from the rooftops, thereby hoping to gain 'relief from its inexorable attacks'. Evidence of this kind was adduced for the purpose of explaining Dostoevsky's habitual use of 'semi-insane characters, and especially epileptics . . . moral lunatics'. Not unexpectedly, the descriptions of epileptic seizures occurring in *The Devils* and *The Idiot* were quoted at length, and with ample commentary, to illustrate the alleged resemblance between inspiration and epilepsy.

Fresh impetus was given to this trend by Havelock Ellis, who, in his collection of essays *The New Spirit*, referred to Dostoevsky's 'profound science of the human heart'. Dostoevsky, he supposed, was 'the most intensely Russian' of all the Russian novelists.

By the turn of the century dissenters from the established view had become rare. Among the big names of the day, Galsworthy, Arnold Bennett, Gosse and Gissing, all became subscribers to the received opinion, and in varying degrees admirers. Bennett bracketed Dostoevsky with 'the lonely Emily'. *The Brothers Karamazov*, which he had probably read in French, 'contained some of the greatest scenes ever encountered in fiction'.[6]

The atmosphere was not made any clearer by the appearance in 1902 of a translation of Merezhkovsky's elaborate antithesis under the title *Tolstoy as Man and Artist, with an Essay on Dostoievsky*. At least one review rated Merezhkovsky's interpretation as unquestionably correct.[7]

A further red herring came from Gissing, who was making much of the Dickensian side of Dostoevsky. The analogies were obvious, and he could not resist finding a direct influence of Dickens on *The Insulted and Injured*. *Crime and Punishment*, as might be expected, was found to contain 'Dickens-like touches in its lighter passages'.[8] It transpired that Dostoevsky was just that much better at Dickens than

Dickens himself. 'It would not have been so but for the defects of education and the social prejudices which forbade his [Dickens's] tragic gift to develop.' Dickens's murders, Gissing felt, were 'too vulgar greatly to impress us, and lacked the touch of high imaginativeness'.

Within a few more years, with the majestic procession of Constance Garnett's translations, the time became ripe for a prophet. And that prophet was of course Middleton Murry. He had read 'all Dostoevsky's major books over three times, first with a glimmer of comprehension and finally with an altogether unprecedented flood of illumination. Suddenly the whole thing fell into pattern.' Writing his book on Dostoevsky he became 'for the first time, the victim of the strong sensation of being hardly more than the amanuensis of a book that wrote itself':[9]

> It was no question of my opinion of Dostoevsky; I had no opinion of Dostoevsky and if I expressed any personal opinions about him in the book, they were certainly exaggerated and probably wrong. All that had happened–I speak, of course, of my sensation only– was [that] the objective 'pattern' of Dostoevsky had declared itself, through me as an instrument.[10]

Middleton Murry's study represents the tense mood of the war years, but it is also the high-water mark of Dostoevsky adulation in this country. His achievement, to do him justice, was to rescue Dostoevsky from what had become to some extent the slums of ordinary fiction. He was shown to be far more than a writer of cheap sensational melodrama. His challenge to his readers was that they should find 'a new attitude towards his [Dostoevsky's] work'. The novels were to be treated as a 'new creation' demanding a 'new criticism'. Which is, after all, what they are.

Having at about this time undergone certain mystical experiences,[11] Murry found himself provided with a category that was right for throwing light on Dostoevsky. This was 'metaphysical obscenity'. Murry discovered that metaphysical obscenity was 'the appointed end of the human striving of the human consciousness'. He was also the first to notice that certain of Dostoevsky's characters might really be no more than hallucinatory projections; perhaps there was no Smerdyakov in reality, just as there was no real devil to taunt Ivan Karamazov. Perhaps both these characters were paranoiac projections.

Middleton Murry's besetting sin was excess. The vast edifice he managed to construct out of Dostoevsky's alleged Christianity is largely irrelevant, and certainly misleading. In this case, that Russian[12] was devastatingly right who said: 'If you want an intelligent Englishman or Frenchman to talk nonsense, let him emit an opinion on Russia; it is a subject which intoxicates him and at once clouds his intellect.'

No doubt influenced to some extent by Murry was E. M. Forster's view. In his *Aspects of the Novel* (1927) he compares George Eliot's Hetty (*Adam Bede*) with Dostoevsky's Dmitri Karamazov. Whereas Hetty stands for a particular world view, Mitya does not *mean* anything. Dmitri Karamazov is 'intermittent', 'distorted out of drawing'. Referring to the passage in the novel where Mitya dreams his freak dream, Forster explains that 'we cannot understand him (Mitya) until we see that he extends, and that the part of him on which Dostoevsky focussed did not lie on that wooden chest where he had the dream or even in dreamland, but in a region where it could be joined by the rest of humanity— Mitya is all of us'. 'Dostoevsky's characters ask us to share something deeper than their experiences.'[13] It is a pity that we have no more than isolated remarks from Forster on the subject of Dostoevsky, for the little we do possess has the makings of a much needed critique.

Dissenting voices were slow to make themselves heard (if we totally ignore isolated remarks in reviews about the 'Slavonic menace to Europe'). Henry James was the exception; his mind was made up from the beginning. Dostoevsky had not been to his taste. James described both Tolstoy and Dostoevsky as 'fluid puddings'. Not tasteless for all that, 'because the amount of their own minds and souls in solution in the broth gives it savour and flavour, thanks to the strong rank quality of their genius and their experience'.[14] Their unforgivable vice was their complete lack of stylistic composition.

By 1912 the solo voice of Henry James was joined by a chorus: Galsworthy, Conrad, and finally, D. H. Lawrence. Although Galsworthy's first reactions had been favourable, on re-reading *The Brothers Karamazov*, he found the novel just did not 'wash'. 'Amazing in places of course; but my God!—what incoherence and verbiage, and what starting of monsters out of holes to make you shudder. It's a mark of these cubistic, blood-bespattered-poster times that Dostoevsky should rule the roost.'[15]

'Terrifically bad and impressive and exasperating' was Conrad's impression after reading the copy of *The Brothers Karamazov* Edward Garnett had sent him. 'I don't know what D. stands for or reveals, but I do know that he is too Russian for me. It sounds to me like some prehistoric mouthings from prehistoric ages. I understand the Russians have just "discovered" him. I wish them joy.'[16] This reaction of Conrad's is surprising when one considers the resemblances some of his characters show to Dostoevsky's, their quality of 'being thrown there', the seething personal complexes which project their own settings. The style of Conrad is not at all unlike Dostoevsky's in places, although the likenesses may be coincidental.

Better known is Lawrence's opinion. Russia fascinated him. His letters to S. S. Koteliansky ('Kot') over a number of years are sufficient to convince one that much of his attention during the years 1915 to 1921 was directed toward a single phenomenon: the Russian cosmos.[17] He could see Russia as a distinctly non-European country just sufficiently infected with the 'virus' of European culture 'to display unique symptoms'. In a preface he wrote for Koteliansky's translation of Shestov's *All Things are Possible*, Lawrence writes:

> European culture is a rootless thing in the Russians. With us it is our very blood and bones, the very nerve and root of our psyche .... With the Russians it is different. They have only been inoculated with the virus of European culture and ethic. The virus works in them like a disease. And, the inflammation and irritation comes forth as literature .... Russian literature after all does not stand on the same footing as European or

Greek or Egyptian art. It is not spontaneous utterance. It is not
the flowering of a race. It is a surgical outcry, horrifying or
marvellous, lacerating at first; but when we get used to it, not
really so profound, not really ultimate, a little extraneous.[18]

The Russians, although Dionysian enough for Lawrence,
were ambivalent. The overwhelming pain, anguish and outcry of Russian literature was, when all said and done, not
really all that significant. But Lawrence could not dismiss
Dostoevsky just like that. His attitude towards Dostoevsky
was far too complicated, and their make-up was too similar
for Lawrence's liking. '. . . What an amazing person he was—
a pure introvert, a purely disintegrating will—there was not
a grain of the passion of love within him—all the passion of
hate, of evil. Yet a great man.'[19] More than once has
Dostoevsky's influence on Lawrence been detected. His
novel *The Trespasser* appeared at about the same time as
Constance Garnett's translation of *The Brothers Karamazov*.
For one reviewer his book seemed to recall 'the best Russian
school' with its 'psychological intensity'. In another review
Lawrence's novel was described as 'poetic realism of a
Dostoevskian order'.

Lawrence must have been stung by reviews like these,
for by this time he had come to regard Dostoevsky as poison.
In a letter to Middleton Murry and Katherine Mansfield
he writes:

> I find I've gone off Dostoievsky and could write about him in
> very cold blood. I didn't care for *The Possessed*: nobody was
> possessed enough really to interest me. They bore me, these
> squirming sorts of people: they teem like insects. . . . They are
> great parables, the novels, but false art. They are only parables.
> All the people are *fallen angels*—even the dirtiest scrubs. This I
> cannot stomach. People are not fallen angels, they are merely
> people.'[20]

In the same letter there follows some detailed criticism of
Dostoevsky's works. And very disappointing it is through its
lack of perspicacity. It is the kind of criticism that sets out
with a particular view, determined to keep to it. Its main
action is to recoil on the critic. Writing to his friend
Koteliansky, Lawrence exclaims:

If I had the energy I should tirade you about Dostoievsky. He has lost his spell over me. . . . Stavrogin is a bore. He was only interesting when he bit off the old man's ear. . . . I am most sick of this divinity-of-man business. People are *not important*; I insist on it. . . . People are so self important. Let them die, silly blighters, fools and twopenny knaves.'[21]

Already Lawrence's and Dostoevsky's brands of 'religion' were irreconcilable. Dostoevsky's Christ was a swindle, an opiate. 'Dostoievsky, like the rest, can nicely stick his head between the feet of Christ, and waggle his behind in the air. And though the behind-wagglings are a revelation, I don't think much even of the feet of Christ as a bluff for the cowards to hide their eyes against.'[22] 'The meek are evil. The pure in heart have base, subtle revulsions . . . the whole Sermon on the Mount becomes a litany of white vice.'[23]

The 'Dostoievsky lot' were all the while 'sinning their way to Jesus'.[24] With slogans of this kind Lawrence was persuading at least a few in his direction, for there has indeed been at least a small turn-over of Lawrence's view up to the present day. Dostoevsky the corruptor, the spiritual masturbator.

> Dostoievsky, the Judas
> with his sham christianity
> epileptically ruined
> the last bit of sanity
> left in the hefty bodies
> of the Russian nobility[25]

By his time, Lawrence believed, the Revolution had already swept aside those 'goody-goods' and 'saintly-saints'. There was now some small hope that 'the sickly air of Dostoievsky and Tchekhov' would be cleared. It is 'because your soul will coruscate, if you think it does' that makes Russian literature so popular. 'No matter how much of a shabby animal you are, you can learn from Dostoievsky and Tchekhov, etc., how to have the most tender, unique, coruscating soul on earth.'[26] Rozanov was the only Russian with whom Lawrence did not become disillusioned; he at

9

least shared his 'phallic vision'. The rest made him heartily sick.

> They have meant an enormous amount to me; Turgenev, Tolstoi, Dostoievsky–mattered almost more than anything, and I thought them the greatest writers of all time. And now with something of a shock, I realise a certain crudity and thick, uncivilised, insensitive stupidity about them, I realise how much finer and purer and more ultimate our own stuff is.[27]

We should not let ourselves be startled at Lawrence's revulsion. It is possible that, with Dostoevsky, revulsion is inevitable and even necessary for a true understanding. At least this aspect brings him into line with many of the more prominent writers and playwrights of our own day.

By the year 1930 there was substantial agreement among the critics that Dostoevsky's influence had irreversibly affected not only English literature but also European and American literature as a whole: Thomas Mann, Gide, T. S. Eliot, Aldous Huxley, Somerset Maugham, Faulkner, to mention only a selection. Neuschäffer[28] has shown in detail, even if ponderously, how Dostoevsky has influenced the English novel in three directions: in character, content and structure. Raskolnikov, Myshkin and Stavrogin types have been tracked down in the works of Conrad, Hugh Walpole, Aldous Huxley, and above all in Lawrence. Virginia Woolf has been described as 'truly Dostoevskyan'. Neuschäffer's thesis is easily exploded, but it certainly contains a grain of truth. More recent traces of Dostoevsky have been discovered in writers as diverse as Beckett, Max Frisch, Iris Murdoch and Ferlinghetti.

At about the same time as Dostoevsky's influence was beginning to be noticed in every quarter, Dostoevsky criticism entered a more sober phase. This is partly to be ascribed to the availability of the wealth of documentary material edited by Russian scholars in the period since the end of the Civil War, when the Tsarist archives were opened to the public. E. H. Carr's study marks the impact of scholarship on the English view of Dostoevsky. In the preface, Carr's work[29] is hailed by D. S. Mirsky as 'an eminently sensible book'–which exactly describes it. Carr's study is vindicated to the extent that it has been impossible since his time to return to the days of take-your-pick enthusiasm and speculation. Ironically, none the less, Carr is not only the beginning but also the end of serious criticism in this country. His success lay in prescribing the limits set by his material.

That the period since the publication of Carr's book has produced so little in the way of original or fresh work on Dostoevsky is of course partly to be ascribed to the disruption of the last war, but mainly, perhaps, to the stagnation of criticism in Soviet Russia. Among the more noteworthy books in recent years have been George Steiner's *Tolstoy or Dostoevsky* (1959), David Magarshack's biography (1962), Marc Slonim's *The Three Loves of Dostoevsky* (1955), Jessie Coulson's presentation of Dostoevsky through the medium of his correspondence (1962)–an unenviable but praiseworthy undertaking–finally, the Soviet émigré Vladimir Seduro's much needed *Dostoevsky in Russian Literary Criticism*: 1846–1956 (1957). Although nearly all Dostoevsky's literary work is now available in translation (if not actually in print), the manuscripts, note-books, fragments, sketches remain inaccessible to all but Russian scholars. The works and articles of the important Russian critics of the 1920s are still awaiting translation.

Meanwhile, a revolution has occurred under our very noses. In 1936 it could truly be said[30] that 'Dostoevsky in England belongs to the intelligentsia, a very small part of the literate population'. In 1966, as a result of the paperback revolution, and the cinema versions, nothing could be further from the truth. During this period, critical interest in Dostoevsky seems to have been in inverse proportion to his popularity. There are plenty of readers in search of solutions and interpretations, but the oracles remain mum.

If Dostoevsky were really defunct, we could all go to his funeral, and there let things decently rest. But there are no signs whatever of decease. The chief danger is that, unless Dostoevsky is rescued by a revival of critical debate, he will succumb to a 'pop-existentialism' and sink beyond reach.

CHARADES

1 *A royal divertissement*

RUSSIA has witnessed so many forms of political unrest that it makes even French history seem dull by comparison. It is a great temptation for the modern historian to look for a natural historical progression linking the various revolutionary episodes in Russia. But there is nothing in common between the Pugachev popular uprising of Catherine's day, the Romantic idealism of the Decembrists in 1825, the gradualism of the Populists of the 1870s, and the fanatical armed conspiracies of the latter years of Alexander II's reign culminating in the latter's assassination. To put any one of these alongside the Petrashevsky Affair of 1849, one of the most grotesque political farces of all time, would be to invite ridicule.

The Petrashevsky conspiracy reads like some abortive melodrama. Its value is for the light it throws on the political atmosphere of the period, on the extent to which the Russian political machine had managed to isolate a vast Empire from the mainstream of European thinking and activity. It was only a combination of the trauma of the Crimean War and the death of the repressive Tsar Nicholas I (who had all but managed to turn Russia into a kind of Ruritania) that allowed a new generation for a few years to get at the dry rot.

In this period the only thinkable thing for the intelligentsia to do was to get out of Russia and to try and influence events from abroad. It is easy to imagine their head-shaking contempt for Petrashevsky and all the other poor fellows who were amateurs when it came to political thinking, and schoolboys when it came to political action. Herzen, the most influential of all the émigrés, characterised the Petrashevsky circle as 'gifted young people, outstandingly clever and extraordinarily well-educated, but nervous, highly-strung and afraid of their own shadows. . . . Something inside them had gone bad.'[1] They were too wrapped up in themselves, Herzen thought:

> Theirs was not the healthy sort of pride which befits a young man full of dreams of a great future . . . not the kind that in former times drove men to accomplish miracles of daring . . . their self-esteem on the contrary is diseased, frustrating all action through the sheer enormity of their pretensions. They are fretful, quick to take offence, impudently overweening, and at the same time completely lacking in self-confidence.[2]

Herzen was convinced it was the atmosphere of suspicion engendered by Nicholas I which had bred this type, this spiteful hypochondriac, with a character like a mimosa; Dostoevsky's Man from Underground 'germinated in a test-tube'. Dostoevsky himself epitomised this type in his novel *The Devils* when he contrasted the natural craving for danger and sensation of the earlier generation of Decembrists with the neurotic, exhausted and complex character of the young men of his own day.[3]

Dostoevsky was in his mid-twenties when he became associated with the Petrashevsky circle, one of hundreds that proliferated in the capital during that period. He was already a writer of some repute, with several stories and short novels to his credit. His interest in the Petrashevsky group could be described as 'experimental'. He was no doctrinaire, and his intelligence and paradoxicality made him immune from political activism of any kind. His friends described him as 'taciturn, with a preference for the confidential tête-à-tête, and a tendency to be secretive'. 'We could all see in him a flaccid, nervous character, capable of great sensitivity.' Here, quite unmistakably, is the author of *White Nights*, *Netochka Nezhvanova*, *A Feeble Heart*, and the other stories of Dostoevsky's 'Petersburg period'.

Dostoevsky had never been exactly a regular participant at the Petrashevsky soirées; if anything, he was rather more closely associated with the 'Durov circle', a group of the same kind, of which more will be said later. It is nevertheless reasonably well established that he became acquainted with

Petrashevsky in 1846. He began to appear regularly at Petrashevsky's Friday-evening gatherings in 1847, though only for a brief period. This meant that he had the unenviable distinction of being one of the founder members, the group reaching sizeable proportions only a year later in 1848. After his arrest (23 April 1849) he explained to the Commission of Enquiry that he had been keeping up a show of friendly relations with Petrashevsky out of mere politeness, putting in token attendances about once a month and no more. On his arrest Dostoevsky was nonplussed at the charge brought against him; the main accusation being that he had taken the unwarranted liberty of reading to the assembled company Belinsky's supposedly red-hot *Letter to Gogol*. Like many others of the thirty-four under arrest he was completely unable to see what all the fuss was about. When all was said and done, the Petrashevsky circle was no secret, the whole of Petersburg knew of its existence. If there was any real suspicion, then why had they not all been arrested long since? The whole affair made sense only as a sequence straight out of a dream play.

The rest of the ugly story is already well known. Twenty-one of those arrested were condemned to death by firing squad. Or rather this was only part of the Tsar's little game. For he had already secretly arranged for their sentences to be commuted to penal servitude. The 'execution' was a public affair, staged on a fairly impressive (though not too grand) scale on the Semyonovsk Square in St. Petersburg. The first batch of prisoners, Petrashevsky, Speshnev and Mombelli, were led up to the scaffold, bound, hooded. The timing was perfect. And just at the precise moment when the order to fire was about to be given, the proceedings were brought to their prearranged halt. The condemned were untied, and an emissary from His Imperial Majesty who had expressly for this purpose driven up in his carriage, read a decree commuting their sentences to imprisonment with hard labour in Siberia. One has to suppose that the whole spectacle was meant to be something more than a bizarre joke, if only because the Tsar was not given to pranks, especially lavishly staged pranks of this order.

14

There exist several eye-witness accounts of the scene so laboriously acted out on that snow-bound square in Petersburg. The best account of all, though, is that of Prince Myshkin in *The Idiot*. The account is simply a dramatisation, some twenty years after the event, of the scene Dostoevsky described in a letter to his brother written on that horrible day. Myshkin's account runs as follows:

This man had once been brought to the scaffold in company with several others, and had had the sentence of death by shooting passed upon him for some political crime. Twenty minutes later he had been reprieved and some other sentence substituted; but the interval between the two sentences, twenty minutes, or at least a quarter of an hour, had been passed in the certainty that within a few minutes he must die. . . . He remembered everything with the most accurate and extraordinary distinctness, and declared that he would never forget a single iota of the experience.

About twenty paces from the scaffold, where he had stood to hear the sentence, were three posts, fixed in the ground, to which to fasten the criminals, of whom there were several. The first three criminals were taken to the posts, dressed in long white tunics, with white caps drawn over their faces, so that they could not see the rifles pointed at them. Then a group of soldiers took their stand opposite to each post. My friend was the eighth on the list, and therefore would have been among the third lot to go up. A priest went about among them with a cross; and there was about five minutes left for him to live.

He said that those five minutes seemed to him a most interminable period, an enormous wealth of time; he seemed to be living in these minutes so many lives there was no need as yet to think of that last moment, so that he made several arrangements, dividing up the time into portions–one for saying farewell to his companions, two minutes for that; then a couple more for thinking over his own life and career and all about himself; and another minute for a last look around. He remembered having divided his time like this quite well. . . . Then, having bade farewell, he embarked upon those two minutes which he had allotted to himself; he knew beforehand what he was going to think about. He wished to put it to himself that here was he, a living, thinking man, and that in three minutes he would be nobody; or if somebody or something, then what and where? . . .

2 *Intellectual boredom*

Most of those associated with Petrashevsky were young men, mainly in their mid-twenties and early thirties. They were Russia's 'lost generation'. Their nerve was gone; fear had been replaced by an insidious malaise. They were ill-at-ease with themselves, and hence with everyone else. Dreams and ideals foundered upon the burdens of social intercourse. Those who found actual life intolerable sought an outlet in schemes of social reconstruction and utopia. They mostly eked out rather poor livelihoods in various government departments; the routine was often crippling. One member of the Petrashevsky circle has described the atmosphere of those times:

> Everyone is to a greater or lesser extent suffering from physical disorder and moral illness. As for me, all this mass of nastiness and ugliness which I am compelled to endure is so demoralising that I am all the time in low spirits and consider myself unfit for anything. I am a sick man, morally crushed at every moment by life; I find it difficult to talk, and am engrossed in my own sorry situation. I even think sometimes that in my case, in all probability, things will never be any different.[4]

Although the Petrashevskyites in general were of the nobility, this status in Russia could mean almost anything from unbridled luxury to abject poverty. The lower end of this class, to which Dostoevsky for instance belonged, lived within a precarious margin just this side of destitution, and counted for next to nothing socially. Others of the circle, including Petrashevsky himself, were relatively well off. The latter were not always sensitive to the feelings of their more impecunious members, a feature brought out rather touchingly and not without bathos by one of the more needy and semi-literate of the circle. His words could have been taken straight from the popular literature of the period, even from Gogol. He complains that whenever he came to their Friday evenings he was made to feel:

simply a martyr. You see, you're all the while treading gingerly so as not to give offence to this fine, rich man, and you simply daren't turn up more than two or three times a year for fear of infringing etiquette, and even then you haven't a clue about half of what is being discussed. And I must say, I simply can't stand being ridiculed for not reading the French and German newspapers in the cafés like the rest of these well-to-do people, though mark you it isn't that I don't know any French. It's like this. You go off to work and they go to the cafés. You rush off to have a meal and a rest after a hard day's work, while they go off to musical evenings or drop in on friends, and then they are parading the Nevsky at three in the morning. That's no life for me. . . . Granted, they are all well-educated young men, but they have no idea of practical matters facing poor folk.[5]

Curious side views such as this put quite a different face on the so-called Petrashevsky 'plot'.

Petrashevsky's companions were concerned principally with intellectual reorientation. They had rejected the German metaphysical struggles of half a generation earlier, and attention was now focussed upon the French socialists: Fourier, Saint-Simon, Proudhon, Louis Blanc. Fourier especially was read with uncritical enthusiasm; perhaps because Fourier too had been a dreamer, with something of the prophet-like, soul-shaking strain which went straight to the heart of the Russian. Unlike Owen, Fourier was not so much concerned with practical economics as with human perfectibility. Petrashevsky himself was so inspired by Fourier's admittedly ingenious scheme–French genius at its most rococo–that it was generally believed[6] that he himself launched a Fourier-type commune, albeit on a very small scale. His peasants were presented with spanking new quarters, but to show their gratitude they had promptly razed them to the ground.

Yet Petrashevsky's own harsh impact with social reality did nothing to dampen his enthusiasm. At his trial he staunchly defended his idol against charges of incitement to insurrection. But authority had taken fright. In France 1848 had already happened, and the cause and effect relationship between intellectual radicalism and revolution was assumed, even if not proven. The Petrashevskyites were victims not of their own deeds but of the panic among those in power. No one could be less like a political revolutionary than Petrashevsky: and the same can be said of the majority of his circle: 'Their primary and fundamental impulse was merely the desire to escape from the intellectual and moral oppression of life in Petersburg under Nicholas I into an ideal world of their own invention. . . . In many respects, they were typical of the Russian *ineptitude* for political life.'[7]

3 *A Friday evening oracle*

Petrashevsky's flat where everyone gathered on Friday evenings was roomy enough, though not particularly cosy: a spacious sitting room, a single battered old divan, chintz upholstery, a few decrepit chairs, not much of a table, and a single tallow candle for illumination. The lack of amenities was probably a deliberate pose.[8] The atmosphere was almost gay; the food good as well as ample. In most respects the Petrashevsky circle could have been any one of a score of similar gatherings. The real difference was in the people who frequented it.

Although he had made an overnight reputation with his 'loaded' imitation encyclopédie *A Pocket Dictionary of Foreign Words*, and although renowned as a collector of banned publications, censor-baiter and mock *provocateur*, Petrashevsky's success depended largely on charisma. He was a poor speaker, and his diatribes were usually halting, repetitious and incoherent. Herzen had been struck by his 'meekness and inexhaustible patience'. 'He bore the bitterest criticism without the least sign of rancour. There was never any suspicion that he was trying to score off those around him . . . he was too deeply engrossed in his own schemes to bother about his own personality.'[9] There can have been no more incongruous sight than this harmless *gamin* tied to the scaffold facing a firing squad.

Not everyone liked Petrashevsky though. Years later Bakunin had to live with him for a time in Siberia, and found him only a troublemaker, 'a pig with a sore head', revelling in scandal for its own sake. 'In all my born days I have never met such an arrant, unscrupulous cynic.'[10]

4 *A splinter group*

'Petrashevsky is a fool, a play-actor and a gas-bag; he will never be anything different.' This was how Dostoevsky saw the situation.[11] It was evident that Petrashevsky was not over-endowed with good sense and tact. His ineptitude drove a small group of visitors to hold their own meetings at Durov's house. This splinter-group later came to be known as 'the Durov circle'.

Actually the idea was not Durov's originally. It was Dostoevsky and the poet Pleshcheyev who first expressed their misgivings when one evening they were in Speshnev's company. With a touch of desperate humour they christened themselves 'the society with a healthy respect for the police'. The date was 12 October 1848. In all they met no more than seven times. Their discussions were of a general nature and on much the same lines as those of Petrashevsky.

Durov's coterie consisted primarily of writers or, more accurately, 'litterateurs' who had had their bellyful of politics. The brothers Dostoevsky, as well as Durov and Palm, declared themselves 'advocates of pure art, which reproduces reality as it really is'. This was to counter Petrashevsky's thesis that literature was devoid of content and that writers would do better to cultivate their minds.[12] The participants were all close friends and were intent on getting some enjoyment out of their Saturday evenings. They were determined to restrict themselves to music and literature. It has been suggested that all this was merely a smoke-screen to deceive the police, but it is difficult to find any clear evidence for this.[13] It was an outsider, a young hot-head named Philippov, who lured them into politics, and finally into anti-government propaganda activity. In the course of a single evening the politically tense atmosphere of the outside world burst into their aestheticism like a tornado. They ended their evening feverishly discussing plans for a printing press designed for lithographing publications for clandestine circulation.[14] There was no opposition other than from

Mikhail Dostoevsky* who, true to form, protested against the impracticability of the scheme, which he considered doomed to disaster from the outset.

There were only two more meetings, after which Durov sent round notes to everyone (17–18 April) informing them that the next meeting had had to be postponed. Only four days later came the mass arrest and an end to everything.

It was at the last but one Saturday soirée that Dostoevsky first read Belinsky's notorious letter to Gogol, which was to become the main incriminating evidence against him at his trial. In this letter Belinsky had savagely and scathingly attacked Gogol for going over to the ruling 'establishment', the patrons of Autocracy and Russian Orthodox Christianity. By special request the reading was repeated a number of days later at Petrashevsky's. Dostoevsky was already renowned for his vivid impassioned reading, and on this occasion apparently it was infused with the requisite fire.

Those who have assumed, as the police did, that Dostoevsky had been intellectually committed to what he had read on these occasions are almost certainly wrong. Dostoevsky lived, and had already been living for the past five years, in a world of fancy and psychological drama where normal people entered only for brief spells of entertainment or edification. Regardless of this, not everyone has interpreted Dostoevsky's defence before the Commission of Enquiry correctly. Some have been repelled by its apparent insincerity.[15] In actual fact, the young novelist may have been more candid than is supposed. He had no reason to swallow Belinsky, nor is there any reason to be found for his supposed antipathy towards Gogol. The likelihood is that Dostoevsky was reading the letter as an actor would. As he himself maintained, he had read it in public only for its literary merit, as 'an outstanding literary monument'. He failed to see how anyone could have been carried away by the *content*.[16]

Dostoevsky at the time of his arrest was very far from being the naïve socialist revolutionary the police presumably took

* One of Dostoevsky's brothers.

him to be. It could only have been the fantastic element and the intriguing possibilities of the Petrashevsky situation that attracted him, never the political theory: 'the commune is more ghastly and more repulsive than any penal settlement'.[17] It is said that at one of the Petrashevsky gatherings, Dostoevsky was challenged as to what he proposed to do if the peasants could be freed only by an uprising. His reply was: 'then let us have an uprising by all means'.[18] Revolution no doubt appealed to him, but at the dramatic and metaphysical levels only (metaphysical rebellion is one of the major motifs of *The Brothers Karamazov*).

Dostoevsky and Durov were regarded by their friends as atheists. Yet, incongruous as it may seem, we have reliable information that they were once seen together at Easter Communion. This could not mean that secretly they were devout churchgoers. Contradictions of this kind are explicable only in terms of the attitude shared by the whole generation of which Feuerbach's *Essence of Christianity* is the epitome. Kirillov the religious atheist in *The Devils*, who keeps a lamp lighted before an ikon, is only another side of the Russian pagan who (this partly deranged character assures us) will in time come to believe in God.

5 *Arrest*

The police had known about Petrashevsky for such a long time that, by the time of his arrest, he had become almost a figure of respect. The difficulty was that there was no evidence against him, and moreover there existed no spy who could be relied on to ferret out the evidence they so badly needed. It was then that a promising young ex-student turned up at the Ministry, and it was he who was singled out for this delicate mission. The danger, as the police bureaucrats saw it, was that Petrashevsky was so inclined to blab deliberately that he could ruin any ordinary spy within a month.

Before very long, there was a most impressive dossier on Petrashevsky and his associates. The laconic and in some ways boyishly naive reports compiled by this zealous apprentice contain enough material to provide a fit sequel to Gogol's *Inspector General*. Parts of them are so incredible that, if we knew less than we did about Petrashevsky, we might suspect some vast leg-pull. It is not entirely impossible however that Petrashevsky was acting out some bizarre comedy with this raw youth, the rules of which were known only to himself. The highlight of Petrashevsky's intimate disclosures is the latter's trap for would-be spies. Suspects would be decoyed by false information that the Friday evening gatherings were really spiritualist séances. If this did not deter, the culprit would be invited to take an active part in a 'séance'. He would be asked to summon up the spirit of a famous cut-throat, with the warning that if he bungled things he would be cut down by whatever weapon the spirit happened to be armed with.

This kind of elaborate joke is not without irony; because, only a few weeks later, Petrashevsky was behind bars. The date of the arrest had been discussed in committee and fixed comfortably in advance. Dostoevsky describes what happened to him in particular. He had been out that day to borrow money from an acquaintance, had returned home about midnight soaked to the skin, and had gone straight to bed feeling 'absolutely bloody'. A short while later he was awakened by a soft, caressing voice: 'Would you mind getting up, please. . . . Take your time. There's no hurry. We can wait till you get dressed.' Secret police methods have a long history in Russia.

The criminal proceedings lasted some five months, by the end of which time every tiresome piece of evidence had been sifted a dozen times. The Monarch was in no mood for botched jobs. For this reason the ringleader was arrested in style, with footman, carriage and four high-up officials into the bargain. There was a General Rostovtsev, who liked to give himself airs. He was Dostoevsky's cross-examiner, and was reduced to frenzy by Dostoevsky's dumb insolence. More than once, he rushed off into an adjoining room screaming that he refused to cross-examine this man any more.[19]

The mock execution had been pre-arranged for 23 December. All, including Tsar Nicholas himself, seem to have breathed a sigh of relief that the farce had successfully run its course. None of the condemned, even in their gloomiest moments, had expected the death sentence. Not even when they were disgorged from the black marias on to that bleak parade ground, not even when they saw before them the scaffold black and stark against the snow, did they awaken to reality. Later in prison the nightmare of those few moments became frozen into trauma. It was on that day that Dostoevsky discovered a new and awful dimension of the human spirit. It is Prince Myshkin who conjures up for us the face of the victim on which the ultimate lesson of existence is written.

6 *The real conspiracy*

Some top officials thought the police had been overhasty. If they had bided their time, some real evidence would have come to light, and lengthy proceedings could have been avoided. Luckily for the Petrashevskyites, patience was not a virtue among the Russian secret police. There did exist some really incriminating evidence, but the police never unearthed it. Had they done so, the execution would have been no mock affair.

The real conspirator was not Petrashevsky, but Speshnev, a member of the Durov splinter group. Speshnev, himself the most enigmatic member of the group, had developed a passion for secret societies, and had studied the history of some of them. He was above all intrigued by the revolutionary potentialities of these societies. With a few members of the Petrashevsky circle he had discussed his plan for a communist secret society which would employ three methods of activating the masses: propaganda, jesuitry and insurrection. All would be organised by a 'central committee'.

The participants in this discussion were sworn to secrecy, and only three days before the mass arrest, the components of a secret printing-press were delivered to Speshnev's house. In their routine search the police found nothing, even though very obvious pieces of printing equipment were in evidence scattered about amongst the furniture. The room was sealed as a matter of routine, but Speshnev's servants managed to lift the door from its hinges and remove the incriminating evidence, without damaging the seal.[20] Speshnev alone of those arrested knew anything of this. The other accomplices got away scot-free after the briefest cross-examination.

7 A nest of devils

If we open *The Devils* at 'The Meeting' (Part II, Chap. 7) we find a veritable parody of the kind of secret meeting Dostoevsky had witnessed more than once in his youth. But nothing in Dostoevsky is ever mere caricature. This chapter opens an entirely new perspective upon revolutionary conspiracy in mid-nineteenth-century Russia: a quasi-genteel past, laced with portents of sinister things to come.

Dostoevsky's satirical novel appeared in 1871. The score of years that had elapsed since the arrest and conviction of the Petrashevskyites had been a time of almost uncontrolled change. The stagnation of civic and political life seemed to evaporate with the death of Tsar Nicholas in 1855; there followed an interval of intoxicating awakening. Within months of the accession of Alexander II, the Tsar of much promise and little achievement, the writers and intelligentsia began to wear their true colours. The new generation were men of action, the nihilistic generation of Turgenev's Bazarov; in extreme cases they were anti-art (Pisarev) and even anti-culture. Chernyshevsky, the new-style political philosopher, was a sensation. He had lent his own brand of laconic grandeur to Bentham and Mill, and had made a clean sweep of the Russian intellectual scene. The 'new men' were by self-acclaim practical, loyal, virulent, sardonic. They had before them the shining heroism of Bakunin, the dedication of Chernyshevsky, and of course the inspiration and encouragement of their tutor-in-exile, Alexander Herzen. Only a few were cynics, and these were scarcely in evidence at this time; they were still back-stage, nursing their dreams in 'dark cellars'. It was in fact only a few months before Dostoevsky started work on the final draft of *The Devils* that the notorious Nechaev affair burst upon a bewildered public. The press reports of the trial made Dostoevsky rethink the entire shape of his novel.

Dostoevsky was a past master at underground intrigue. He was drawn to it by his passion for paradox and queer goings-on. Virginsky's 'meeting' has all the necessary ingredients: rudeness, reserve, hypersensitivity, squeamishness, violence, and not least, farce. Dostoevsky obviously revelled in it. Except for the personnel, the nonsensical sequence of events cannot have been very far different from what Dostoevsky himself had been closely acquainted with in his younger days in Petersburg. Pyotr Verkhovensky becomes bored with all the garrulousness: 'Haven't we any playing cards?' he sniggers. 'I'll venture just one question,' begins the lame teacher with studied politeness, 'I should like to know, are we at some sort of meeting, or are we simply a gathering of ordinary mortals paying a social call? I simply ask for the sake of routine enquiry and so as not to remain in ignorance.' Even Lyamshin, the Jewish pianist brought in to provide light entertainment, may not have been entirely foreign to Dostoevsky's experience. The Durov splinter group too had its performers who, like Lyamshin, were there only to divert police suspicion.

All this is only a prologue to the appalling revelation the novelist has in store for us. Verkhovensky the craftsman of clandestine power puts his pawns to the test. He turns on the lame man: 'Yes or no? Would you inform on us or not?' – 'Of course, I wouldn't.' 'And no one would, of course not,' the rest join in. But the unanimous pledge from the company is not enough for this ruthless 'expert'. 'Allow me to appeal to *you*, Mr. Major [the host]. Would you inform or not? . . . Note that I appeal to you on purpose.' – 'I won't inform.' 'But even if you knew that someone meant to rob and murder someone else, an ordinary mortal, then would you inform?' – 'Yes, of course, but that's a private matter, while the other would be political treachery. I have never been an agent of the Secret Police.' The rest try to play for time: 'It's an unnecessary question. . . . There are no informers here.' Shatov rises as if to leave. 'That is Shatov. What are you getting up for?' Neither Shatov nor Stavrogin are willing to undergo this simple but effective test.

There are some surprising resemblances between Dostoevsky's characters and the people he met at Petrashevsky's place. Virginsky, for instance, reminds us of Mombelli, an idealist whom Speshnev used for his own more sinister ends. In the novel Virginsky is characterised as a 'universal humanity man'. 'A pure-hearted fellow, ten times purer than you or I' is Verkhovensky's way of sneering at such people. Liputin, another of the characters, bears a striking resemblance to Petrashevsky. In the first place he is 'a true Fourierist'; but he is also a rogue who has to be closely watched ('he is indispensable to us up to a point, but he needs strict supervision'). The Liputin–Petrashevsky 'hero' has his bags ready packed and hidden under his bed in readiness for a quick getaway. In court Liputin would have protested his innocence just as disarmingly as Petrashevsky had done.

Only the events in the novel belong to the early seventies, the years during which Dostoevsky was completing his work on *The Devils*. The crucial incident is Shatov's murder. We know it to be based on a newspaper report Dostoevsky happened to light upon while staying in Dresden. The murderer was Nechaev, one of the new-style fanatical revolutionaries; the real-life victim was a student called Ivanov (in the rough drafts of the novel that was Shatov's name too). This newspaper cutting was all Dostoevsky needed. Suddenly a whole train of events came to life.

> I knew nothing about Nechaev, or Ivanov, or the circumstances of this murder, and never knew more than what I read in the papers. Even if I had known, I would not have plagiarised. I take only the fact as it occurred. My fantasy can be very different indeed from actual reality, and my Pyotr Verkhovensky may resemble Nechaev not the least bit, but as I see it . . . my imagination has created the character, the very type that tallies with an evil occurrence such as this.[21]

The 'Nechaev Affair' can be summarised as follows: In September 1869 Nechaev arrived in Moscow straight from Geneva. He immediately contacted an acquaintance by the name of Uspensky; he had met him several months earlier before going abroad. After protracted discussions on what should be done to help the masses, and to counteract government measures, Nechaev suddenly changed his tack, and tried to make Uspensky see the urgency of a secret society for the purpose of actively fomenting rebellion and anarchy. A

short time later, Nechaev began to cultivate the acquaintance
of students from the Petrovsky Institute, in particular a
fellow called Ivanov. The rest of his associates were profes-
sionals. Nechaev made out that he had been specially
delegated by the International Revolutionary Committee in
Geneva to instigate a nation-wide revolt in Russia. In fact, a
date for a general uprising had already been fixed: 19 Feb-
ruary 1870. Meanwhile in November of the previous year the
corpse of a young man had been hauled out of an ornamental
pool in the Petrovsky park. The body had heavy stones tied
about the neck and feet. The police investigated what was
already obviously a murder and very quickly identified the
victim. It was only somewhat later that it occurred to the
police to investigate a possible link with Ivanov's fellow
students. Their main clue was the apparent utter lack of
motive for the crime. The only possibility was revenge. The
whole affair gradually came into focus, and eventually came
to make sense. Meanwhile however Nechaev had fled the
country. All traceable suspects were arrested, and cross-
examination revealed that the murder victim, Ivanov, had
once been 'found guilty of insubordination' by the 'Committee'. He had been lured into the cellars of the Academy on
the pretext that a secret printing press was going to be dug
up. Ivanov's comrades seized him by the throat, but before
they could strangle him, Nechaev grabbed a revolver from
someone and shot him through the head.[22]

There are obvious differences in detail between the
Nechaev episode and the events in the novel. But these are
not really significant. It is the psychological resemblance
between Nechaev and Verkhovensky that is really striking;
all the more remarkable because deriving largely from the
novelist's intuition. One could even argue that Verkhovensky
is a more complete character than Nechaev, an archetype
to which the latter only approximates. There was little
Dostoevsky needed to learn about the motivations and make-
up of such people; especially their maniacal capacity for
destroying the personalities of others.[23]

Intuition however is not the only explanation for the
likeness. Years before, Dostoevsky had fallen under the

influence of such a man. This was no other than Speshnev, with whose name we are already familiar. Speshnev was probably the richest member of the Petrashevsky circle, and, as Dostoevsky was perpetually in need of money, it is not surprising that he soon got into Speshnev's debt. Although the sum borrowed was as much as 500 roubles, Speshnev waived the whole question of repayment. From that very instant, Dostoevsky developed something like a persecution mania. He became excessively touchy and petulant, and the whole matter of the loan assumed an occult significance, very nearly driving him out of his mind: 'From now on, I am his for good, and shall never escape from his clutches. Never again shall I be in a position to return the money, and for his part he will never accept repayment. He's like that. Can you understand that from this time onwards I had my own Mephistopheles?'[24] At this time, Dostoevsky was not unlike his own character Raskolnikov pursued by his own wraith-like shadow Svidrigailov. Dostoevsky's neurosis produced a great change in him even in the short space of two or three weeks; with physical symptoms as well as a good deal of hypochondria.

No ordinary loan could have caused a transformation such as this, for Dostoevsky was seldom out of debt. If we look closer at Speshnev we discern the 'man of power' whose near relations are Stavrogin and Verkhovensky. The similarity has not gone unnoticed. (The resemblance is so striking and so obvious that it is impossible to imagine how an academic dispute arose in Moscow in the 1920s over a claim that Stavrogin was a literary characterisation of Bakunin. The latter was a firebrand and idealist, whilst Stavrogin remains a cold cynic.) Ironically, one of the letters Bakunin wrote from exile in Irkutsk, containing a sketch of Speshnev, has survived. The contours are so extraordinary, that out of context they might be taken for a rough sketch of Stavrogin:

> Speshnev is a man outstanding in many respects: clever, rich, cultivated, goodlooking, of unusually noble appearance, far from repulsive, although calm and cold, inspiring confidence, like any controlled power, a gentleman from head to toe. Men

could easily be repelled by him; he is too passionless, and too
self-satisfied, as though not requiring the affection of anyone.
Women however, young and old, married and unmarried alike
have been and, if so he wishes it, will go on being crazy about
him. Women are not put off by his trace of charlatanry, and he
is really affected; he is very good at assuming an air of thought-
ful, calm impenetrability. The story of his youth is a novel in
itself. He had scarcely left school, when he met a young and
beautiful Polish girl, who left her husband and children for his
sake, allowed herself to be taken abroad with him, bore him a
son, and then began to suffer from jealousy until finally in a fit
of jealousy she poisoned herself.[25]

All those who knew Speshnev testify to his prodigious personal influence and magnetic power.

Speshnev was not the only inscrutable character. There
was one other: a man called Chernosvitov, a businessman
from Siberia. He was not a regular member of the Petrashevsky circle, and thus escaped the notice of the police. He was
by all accounts a very wealthy director of a gold-mining
company syndicate, and a man of extraordinary intelligence
and wit. He saw himself as a radical and a man of action.
For him liberalism and socialism were 'as near as damn it'.
His portrait reveals the intense alertness of a man several
moves ahead of his opponents, hands and gestures poised for
action.[26] In Petrashevsky's salon Chernosvitov was an outstanding success. With his endless flow of wit, subtlety,
debate, threaded with a counterpoint of scurrility, he
seemed to have something for everybody. Even the supercilious Speshnev was impressed.[27] In his assessment of the
Petrashevsky circle on the other hand Chernosvitov was less
flattering: 'I did not find my equal there. At first I was
interested in Dostoevsky, the fact that he was a writer and all
that . . . but it all turned out to be rather unsatisfying.'[28]
Dostoevsky with his weakness for the 'paradoxalist' must
have been highly gratified by this phenomenon from the
other side of the Urals. We know that he was astounded at
Chernosvitov's command of Russian style. Dostoevsky
remarked on one occasion: 'The devil only knows; this
fellow speaks Russian just as well as Gogol writes it.'[29]

Needless to say, the circle suspected Chernosvitov of being an *agent provocateur*. A comic situation arose in which Speshnev and Chernosvitov were each trying their most skilful manœuvres to find out if the other had links with any secret organisation, political or otherwise. The latter suspected Speshnev of being the ring-leader of a clandestine society operating from the very heart of Russia. Petrashevsky was for denying this on Speshnev's behalf, but the latter decided he would put out a red herring to see how Chernosvitov would react, by letting him into the spurious confidence that he was the head of a communist organisation. For his part, Speshnev was quite convinced that the buffoon from Siberia was a kind of emissary from some underground league, and that he was in the capital only nominally on business, but really on a 'recruiting campaign'. After a number of exchange reconnaissances, Chernosvitov casually came forward with the startling news that in Perm Province there were 400,000 workers who could be supplied with arms at very short notice and who were simply 'dry tinder' for insurrection. He immediately went on to discuss with Speshnev (and Petrashevsky who happened to be present) a plan for a new, and this time well-organised, Pugachev-type *coup* in Eastern Siberia and the Urals. An armed division would be sent by the government to Central Siberia as soon as trouble was reported, and would be cut off from east and west by specially trained guerillas, and destroyed. The lower Volga and Don could then easily be overrun, and finally a link-up established with urban revolts in Moscow and the capital.[30]

The comic potentialities of the Petrashevsky circle were not wasted on Dostoevsky. It will already be obvious that Verkhovensky is a successful compound of aspects of a number of real-life characters, though of course a character in his own right besides. In his skilled blend of farce, intimidation and incognito, Verkhovensky is perhaps nearest of all to Chernosvitov, though extending the dimensions in every direction. In many ways Nechaev is almost a rustic by comparison with Verkhovensky, a mature fruit of what was already germinating in Dostoevsky as early as 1848. In all his years in Siberia, and subsequently in the gambling houses of the German spas, the novelist must have been in a sense living with this phenomenon which would every day grow in monstrosity, ludicrousness and sheer devilry. In the pages of the *Diary of a Writer* we come across a strange admission:

> And how on earth do you know that the Petrashevskyites could not have been a bunch of Nechaevs . . . if things had turned out that way? Of course, at the time it was impossible to tell how things would go. The time was not ripe. But allow me to say one thing on my own behalf: I could probably never have been like Nechaev himself but I will not swear that I could not have been one of his sort . . . in my younger days.

It would hardly be worth the attempt to try and find exact historical counterparts for Dostoevsky's 'devils': Stavrogin, Verkhovensky (Pyotr), Kirillov, Shigalev, etc. Dostoevsky was writing a novel, not a history. Yet this comedy of conspiracy is not entirely straight out of Dostoevsky's own imagination. Many of the ingredients were well within his own direct experience. In the first place, Verkhovensky's plan for an organised riot at the Shpigulin factory resembles Chernosvitov's scheme even down to the finer details:

> There are Skoptsi* here in the neighbourhood – they're curious people . . . of that later, though . . . Ah, here's another anecdote. There's an infantry regiment here in the district. I was drinking last Friday with the officers. We've three friends among them, *vous comprenez*? They were discussing atheism and I need hardly say, they made short work of God. They were squealing with delight. . . . Well, what else have I to tell you? The Shpigulin factory's interesting; as you know there are 500 workmen in it, it's a hotbed of cholera, it's not been cleaned for fifteen years and the factory hands are swindled. The owners are millionaires. I assure you that some among the hands have an idea of the Internationale. What, you smile? You'll see – only give me ever so little time! I've asked you to fix the time already and now I ask you again. . . .

It is worth noting, too, that Dostoevsky expressly underlines Verkhovensky's indifference to theory. The latter, with

---

* A religious sect, referred to in Chapter IV, *Roots*, p. 65.

deliberate indiscretion, confuses Shigalev's theories with those of Fourier. Shigalev is furious; he will not be associated with 'that mawkish theoretical twaddler'. Verkhovensky finds a debonair way of insulting this most extreme of anarchists, whom he sees as just another theorist. He is cynically contemptuous of shigalevism (a philosophy of mass murder), a theory as hidebound as Fourier. Pyotr Verkhovensky, ironically the harmless eccentric 'dropped from the moon', is a prototype of the mid-twentieth century totalitarian opportunist. His likeness was already to be found in Europe in the person of Lassalle, the socialist who had cultivated useful aristocratic connections and was capable of intimidating Bismarck himself; according to Marx, the self-assured man without scruples, 'the everlasting chatterbox with a falsetto voice, unlovely demonstrative gestures, and a way of putting you right about things'. But even Lassalle is mild and gentlemanly compared with Verkhovensky. This most diabolical of all Dostoevsky's devils reminds us of the modern central-committee man who picks up the telephone receiver, nonchalantly orders the deportation of half a million inconveniently settled inhabitants, gets the appropriate bureau to make yet another statistical entry on the appropriate graph and goes off to finish a game of chess. We are reminded of the Krupp-like monopolist in Auden and Isherwood's *On the Frontier*[31] who despises not only his employees but even the Leader; 'Nature is not interested in underlings—in the lazy, the inefficient, the self-indulgent, the People. . . . The world has never been governed by the People or by the merely rich, and it never will be. It is governed by men like myself. . . . Yes, for the man of power, there can now be but one aim, absolute control of mankind.' Verkhovensky asks his confederates:

Which do you prefer: the slow way, which consists in the composition of socialistic romances and the academic ordering of the destinies of humanity a thousand years hence . . . or do you, whatever it may imply, prefer a quicker way which will at last untie your hands, and will let mankind make its own social organisation in freedom, and in action, not on paper? They shout 'a hundred million heads'; that may be only a metaphor;

but why be afraid of it, if with the slow day-dreams on paper, despotism in the course of some hundred years will devour not a hundred million but five hundred million heads.

All this is an unmistakable anticipation of Russia under Stalin, and much else in our own century.

Finally, a word about Verkhovensky's 'neo-Pugachevism'. With this the Russian revolutionary trend has at last come full circle. Pugachev, the semi-legendary character of eighteenth-century Russia, was clearly in Chernosvitov's mind (not the crude flash-in-the-pan of history, but the archetype). A large-scale popular uprising was out of the question; Verkhovensky would have been no match for the 'final solution' proposed by Chernosvitov, the new Pugachev. But Verkhovensky has his positive side; he is the proclaimer of a legend:

> The people must believe that we know what we are after. . . . If only we had more time! That's the only trouble, we have no time. We will proclaim destruction. . . . Why is it, why has that idea such a fascination? But we must have a little exercise; we must. We'll set fires going. . . . We'll set legends going. Every scurvy 'group' will be of use. Out of those very groups I'll pick you out fellows so keen they'll not shrink from shootings, and be grateful for the honour of a job, too. And there will be an upheaval! There's going to be an upset as the world has never seen before. . . . Russia will be overwhelmed with darkness, the earth will weep for its old gods. . . . Well, then we shall bring forward . . . whom? . . . No other than Ivan the Tsarevich.

Stavrogin is to be this dionysian figure, the deity, whose shadow will stalk the length and breadth of Russia, but will remain 'hidden'. Here is the final perversion of Shatov's god born of the Russian soil. Verkhovensky goes on: 'You are beautiful and proud as a god', he tells Stavrogin. 'You are seeking nothing for yourself, with the halo of a victim around you, "in hiding". The great thing is the legend. You will conquer them, you will have only to look and you will conquer them.'

The flint-hard brutality of Dostoevsky's devils scarcely shocks people alive today; but to Dostoevsky's own generation it could have made little sense. Bakunin, Nechaev,

Lassalle, and even the hardened regicides of the eighties pale into insignificance before the ultima ratio so accurately forecast by Dostoevsky. Meanwhile we can begin to appreciate the full impact of the shock Dostoevsky received when over his cup of coffee in Dresden his eye fell upon that newspaper report. We have not done with the' devils', however, but shall be returning to them later.

DESCENT FROM REALITY

Notes from Underground could almost count as a work of our own century. It really belongs to the Literature of the Absurd, and in many surprising ways it anticipates Musil, Kafka and Camus. At the same time, Dostoevsky has provided us with a kind of prolegomenon to his major novels, with intimations of all their more important motifs. The first part especially is like a sponge which never reaches saturation. After twenty, after fifty readings, *Notes from Underground* goes on revealing unsuspected facets, further tantalising clues; but the core is still beyond our grasp.

Not surprisingly, *Notes from Underground* was not one of Dostoevsky's successes. The public preferred *The Insulted and Injured* and *Notes from the House of the Dead* which had appeared not long before. Originally, Dostoevsky had planned to write only a polemical attack against the new radicals of the sixties; he had returned from exile only four years before, and at that time they seemed firmly entrenched. He especially wanted to demolish those ideas taken over from the English Utilitarians, then fashionable. Before long he found himself writing a full-length novel: 'I don't know if it's going to be a load of trash,' he tells his brother, 'but personally I have great hopes for this novel. It will be a work of considerable power and frankness, and there will be plenty of plain speaking. It may not look too good on paper, but it will have its desired effect all right. . . .'

Notes from Underground consists of two parts, different both in length and in mode of composition. Part I, entitled 'The Dark Cellar', is entirely monologue, a highly concentrated fabric of kaleidoscoping ideas, satirical slant, psychological analysis, irony and shrewd observation. Part II, 'A Propos of the Wet Snow', is considerably longer, still largely monologue although in texture more akin to the narrative of a conventional novel.

The contrast between the first and second parts is in the opinion of the present writer highly significant. The *Notes* are primarily occupied with the problem of reality, real life. 'The Dark Cellar', with its tight-packed narrative, is a *metaphysical* or *ontological* consideration of reality; 'A Propos of the Wet Snow' broaches the same problem *aesthetically*. It is only in the final paragraph that the two views coalesce:

> Come, look into it more closely! Why, we do not even know where we are to find real life, or what it is, or what it is called. Leave us alone without any books, and we shall at once get confused, lose ourselves in a maze, we shall not know what to cling to, what to hold on to, what to love and what to hate, what to respect and what to despise. We even find it hard to be men, men of *real* flesh and blood, *our own* flesh and blood. We are ashamed of it. We think it a disgrace. And we do our best to be some theoretical 'average' men.*

The first thing to be clear about regarding the Man from Underground is that he is not what he has sometimes been supposed to be: a social outcast, or as he has been more recently termed, an outsider. He may seem on first acquaintance a bundle of traits which could be loosely labelled psychopathic or, at the very least, abnormal. It is only gradually that this blatantly perverse human being begins to resemble *us*. Not you or me particularly, but *we* as our modern environment (or what the Man from Underground would call modern civilisation) has determined our existence. To have urged this only twenty years ago would have seemed near preposterous. It is only comparatively recently that writers such as Pinter in this country, for example, seem really to be concerned with Everyman. If one can accustom oneself to reading *Notes from Underground* in this retrospective light, it soon becomes evident that the narrator in his own extravagant manner is pointing with his finger along some of the major cracks in the fabric of modern society.

Notes from Underground begins with a section which is hardly more than a prologue. The Man from Underground tells the

---

* The quotations used in this essay are all taken directly from David Magarshack's translation *A Gentle Creature and Other Stories* by Fyodor Dostoevsky, London, 1950.

reader about himself. 'I am a sick man. . . . I am a spiteful man. No, I am not a pleasant man at all.' We very soon learn that his chief drawback is a lack of talent for anything at all; not even for spitefulness, of which he might seem to possess more than a moderate endowment:

> Not only did I not become spiteful, I did not even know how to become anything, either spiteful or good, either a blackguard or an honest man, either a hero or an insect. And now I've been spending the last four years of my life in my funk-hole, consoling myself with the rather spiteful, though entirely useless, reflection that an intelligent man cannot possibly become anything in particular and that only a fool succeeds in becoming anything.

In the very next sentence comes the crux of the *Notes* and one of its major paradoxes: highly civilised man necessarily lacks character, whereas a man of character must essentially be lacking in imagination, or as the narrator put it: 'A man of the nineteenth century must be, and is indeed morally bound to be, above all a characterless person; a man of character, on the other hand, a man of action, is mostly a fellow with a very circumscribed imagination.' It is quite easy to be duped by the Man from Underground into supposing that the final laugh is on the ordinary man of limited awareness, when in actual fact it is modern man with his passion for the 'sublime and beautiful' who is well on the way first to spiritual, then to total biological extinction. For a test-tube man (little more than a joke was intended by Dostoevsky's character) may well have some form of being, but of whatever nature it may be, it is not *human*.

It is in Section II that the ontological critique begins. The initial premiss, we learn, is that consciousness is a form of sickness.

> I assure you, gentlemen, that to be too acutely conscious is a disease, a real, honest-to-goodness disease. It would have been quite sufficient for the business of everyday life to possess the ordinary human consciousness, that is to say, half or even a quarter of the share which falls to the lot of an intelligent man of our unhappy nineteenth century who, besides, has the double misfortune of living in Petersburg, the most abstract and premeditated city in the world. . . . It would have been quite

sufficient, for instance, to possess the sort of consciousness with which the so-called plain men and men of action are endowed.

At this stage he holds up to our gaze another major paradox: heightened cultivation of the sublime ideal only plunges one into the mire. We find no clue to this riddle in the *Notes*, and we have to wait for Dmitri Karamazov, who discerns the artificiality of the division beautiful/ugly or sublime/ignominious. There is in reality only a continuum, which Dmitri naturally finds exhilarating, yet sheer hell to live with.

'Intensified consciousness' has already compelled the Man from Underground to a realisation that he is a blackguard, a damnable admission for a sensitive, intelligent man; 'as though it were any consolation to the blackguard that he actually is a blackguard'. Just then we seem to be drawn abruptly into what looks like a side track, which soon seems to become the major issue. At the root of the malady of modern man is his own major discovery, the laws of nature.

> . . . what hurt most of all was that though innocent I was guilty and, as it were, guilty according to the laws of nature. . . . For I should most certainly not have known what to do with my magnanimity–neither to forgive, since the man who would have slapped my face, would most probably have done it in obedience to the laws of nature; nor to forget, since even though it is the law of nature, it hurts all the same.

One aspect of the predicament of conscious man is that his existence is unbounded, and purposive activity becomes difficult or impossible. The 'stone wall', which represents the circumscribed ordinary consciousness, is the theme of Section III.

> Before such a stone wall such people, that is to say, plain men and men of action, as a rule capitulate at once. To them a stone wall is not a challenge, as it is, for instance, to us thinking men who, because we are thinking men, do nothing. . . . No, they capitulate in all sincerity. A stone wall exerts a calming influence upon them, a sort of final and morally decisive influence, and perhaps even a mystic one.

The Man from Underground can never at any stage be taken absolutely seriously, but, in the light of what has gone before, it would seem that he is as serious as he ever can be when he says:

> Well, that sort of plain man I consider to be the real, normal man, such as his tender mother nature herself wanted to see him when she so lovingly brought him forth from the earth. I envy such a man with all the strength of my embittered heart. He is stupid – I am not disputing that. But perhaps the normal man should be stupid. How are you to know? Which brings us round to another facet of a paradox already discussed: the conscious man of great sensibility is no man at all – but a *mouse*. I grant you it is an intensely conscious mouse, but it's a mouse all the same, whereas the other is a man. . . .

And one further paradox before the reader leaves this section. Although it is men of advanced consciousness who have elaborated the laws of nature and mathematics, it is precisely these that constitute the 'stonewall' which seems to have such a calming influence, to be so categorical to the mentality of the plain man. 'When, for instance, it is proved to you that you are descended from a monkey, then it's no use pulling a long face about it: you just have to accept it.' When the Man from Underground asks: 'Is it not much better to understand everything, to be aware of everything, to be conscious of all the impossibilities and stone walls?' we glimpse the tragedy of the situation. For there would never have been any stone walls or mathematical impossibilities if scientific man had not dreamt them up:

> To reach by way of the most irrefutable logical combinations the most hideous conclusions on the eternal theme that it is somehow your own fault that there is a stone wall, though again it is abundantly clear that it is not your fault at all, and therefore to abandon yourself sensuously to doing nothing silently and gnashing your teeth impotently, hugging the illusion that there isn't really anyone you can be angry with; that there is really no object for your anger and that perhaps there never will be an object for it. . . .

The following section, together with Section V, is partly an 'interlude' in which the narrator indulges his sense of fun and partly a 'polyphonic' section to the second part of the novel, since the theme is each time 'aesthetic man'.

Section VI is a development of motifs already announced: 'The legitimate result of consciousness is to make all action impossible, or–to put it differently–consciousness leads to thumb-twiddling.' We find further clarification of the behavioural processes of the plain man. It seems that owing to his arrested mental development the latter mistakes secondary causes for primary: 'in this way they persuade themselves much more easily and quickly than other people that they have found a firm basis for whatever business they have in hand and, as a result, they are no longer worried, and that is really the main thing.' The 'man of intense consciousness' can unhappily never locate any primary causes; they all seem secondary, an infinite regression of secondary causes. Everything dissolves or disintegrates on examination 'as a result of those damned laws of consciousness. One look and the object disappears in thin air, your reasons evaporate. . . .'

So far all has been mere reconnoitring. It is only in Sections VII to IX that we sail hard against a fierce current, as near as we ever do to the 'core' of the monologue. In the first part of this voyage the opposing principles of the laws of nature and individual human freedom are pressed gradually closer and closer together, creating such a tension that one feels the monologue must at any moment snap. The process begins with a brilliant but straightforward critique of the utilitarian doctrine advanced by the British Philosophical Radicals, notably Bentham and J. S. Mill and taken over, although not quite lock, stock and barrel, by the Russian radicals of the sixties, Chernyshevsky, Dobrolyubov, etc.

> Oh, tell me who was it first said, who was it first proclaimed that the only reason man behaves dishonourably is because he does not know his own interests, and that if he were enlightened, if his eyes were opened to his real normal interests, he would at once cease behaving dishonourably and would at once become good and honourable because, being enlightened and knowing what is good for him, he would see that his advantage lay in doing good, and of course it is well known that no man ever knowingly acts against his own interests and therefore he would, as it were, willy-nilly start doing good.

Who was the 'innocent babe' who put forward such green
theories as this? Such a system simply does not stand up to a
few moments' reflection. 'To begin with, when in the course
of all these thousands of years has man ever acted in accordance with his own interests?' All statistical computations of
the collective good leave out one important item, which
upsets the entire calculation, *man's urge and capacity for doing
exactly as he pleases.*

> He will talk to you, passionately and vehemently, all about
> real and normal human interests; he will scornfully reproach
> the shortsighted fools for not understanding their own advan-
> tages, nor the real meaning of virtue, and–exactly a quarter of
> an hour later, without any sudden or external cause but just
> because of some inner impulse which is stronger than any of his
> own interests, he will do something quite different, that is to
> say, he will do something exactly contrary to what he has been
> saying himself: against the laws of reason and against his own
> interests, in short, against everything. . . .

The Man from Underground seems to have made considerable headway already, but his attack, it seems, is still
only at the beginning. If one looks at the matter in a different
way, one is easily persuaded that man is actually improving
morally. At this juncture Buckle's theory that civilisation
softens man, who consequently becomes less bloodthirsty and
less liable to engage in wars, comes under attack. All that
civilisation has done, we are told, is 'to develop in man the
many-sidedness of his sensations, and nothing, absolutely
nothing more'. Which leaves man more deadly than before.
'The most subtle shedders of blood' are not the Attilas and
Stenka Razins but civilised men. 'Civilisation has made man,
if not more bloodthirsty, then certainly more hideously and
more contemptibly bloodthirsty.' In the past he looked on
bloodshed as an act of justice and exterminated those he
thought necessary to exterminate with a clear conscience:
but now we consider bloodshed an abomination and we
engage in this abomination more than ever.' Even re-
education and conditioning may succeed, up to a point,
Planned Utopia (the 'crystal palace') may be attained. But
all to no avail. For just as soon as all is set fair for a new

Golden Age 'suddenly and without the slightest possible reason a gentleman of an ignoble or rather a reactionary and sardonic countenance' would arise amid 'all that future reign of universal common sense and, gripping his sides firmly with his hands', would say to us all: "Well, gentlemen, what about giving all this common sense a mighty kick and letting it scatter in the dust before our feet simply to send all these logarithms to the devil so that we can live according to our foolish will?" That wouldn't matter, either, but for the regrettable fact that he would certainly find followers: *for man is made like that.*' The last few words have been italicised because they bring us once again face to face with one of the major concerns of the Man from Underground. He is all the while trying to capture and isolate what is essentially *human*; and he has decided that scientific laws and method are non-human. The fundamental truth is that man is wilful, capricious, man wants to do as he pleases. Not only this but he '*positively should*'. 'All man wants is an absolutely *free* choice, however dear that freedom may cost him and wherever it may lead him to.' Man has always been and will always be like this. The only pity (and this is implicit in the Man from Underground's argument) is that modern man is much cleverer, more consciously aware than his forebears, and this together with his newly acquired technological means makes him potentially more dangerous and harmful. He may even do something incredibly stupid and wicked simply in order to prove that he is still his own arbiter. At this point the way is open to the theme of *Crime and Punishment*, but the Man from Underground instead presses further his main argument.

I repeat for the hundredth time that there is one case, one case only, when man can deliberately and consciously desire something that is injurious, stupid, even outrageously stupid, just because he wants *to have the right* to desire for himself what is very stupid and not to be bound by obligation to desire only what is sensible. For this outrageously stupid thing, gentlemen, this whim of ours, may really be accounted more valuable by us than anything else on earth, especially in certain cases. And in particular it may be more valuable than any good even when it is obviously bad for us and contradicts the soundest conclusions of our reason as to what is to our advantage, for at all events it preserves what is most precious and most important to us, namely, our personality and our individuality.

It is this instinctive desire to preserve and assert personality and individuality which leads men to their greatest excesses and foibles. Raskolnikov plots and carries out a murder to assert his freedom. Kirillov (in *The Devils*) shoots himself to prove that he is God. Stavrogin dreams of the crime which will outrage humanity for all time. One thing you *cannot* say about man is that he is sensible. 'The best definition of man is – a creature who walks on two legs, and is ungrateful.'

> He will, man will, out of sheer ingratitude, out of sheer desire to injure you personally, play a dirty trick on you. He would even risk his cakes and ale and deliberately set his heart on the most deadly trash, the most uneconomic absurdity, and do it, if you please, for the sole purpose of infusing into this positive good sense his *deadly fantastic element* [my italics]. Mathematical calculations drive him into a rage. If necessary, rather than accept the scientific evidence that he is no more than an organ-stop in some intricately predictable system, he will even go out of his mind just to prove his point.

Dostoevsky's insight at this point is impressive, for it has been established in our own time that certain cases of schizophrenia are self-determined, a curious uncontrolled kind of play-acting, in which it can almost literally be said that the insane person has lost his reason on purpose.

In Section IX the conclusions are faced up to. Firstly, is there the slightest reason for believing that man *should* be remade? Is there any reason for believing that the laws of logic and science are applicable to human behaviour? Not the least, asserts Dostoevsky's character. If that is the case, we must try and find out what man positively is. In the first place, man is a striver after goals, but possessing no taste for *attaining* goals. It could even be that man is 'instinctively afraid of reaching the goal and completing the building he is erecting': 'The excellent ants began with the ant-hill and with the ant-hill they will almost certainly end, which does great credit to their steadfastness and perseverance. But man is a frivolous and unaccountable creature, and perhaps, like a chess-player, he is only fond of the process of achieving his aim, but not of the aim itself.' The whole of life may be no more than an incessant striving, and a dread of achieving. 'Twice-two-makes-four is not life, gentlemen. It is the beginning of death.' Man is thus, when all is said and done, a comical creature, and perhaps there is some joke behind it all. There is plenty of evidence too that man prefers suffering to well-being. In him is a propensity not only for suffering, but even for chaos and self-destruction: 'Whether it is good or bad, it is sometimes very pleasant to smash things, too.' And finally, the wheel comes full circle when it might even be argued that suffering is the origin of consciousness.

The next section, Section X, was considered by Dostoevsky to be the key section of the novel. Unfortunately it has been so badly mangled by the censor that it lacks coherence and makes incomplete sense. It was certainly intended to be the culmination of the ontological critique. The Man from Underground finally rejects the vision of Utopia, the Crystal Palace, if only because he will not be permitted there to stick his tongue out. The only way he can be persuaded to accept the Welfare State is for his desires to be destroyed and his ideals eradicated, and for him to be shown something better. It is from this point that the legend of the Grand Inquisitor in *The Brothers Karamazov* logically begins. The Inquisitor saves the multitudes from themselves by holding up to them the Mystery, the Miracle and the Authority. It is only by this cynical yet humanitarian device that the ageing cardinal's subjects have become like sheep.

In the closing section of 'The Dark Cellar' our obtuse monologist covers his retreat, using every device capable of disquieting his reader, without however at this stage wanting to alienate him entirely. There are throw-away remarks of the most provocative kind, as if purposely saved up for the occasion. One of these has been reckoned to be among Dostoevsky's most profound observations:

> There are certain things in a man's past which he does not divulge to everybody but, perhaps, only to his friends. Again there are certain things he will not divulge even to his friends;

he will divulge them perhaps only to himself, and that, too, as a secret. But, finally, there are things which he is afraid to divulge even to himself, and every decent man has quite an accumulation of such things in his mind. I can put it even this way: the more decent a man is, the larger will the number of such things be. . . .

Now, this melancholy comment is ostensibly a digression on the subject of public confessions, whereas in fact it is a cleverly arranged 'bridge passage' between the two parts of the novel. And more besides. Notice the way in which the author has partly, although not entirely, resolved one of the key dilemmas: the ordinary man has the advantage of being more real, more like what a human being ought to be, but the superior man, although ineffectual and ridiculous in real life, has the satisfaction of being able to observe and scorn the limitations, even stupidity of his opposite number. The formula: 'the more decent a man is, the larger will the number of such things be' is a different way of viewing this dilemma and at the same time lifts the problem out of the moral and metaphysical domain into the aesthetic. The criterion is from now on *decency*. Decent man is limited man, and we must not imagine that in Part II: 'A Propos of the Wet Snow' the Man from Underground is getting the better of his ordinary-men antagonists any more than he did in his earlier monologue. But what does emerge—and this is the most significant development in the *Notes*—is a third stage, which takes the dilemma on to a hitherto unseen plane, and thus begins a developmental line, leading from the prostitute in 'A Propos of the Wet Snow' through Sonya Marmeladova in *Crime and Punishment* (also a prostitute), to Grushenka (another prostitute) and Dmitri Karamazov. In the last analysis true humanity requires a greater vehicle than the ordinary, decent plain man, for it must be able to recognise and at the same moment accommodate with compassion the superior intelligence and sensibility of highly conscious modern man, yet avoid the intellectual and spiritual pitfalls by virtue of its own incapacity for self-conscious ratiocination. The measure of truly human being is neither the conventional, decent ordinary man nor the hypercritical and sensitive product of modern urban civilisation, but one that includes but also far surpasses both these types. This latter must possess the intuitive qualities of wisdom and understanding, the moral virtues of humility, courage and compassion; and above all, must be a vehicle of the 'living life'.

It is by no means evident that Dostoevsky had all this consciously worked out by the time he composed the *Notes from Underground*, although he certainly had by the time he wrote *The Brothers Karamazov*. Was it not rather that he himself was working towards his final realisation by those very intuitive qualities which of necessity operate largely in the unconscious? 'A Propos of the Wet Snow' speaks for itself. Read in conjunction with the first part, 'The Dark Cellar', it can be seen to develop the same theme, not intellectually this time, but aesthetically.

Although the Man from Underground believes that he is morally superior to the 'decent' man ('For my part, I have merely carried to extremes in my life what you have not even dared to carry half-way'), it is easy to see that he is no more than their antithesis. His being out of touch with real life produces cruelty, bookish cruelty. He is wicked, because in order to be good he would require an approving audience; like Satan, he cries: 'They–they won't let me–I–I can't be good.' He is humiliated by Lisa's genuine superiority:

> I was so used to imagining everything and to thinking of everything as it happened in books, and to picturing myself everything in the world as I had previously made it up in my dreams, that at first I could not grasp the meaning of this occurrence. What occurred to me was this: Lisa, humiliated and crushed by me, understood much more than I imagined. . . . I wanted to be left alone in my funk-hole. 'Real life'–so unaccustomed was I to it–had crushed me so much that I found it difficult to breathe.

In losing his taste for living, he has gradually turned into an 'anti-hero'. But, once again, he swiftly turns on the reader and reminds him that we are all anti-heroes, so greatly have we lost touch with life.

We are cripples, every one of us – more or less. We have lost touch so much that occasionally we cannot help feeling a sort of disgust with 'real life', and that is why we are so angry when people remind us of it. Why, we have gone so far that we look upon 'real life' almost as a sort of burden, and we are all agreed that 'life' as we find it in books is much better. . . . We are stillborn, and for a long time we have been begotten not by living fathers, and that's just what we seem to like more and more. We are getting a taste for it; soon we shall be inventing some way of being somehow or other begotten by an idea.

The following essay is an attempt to explore Dostoevsky's own search for the 'real life', his own roots, in the period after his return from Siberia, and the form that this quest assumed during the course of the great creative period of his life.

ROOTS

In marked contrast with the general scurrilous tone of his monologue the Man from Underground lets fly a number of radical criticisms at modern (synonymous with 'Western') man. Some of these criticisms are among the most fundamental ever raised. Why, he asks in his 'epilogue', do we get so hot under the collar when people remind us of our ill-concealed disgust for the real, honest, unexpurgated life? The Russians have a concept 'the living life', partly liturgical in origin, and difficult to translate into Western European idiom. It is the 'living life' that this Petersburg Man from Underground is talking about, and it is the basic ingredient that we have ignored to our cost.

> Why, we don't even know how to come by real life any more, we have no idea what it is, or how to identify it. Take away our books of reference, and we at once get confused, lose ourselves in a maze, not knowing what to cling to, what to hold on to, what to love and what to hate, what to respect and what to despise. It is even a problem for us to be what we are, men of real flesh and blood, *our own* flesh and blood. We are ashamed somehow. We think it a disgrace. And we do our best to be some theoretical 'average' man.

The whole tenor of his monologue, even his misanthropy, derives from uprootedness, a disease whose diagnosis is nowadays so frequent as to be tiresome. 'We are still-born, and for a long time we have been begotten not by living fathers, and that's just what we seem to like more and more. We are getting a taste for it; soon we shall be inventing some way of being somehow or other begotten by an idea.' Dostoevsky has found a new theme, an important theme which is to find a place in all his subsequent novels. In a sense, his major novels are *about* uprootedness, if indeed they can be claimed to be *about* anything.

48

What is meant by roots? Simone Weil has luckily given us the perfect definition:[1]

> A human being has roots by virtue of his real, active and natural participation in the life of a community which preserves in living shape certain particular treasures of the past and certain expectations for the future. This participation is a natural one, in the sense that it is automatically brought about by place, conditions of birth, occupation and social surroundings. Every human being needs to have multiple roots. It is necessary for him to draw wellnigh the whole of his moral, intellectual and spiritual life by way of the environment of which he forms a natural part.

The wistful note is familiar. No recent treatment of the theme is without it.

The problem of roots and rootlessness is not confined to technologically advanced societies. In his comparative study of extant myths, Mircea Eliade has used the term *autochthony* for a feature he finds universally distributed and clearly related to the Earth Mother myth: 'It is in this sense that autochthony should be understood; men feel that they are *people of the place*, and this is a feeling of cosmic relatedness deeper than that of familial and ancestral solidarity.'[2] It is no mere passing phase, all this talk of and preoccupation with roots. In Chinese culture, to cite a case of some significance, race and soil share a fundamental indivisible unity. The notion of a close identification between a country and its inhabitants was at certain periods of Chinese history so firmly believed in,[3] that it remained right at the heart of religious institutions and civic rights.

In the context of our mid-twentieth-century preoccupation with uprootedness and rootlessness as major social and ethical ills, new concepts have crept into our vocabulary. These range from the startling idea of 'retribalisation'[4] to more general, often historical, attempts to trace the severance of European man from his roots. As to whether there was any single moment at which this alleged severance occurred one is entitled to have one's doubts, but the problem was certainly acute in Russia by the second quarter of the last century. Pechorin, the 'hero of our time' in Lermontov's novel of that name, was certainly the prototype of generation after generation who were to suffer from loss of identity. Dostoevsky's Man from Underground is a fairly sophisticated exponent. The Russian malaise, not so very different from its European variants, has only recently found a new kind of resolution in Pasternak's Zhivago, but in a manner in which only the most advanced of our own age is capable of comprehending, let alone coming to terms with.

1 *Dostoevsky autochthonist*

'Autochthonism' in Russia, like a number of other cognate 'isms', has its origins in the honeycomb of Herder's theories. His idea of nationhood was early imported into Russia. Herder proposed nationhood as a purely and strictly cultural entity, the belief in the value of belonging to a particular group or culture. Transposed into Russia, it soon took on the extravagant forms of Slavophilism. The supposedly glorious past, already familiar to European opera audiences through the works of Glinka, Mussorgsky and Borodin, was over-idealised to the point of absurdity. The early slavophiles sometimes romanticised obsolete institutions such as serfdom, and deserved a good deal of the obloquy they provoked.

By the late 1850s Slavophilism was beginning to be replaced by mutually antagonistic movements which regarded themselves as more sophisticated, with more respect both for history and political theory. The first of these was a group of writers and journalists whose movement quickly acquired the label *narodnost'*, a noun almost impossible to translate. 'Nationism' would do if such a word were possible in English ('nationalism', on the other hand, is misleading on account of its bellicose overtones). *Narodnost'* is nothing other than the cult of the nation in the Herderian sense of the word. The movement's originators were either disillusioned or embarrassed by the excesses of the Slavophiles, and wanted to work out their own enthusiasm for their 'native soil' in their own superior way.[5] Out of *narodnost'* or 'nation-ism' there arose imperceptibly a new movement which can best be translated as *autochthonism*.[6] It based itself squarely upon the *pochva* or 'soil' and its followers became known as *pochvenniki*, that is, 'autochthonists'. No satisfactory definition of the movement's central idea has been given, although its concern was with the question of 'grass roots' and the very problem of uprooted-ness already discussed. The *pochvenniki* belong inextricably to the early 1860s, the time of the emancipation of the serfs and its attendant social disruption, the period of massive invasion from the West of liberalism, utilitarianism, socialism which threatened to overwhelm the still tender and volatile intelligentsia, the decade during which the most recently established social institutions were either rapidly decaying or being transformed. To this period belong *Crime and Punishment* and Turgenev's *Fathers and Children*, as well as numerous other 'significant' works. The *pochvenniki* were, in what they felt to be a sensible way, trying to stem the tide of social disintegration. Its chief exponents were the literary critic Apollon Grigoriev, the journalist Nikolay Strakhov, and, for a very brief period, Dostoevsky himself. Their organ was the journal *Vremya* (*Time*), published and edited by Dostoevsky's brother, Mikhail.[7]

Not all the pochvenniks were professional writers or journalists. The movement soon attracted fanatics, one of whom was certainly psychotic and not at all unlike a character of Dostoevsky's early work. Its policy found wide support, and *Time* almost immediately attracted many sub-scriptions. The journal ran for two years; it was suppressed after the publication of a provocative article opposing government action over the Polish question. Its successor, *Epoch*, ended almost as soon as it began with the death of Mikhail Dostoevsky, the indispensable man behind the scenes.

Russian Autochthonism began with the work of Apollon Grigoriev. The idea itself was, as we have already seen, not original. But Grigoriev did not hesitate to work it into his own shape. His own particular brand of 'philosophy of the soil' evolved out of his critical method, which he called 'organic criticism'. This new method was to be a refinement and corrective of the 'historical' criticism engendered by Belinsky and his generation. Grigoriev never quite managed to define 'organic criticism'. In one place, he described it as 'an outlook on art as a synthetic, integral, direct and intuitive understanding of life, as distinct from science which was no more than analytical knowledge based upon data'.[9] A great deal was made of the plant analogy. The plant has its own biography, and is extended in time; like a plant, literature too has its roots in the past, in its own genesis, and is all the while extending its branches into the future. 'From the external aspect of a plant you arrive eventually at the roots.'[10] In the same way as a plant, an art or literature must thrive in its own soil. How can one look at a work of art or poetry purely from the aesthetic point of view, when it has all the growing properties of a plant organism? 'Literature visibly grows.'[11] In literature, the analogy of the idea is the flower; 'everything ideal is nothing other than the flower of reality'.[12] Grigoriev was thinking not of the life studied by the botanists and zoologists, but of the 'living life' asserted by the Man from Underground.

Grigoriev's writings were seldom blessed with lucidity, and his recurrent inspirational tone laid him wide open to ridicule. In private life by contrast, he was genial, viva-cious, and his sense of fun came as a surprise to some. He was at his gayest when playing the guitar and delighting his friends and co-revellers with a rich repertoire of Russian folksong. The majority of his contemporaries drove him to fury with their hardened scepticism and irreverence: 'As long as there are Dobrolyubovs[13] it is impossible for an honest writer with any self-respect to do his job properly.'[14]

Dostoevsky admired Grigoriev's Russianness. For a brief spell he became one of Dostoevsky's close friends. Dostoevsky was no easy companion, but his new friend was theatrically hypersensitive, impulsive and pig-headed. Special allowances were made for him: 'he is capricious and impetuous, like a raving poet'. He had to be wheedled and tricked into doing things, and no one seemed to be able to save him from his own undoing. For Dostoevsky, he typified 'the man of the soil, rugged, and the most Russian of all his contemporaries'.[15] Those who have spotted a connection between him and Shatov in his later novel *The Devils* are probably not mistaken.

Fet, the poet, recalls the time when he was sharing digs with Grigoriev, and one day the latter came home dressed in simple folk costume. He threw himself on the ground declaiming an absurdly patriotic poem.[16] This was Grigoriev's peculiarly ecstatic brand of autochthonism. Life and art were the same process. Life expected to be given form in men the conscious artists. There was, he believed, no such thing as humanity or mankind; they were abstractions. The only realities were 'races, families, individuals, etc.'[17] Literature he called 'the voice of a particular soil'.[18] Russian folksong and idiom he envisaged as an organic growth, layer upon layer, each layer added by successive generations. Song he held to be the most fundamental of art forms; 'song is not merely the plant, but the soil itself'. 'Our folk song is no mere bundle of archives, but a living thing as far as ordinary people are concerned.'

For Grigoriev, then, autochthony was neither predominantly social, historical nor cultural; it was certainly not political. Sometimes it amounted to nothing more than a vague feeling for the Russian grass roots. As such he was the movement's founder.

Dostoevsky's own connection with the movement was primarily through the highly gifted Nikolay Strakhov. This beguiling armchair philosopher dominated Dostoevsky's intellectual horizon during the half-dozen years immediately following his return from Siberia. It has been persuasively argued[19] that Dostoevsky drew the depths of his metaphysical insight from this man. The influence could coincide with a period in which Dostoevsky dropped his preoccupation with the theories of milieu and environment apparent in *The Insulted and Injured*, and replaced it with the idea of unconditional individual freedom first appearing in *Notes from Underground* and almost certainly arising from his protracted discussions with Strakhov. They even travelled abroad together, but their entire trip was one interminable dialogue, from which they were apparently reluctant to be interrupted by intrusions.

If Grigoriev provided the foundation, Strakhov erected the superstructure. It was Strakhov who first used the term *pochvennichestvo* 'autochthonism'.[20] Originally it may have been a corollary to his critique of utilitarianism. It was the latter that was taken up and expounded with such brilliance by Dostoevsky's Man from Underground; and like him, Strakhov gushed ideas. 'We are none of us cogs in a machine; each of us is a character in that comedy or tragedy we call life.'[21] There is a streak of Epictetan stoicism in him, and his special irony is part of it. In Strakhov we catch glimpses of the 'ungrateful man' of his time who prefers a hencoop to a Crystal Palace, and who proposes 'giving all this common sense a mighty kick and letting it scatter in the dust before our feet'.[22] The theme of inscrutable and unpredictable man, possessed of a 'deadly fantastic element', is probably Strakhov's.

The pochvenniks' journal *Time* was already under scathing attack from the radicals, particularly Dobrolyubov, the most formidable of them all. In one article Dostoevsky takes up Strakhov's anti-utilitarianism: 'Man possesses his own independent organic life.' Beauty in the final count is more useful than utility, for it is the ultimate goal of existence; 'beauty will save the world' is a motto of more than one of Dostoevsky's later characters. Meanwhile the public image of autochthonism, lumped together with all the earlier national and slavophile movements, had become an object of journalistic fun. Antonovich, the radicals' chief parodist, did the obvious:

> We have cut ourselves off from the soil, from the womb of our beloved mother, ancient Russia, . . . dolled out in tight German clothes, we drink water in place of homely kvas. It's kvas that's lacking! The Romans fortified themselves with it, and were able to bring the whole world to its knees. If only we had gone on drinking kvas, we should long ago have united all the Slav peoples into one large and brotherly family and then our land would have waxed great and abundant.[23]

The autochthonists did not quite deserve ridicule such as this.

The pochvenniks were either not able or not interested in giving as good as they got. They were either deeply engrossed in their own thoughts or else trying to sort out their financial affairs. They had little energy left for anything more.

Strakhov has left us a description of Dostoevsky during this period:

> He was constantly absorbed in something taking place within him. He was bursting with ideas and it was always difficult for him to detach himself from this preoccupation and to get down to writing. To all appearances a man of leisure, he never actually stopped working. . . . Thoughts boiled up within him, ceaselessly, new images were forming, projects for new works, while earlier projects went on growing and maturing.[24]

Dostoevsky's own particular fascination for folk types of course antedates his acquaintance with the pochvenniks. One should not, however, base too much on his *Notes from the House of the Dead*, for almost all of this was written after his return from exile. There is, though, a single letter of 1854 to his brother Mikhail in which he portrays the 'profound, forceful and fine' characters he had encountered among his fellow convicts. 'What a pleasure it would give one to seek out the gold hidden beneath their rough bark.' Two years later, he wrote to Maykov: 'I have such a kinship with everything Russian that even the convicts did not frighten me,–they were the real Russian people, my brothers in misfortune, and I was fortunate more than once even to find magnanimity in the cut-throat's heart, for the very reason that I could understand it; for I was a Russian myself.'[25]

A theme that runs through Dostoevsky's non-literary contributions to *Time* is the rift between the cultivated minority and the ordinary people. We find it in the *House of the Dead*, where the convicts despise their squire-convict for wanting to soil his hands with manual 'dirty' tasks when he could quite easily get out of them. The ordinary convicts felt that here was a man ingratiating himself with them. It was painfully difficult for him to find acceptance among the people. 'Even if you were on familiar terms with them all your life, and had been for forty years in close everyday touch with them you would never really get to close quarters with them.' In *Time* Dostoevsky accuses the slavophiles of ivory-tower idealism: 'The ordinary man will chat with you, confide in you, joke with you; he will even weep in your presence . . . but he will never regard you as one of his own.'[26] The only ultimate solution was for the intelligentsia to become like the ordinary people. Not only should the intelligentsia be prepared to sit at the feet of the common folk, but should do this very thing *before* setting themselves up as their mentors, since teaching with a patronising streak would never win their respect.

In places Dostoevsky appears to be adapting Grigoriev's theory of art, although he would seem to be distorting it rather clumsily. The whole approach seems entirely out of place in Dostoevsky's hands. The important fact to be noted however is that his interest in aesthetics dates from this time, and by the time of his last three major novels it assumes a central position.[27] It is Dmitri Karamazov who becomes the 'bearer', the embodiment of the aesthetic idea.

With the suppression of *Time* Dostoevsky's journalistic activity ceased for the time being. His *Notes from Underground* appeared in part in *Epoch*, the journal's successor. The Man from Underground is pre-eminently a member of the intelligentsia, even if a 'retired' one. His education is European, he suffers from the 'disease' of consciousness, is overoccupied with himself, and cannot identify his roots, 'renouncing the soil and native roots, as they say nowadays'. He sees himself the insubstantial creature of an 'abstract civilisation', and worse, an inhabitant ('the double misfortune' as he calls it) of the most abstract place in the world – the city of St. Petersburg. His bitter complaint is that he, in common with others like him, has 'lost the art of living'. Life has ceased to be the fully organic 'living life'. He suspects he was not born naturally but in a test-tube or retort. Defying the liberal empiricists, he argues that 'human nature acts as a whole, and all that is in it, conscious or unconscious, could well be a pack of lies, but at least it lives'. The second part of the *Notes* consists of a parable illustrating the impossibility of genuine human intercourse between beings who have lost their reality.

Like all else in Dostoevsky the Man from Underground evolves and takes on new shapes. Autochthonism likewise. Dostoevsky's imagination was too volcanic to allow for fixed

views and outlooks. Our next task will be to trace at least a
few of the ramifications in the work of the last fifteen years of
his life.

2 'A great idea'

It has been claimed that in Russia the power of abstract
ideas is so great that at times concrete actuality has become
submerged by them. This is as true in the era of Marxist-
Leninist dogmatics as in almost any decade of the last century.

The 'folk' is a definite entity. But 'folk types' are abstractions. Dostoevsky left behind his raw impressions of the
convicts he portrays in the *House of the Dead*. Flesh and blood
turns to the vapour of an ideal. Only the 'form' remains,
'the skeleton of its spirit'.[28]

We begin to find rationalisations of the cruder sides of the
ordinary man. 'Don't judge the people by the nasty behaviour of which they are often guilty, but by its great and
holy deeds, by virtue of which they still go on breathing life
in spite of all the crudeness.'[29] Like his disciple Rozanov,
Dostoevsky is inclined to accept the folk 'not as it really is,
but as it wishes to become'.[30] This attitude of some ten years
after is in marked contrast with his earlier view that the
people should never be over-idealised, but accepted at face
value with all their sincerity, kindness, meekness and of
course cruelty. In Siberia he was sure that the 'filth' was
skin deep and would disappear of its own accord in time.

There is nevertheless one character who offsets much of
the flagrant adulation of the folk in the pages of the *Diary of
a Writer*. This is Makar Dolgoruky of the novel *The Raw
Youth*. He is of crucial importance. Makar, it will be remembered, is the peasant foster-father of Versilov's illegitimate
son, the raw youth of the novel. Makar arrives on the scene
only very late in the novel to salvage a rapidly deteriorating
situation. Whereas the other major characters are clearly
of the abstract imported European civilisation, Makar by
sharp contrast is essentially a man of firm and deep roots.
A tramp indeed, but as the raw youth reminds them, less of a
tramp than any of them: 'it is he who has a firm footing in
life, while we all the rest of us have no definite standpoint at

all . . .'. This foster-father from another planet embodies the ideal folk virtues: 'extraordinary pure-heartedness and freedom from amour-propre', 'gaiety of heart', 'seemliness', along with the equally indigenous 'sly subtlety'. Compare him with that other famous folk ideal, Platon Karataev of *War and Peace*, and one notices just how remote from reality and tangibility is Tolstoy's ideal peasant. Makar Dolgoruky, on the other hand, stinks of the peasant pilgrim–Dostoevsky goes out of his way to get this effect. Makar is concrete and palpable, the rest of the characters in the book, with two exceptions, make no impact upon our senses whatever. Makar's fondness for stories, usually tall stories, was another important ingredient:

> I'm not familiar with any of these stories [the young narrator admits], but I believe he told them all wrong, adapting them for the most part from the traditions current among the peasantry. It was simply impossible to accept some of his versions, but together with distortions or even inventions there were continual flashes of something wonderfully complete, full of peasant feeling, and always touching. . . . I frankly confess it was almost impossible to listen to the story without tears, not simply on account of sentimentality, but through a sort of strange ecstasy:

As we shall see elsewhere, story-telling in Dostoevsky has two aspects, good or bad, not according to whether the stories are true or false, but mainly according to their *aesthetic* truth. Fyodor Karamazov was also a prize story-teller, but in a bad sense. Makar Dolgoruky's stories, no less tall, are minor works of art and therefore true and valid.

The author of *The Diary of a Writer* takes a fresh look at the slavophiles.[31] They have come a long way since the early 1860s, having become more political and pragmatic, turning their attention to present realities, while managing to preserve their former Russian Orthodox idealism. There were still the kvas advocates, but there were now economists besides. There were also a few politically militant panslavists. There was a fourth group, to which Dostoevsky loosely belonged. They were protagonists of the 'spiritual reunion' of all those who believed Russia to be in possession of some 'new, whole and still unheard word' to give to the whole world. This was Chaadaev's 'third world idea' refurbished. And Dostoevsky turns to jingoism: 'wholeness and the spiritual indivisibility of the millions of our (Russian) people' must be thought of in the light of 'their most intimate relationship with the sovereign'.[32]

The 'religious panslavism' subscribed to at a certain period by Dostoevsky is not, as some believe, just another form of Russian Tsarist Imperialism with its acquisitive eye on the Balkans and Eastern Mediterranean. It was based on a genuine belief that Europe was in need of regeneration, that the time was ripe for the renewal of the Christian Church in the 'Third Rome'. There is even some doubt as to whether Dostoevsky was ever *un*ironically committed to this design. Dostoevsky must never be taken at face value; and even what one supposes to be *his* diary is, one should note, entitled *The Diary of a Writer*. If it is asked: Whose diary is it then if not Dostoevsky's? The answer cannot be framed simply, for the 'third world idea' so pompously extolled in the Diary is given one of the most paradoxical twists of all by Versilov, the ambiguous father in *The Raw Youth*.

Europe [claims Versilov] has created a noble type of Frenchman, Englishman and German; of the man of the future she scarcely has any idea at present. And, I fancy, she has not wanted to know. And this one can well imagine; they are not free and we are. . . . Take note, my dear, of a strange fact: every Frenchman can serve not only his mother country but the whole of humanity, but only on condition that he remains French to the utmost possible degree. And it's just the same for the Englishman and the German. Only to the Russian, even in our own day, has been vouchsafed the capacity to become pre-eminently Russian only when he is being most European, and this is true even in our own day, that is, long before the millennium has been attained. That is the most essential difference between us Russians and the rest, and in that respect the situation in Russia is as nowhere else. In France I am a Frenchman, with a German I become German, with the ancient Greeks I am a Greek, and by that very fact I am most typically Russian. By that very fact I am a true Russian, and am most truly serving Russia, for I am bringing out her leading idea. I am a pioneer of that idea. . . . To the Russian, Europe is as precious as Russia: every stone is cherished and dear. Europe is as much our fatherland as Russia. . . . Only Russia lives not for herself, but for an idea. . . .

The really successful thing about Versilov from a technical point of view is that neither the reader, nor his son Arkady for that matter, can ever be quite certain that Versilov is not simply *sneering* or, at the very least, being supercilious.

Versilov's 'idea' is only an ironic variant of that put forward in Dostoevsky's celebrated Pushkin Speech,[33] one of his last utterances. But can one even be absolutely sure that the Pushkin Speech, the climax of Dostoevsky's career, was entirely free from dramaturgic projection? To express this doubt in a slightly different form: Was Dostoevsky ever simply himself? Was he ever perfectly aware, as most people are, when they are being sincere and when acting a part? It is not possible to view the Pushkin Speech as yet another projection of Versilov, this time in a real public setting on the rostrum before a large audience? The reader may be objecting that all these conjectures are over-subtle and without foundation. But before taking a firm stand on this, my reader ought to compare the *tone* of Versilov's and the Pushkin Speech; they are remarkably and disturbingly similar. Dostoevsky had found the right eloquence for the occasion:

> We have absorbed into our soul the spirits of other nations, not as enemies but as friends, with complete love . . . we have openly declared our readiness and inclination . . . towards a universal reunion embracing all mankind. . . . Yes, the destiny of the Russian is incontestably all-European and universal. . . . O, those nations of Europe, they do not realise how dear they are to us![34]

But what if Europe was unwilling to accept Russia's 'great idea'? Was it to be imposed upon them by force? The idealism, sincere or artificial, of the Pushkin Speech is one thing, but Dostoevsky's correspondence with Pobedonostsev is another. There were times when Dostoevsky was possessed by ideas, and it was at such moments that they became their own mockeries and perversions. After all, this is mainly what his novel *The Devils* was about. But it is equally necessary not to abandon oneself to the other extreme, like Stavrogin, for whom there remained only one solution – suicide. Dostoevsky must at times have been aware of the precarious balancing act he was engaged in for a good part of his life. One should not take too seriously those who claim Dostoevsky for Christianity, or for anarchy and destruction, or for cruelty, authoritarianism, humanitarianism, or anything else. Dostoevsky's task was to prevent himself being claimed, and to go on discovering, without hindrance, whatever the consequences.

3 *Mystical autochthony*

During the 1870s, the last decade of Dostoevsky's life, a new political force had come into being in Russia. Its members called themselves *narodniks*, 'populists'. The founder of populism was Lavrov. In his *Historical Letters* Lavrov claimed that every educated man had obligations towards the common man, who was the pillar supporting all that was possible in the way of enlightened endeavour and artistic achievement. . . . The whole 'temple of culture', as he put it, was built on foundations prepared by manual labour. For this reason everyone who regarded himself as a member of the intelligentsia was obliged to repay his debt to the people by taking part in the foundation of a social order capable of providing cultural and welfare amenities for everyone instead of for a privileged minority.

Populism had an immediate success, attracting a wide assortment of young people of both sexes, of every political colour and conviction. Lavrov's 'method' took the form of peaceful propaganda, which he supposed would catch on and spread like a bush fire. A massive 'crusade to the people' was planned and thousands of fire-in-the-belly idealists recruited. Going from village to village they took every kind of manual occupation they could find, working as craftsman's mates, hospital orderlies and operatives in factories. Out of this ferment sprang terrorist organisations, first *Land and*

Freedom, and later the truly fanatical *Party of the Popular Will*. It was these developments that Dostoevsky foresaw and satirised in his *Devils*.[35]

Out of populism, later revived on a sounder theoretical basis by Mikhailovsky, grew the Russian Marxist faith in the common man, the people, the *narod* 'a mysterious and compelling force which holds the secret of life and is the repository of some special truth'. Berdyaev's now oddly sounding sentiments were in similar and related forms quite usual among the Marxist intelligentsia. There was more than a tinge of religious faith: 'in the people the intelligentsia rediscovered the God they had lost'.[36] Marxism had its extreme right and extreme left. But deist and atheist, the pious and the sceptical found much common ground:

> There is the same idealisation of the people and reactionary hostility towards culture, there is a similar inhibition of the personal principle and the cultivation of personality, responsibility and honour, a similar incapacity for spiritual autonomy, a similar intolerance, a similar seeking for truth outside rather than within oneself; the disease of the national soul is manifest at either pole.[37]

All this is a far cry from post-Stalinist Russia, and it is not difficult to pinpoint Berdyaev's long obsolete Marxism. Our concern at this point is only with the beginnings, and Berdyaev was right about these. The Marxist and populist *élans* found their focus in Lenin.

Dostoevsky was a populist apart. His own brand derives from his *pochvennik* period. Berdyaev has claimed for it the special title 'religious populism': 'By the people, Dostoevsky understood the mystical organism, the soul of the nation, as a great and mysterious whole.' The suggestion is that Dostoevsky took his 'folk truth' not from the peasant, or from any social type in particular, but from the depths of his own being. 'Dostoevsky was more "popular" than the people themselves.'[38] There was nothing sanctimonious about Dostoevsky's adulation of the peasant. He had lived with them and knew the reckless power, whether for good or evil, that might at any moment manifest itself:

forgetful of all limits, the need to go beyond the limits, the need for a sensation which can freeze the heart with terror, the kind to be experienced at the edge of the precipice, half hanging over the edge and glancing downwards. . . . It is the need for negation which is implanted in man . . . the need to deny everything, the things most sacred, the most sublime ideal. . . . One is struck by the haste with which Russia aspires to express itself in evil and good alike—whether in love, drink, debauchery, pride or envy—the Russian abandons himself to it without reserve, ready to burst everything and to deny all: his family, his traditions, God himself.

The first work in which we find religious populism (as distinct from *pochvennichestvo*) is *The Devils*, and the character in which this is concentrated is Shatov. In the rough drafts of the novel Shatov is a rudimentary Stavrogin, a bearer of Russia's sin; he is at this stage no 'god-bearer' but the embodiment of *shatost'* 'precariousness'. In the rough drafts of the novel the actual 'bearer of the Russian Orthodox idea' is Golubov, a character with no future at all in the actual novel. He foreshadows Zosima in *The Brothers Karamazov*, although it is clear that Dostoevsky was not yet ready to take on a character of such dimensions. Golubov was to represent the ideal Russian. His motto is 'paradise attainable on earth'. 'Paradise', he maintains, 'is in existence right now and the world has already been created to perfection. Everything in the world is joy.' His task was evidently to convert Stavrogin to belief in God. His philosophy is religious populism: 'You will have to show more humility; stop looking on yourself as something, and then you will gain salvation and peace.' It is not difficult to observe the way in which Golubov is distilled into no less than three persons: Shatov (the God-bearer of the actual novel), Tikhon (the saintly former archbishop), and Kirillov (the 'paradise on earth' motif). For a resynthesis we have to wait until *The Brothers Karamazov*.

The abandonment of Golubov leaves much ground for speculation, especially as Shatov takes on his actual physical characteristics. Berdyaev thought that Dostoevsky could identify himself better with Shatov than Golubov in his hesitation at accepting the God of Christianity. The truth was probably a great deal more complicated than this. Berdyaev may have been right nevertheless in supposing that Dostoevsky was passing through a phase of 'pagan particularism',[39] the conception of a tribal god. Shatov addresses Stavrogin:

> Do you know which is at the present moment the only God-fearing people in the whole world, getting ready to renew and save the world in the name of the new god, the people to whom the keys of life and of the new gospel are given? . . . Up till now each people has been no more than a people; the time has now arrived for everyone to have his own particular god and rigorously to exclude all other gods whatsoever.

A people without its own god is, according to Shatov, no longer a great people but only an ethnographical unit. The one great 'God-bearing people' has already arrived on the scene; and this can only be the Russian people. Berdyaev believed that 'the antinomies, temptations and iniquities' of the Russian messianic idea are summed up in Shatov's person.

The quirk of Russian messianism is that Christ easily particularises into the 'Russian Christ', a peasant god-man. It will not be out of place here to take a further look at this 'pagan tendency in the very bosom of Russian Orthodox Christianity'.[40] Before the Revolution, and possibly since, pagan particularism was a fairly important ethnic, social and even political problem. In pre-revolutionary Russia there were a number of sects on the fringes of the Orthodox faith, some of which cultivated a blend of asceticism and bacchantic ecstasy. Just as European Russia shades off into Asia, so the parish priest merges into the dervish and shaman. In his work on these sects Rozanov is astonished 'to observe the combination of these broken-off pieces of Orthodox christianity with their current of religious convulsionism, having not a thing in common with a single christian church'.[41] Whirling dances were their means of attaining ecstasy; and apparently they were discovered by these sects and not borrowed from ancient practices or those prevailing in the orient.

The less unorthodox sects were the Old Believers and the

dissenters or Raskolniks. The name Raskolnikov is a particularly apt pun on the latter, in that the Raskol Schism represented a form of manicheism, the ascent towards an ideal, an effort towards the best and the supreme, but in addition posited the goal of perfection on the human scale of being. The 'Raskol' ideal is Nietzschean revolt, or rather the striving towards the man-god. Completely outside the orbit of the Russian Church are the *Skoptsy*, renowned for abominable acts of self-mutilation, the *Dukhobors* who, like Golubov (the character in Dostoevsky's notebooks), believe that paradise is already attained, the *Molokany*, and the *Khlysty* who combine in their worship and techniques of ecstasy a deep Russian Orthodox faith with incompatible bacchanalia. The word *khlyst* is interesting etymologically, fusing* as it does the Russian words *Khristos* 'Christ' and *khlyst* 'a whip or scourge'. They were scorned both for their savage sado-masochistic practices and their magic ritual sacrifices. In common with the *Skoptsy* they had their own 'tribal' or sectarian Christ. On account of their unique combination of purity, asceticism and pagan excesses they have been called 'gnostic quakers', if such a thing is imaginable.

Especially fascinated by these sects was Rozanov, the 'pup out of the Dostoevsky kennel', as he was once called. Rozanov was attracted to them for a variety of reasons. The first and foremost of these was that these sects contained for him explanations both of what was lacking in the Orthodox Church and of what could be observed as actuality. He could not close his eyes to the most patent simple bond between the priest and congregation in any Russian church which was stronger than any affiliation to Christendom. Moreover, since the time of the Petrine Reform[42] the true life of Russian popular religion had gone out of Russia: 'As regards the religious life of Russia not only are we ignorant of the facts, but even the very documents relevant to it can only be obtained in London.'[43] 'The religious spirit has dried up and Russia has been maimed.' Hence Rozanov's desire to come into contact with the lunatic fringe which were

* the /r/ of *Khristos* and the /l/ of *khlyst* are 'fused' by the linguistically well-established process l/r metathesis.

regarded as greater nuisances than gypsies. Only in these sects could he detect any of the ecstatic religiosity of which there was no sign any longer in the 'official' Church liturgy.

All these sects had developed Christianity in their own particular ways. Any member of the *Khlysty* could become a Christ or *khlyst*; the historical Christ was not different from themselves in kind but only in degree; they described him as a big God among lesser ones. They saw themselves in an immediate sense as 'God's people' (*Bozhiyi Lyudi*). The *Skoptsy* made much of the practice of receiving and giving blows on the face. 'The more a man can bear, the more filled he is with divine strength.' The one who receives the blow 'keeps silence so that on the morrow he may have the possibility of proudly telling his offender: "My God is greater" meaning "in me there is more God than in you".'[44] Incidentally, the reader may recall that this was the very same attitude cultivated as a virtue both by Prince Myshkin and Stavrogin in *The Devils*. We know extremely little of Dostoevsky's interest in the sects, and perhaps a great deal remains to be deduced. It is most likely though that, like Rozanov, he was not so much interested in their rituals or even their creeds as in the essence and form of their religiosity.

'Perhaps God is only my mood', writes Rozanov. 'My God is my own special God. He is my God and nothing more. . . . My God is my own boundless intimacy, my limitless individuality.'[45] Prayer for him was the *dance* of prayer:

'I am about to begin the great dance of prayer. With pipes, music, the lot: And there are going to be no holds barred, simply because everything will be sought in prayer. We shall be permitted anything, because after all our prayers are offered to God. But we shall not go to excess, we shall hold ourselves in check, and stop at the Karamazov limit; for in our dancing we shall be keeping God constantly in mind and won't want to anger him.'[46]

Insanity? At least, D. H. Lawrence did not think so; he regarded Rozanov with some respect, as one of the really honest Russians, with more honesty in his little finger than Dostoevsky and Tolstoy put together.

My belief, as I have stated elsewhere, is that Lawrence misjudged Dostoevsky, for the latter was by no means the naïve Orthodox churchgoer Lawrence took him to be. It is very easy to equate Dostoevsky's ideal with Zosima's, but there is no firm evidence for making such an equation. What evidence there is points to his holding a fanatical and atavistic view of Christianity which sometimes threatened to get the better of him. Dmitri Karamazov is no less Dostoevsky's darling than Zosima; and it must be remembered that Dmitri's love of God is overtly bacchantic and dionysian. Entering into Dmitri's profound, one is tempted to say chthonic, conception of the Logos we share his bewilderment; there are chasms all around him into which he was in danger of leaping or falling inadvertently. Dostoevsky likewise, for his author must have faced the same dangers. Perhaps *shatost'* is the right description: *precariousness*.

Vyacheslav Ivanov discovered what he claimed to be the true mythical roots of Dostoevsky's work. 'Dostoevsky's mystical realism, which has its roots in the ancient conception of a living Earth Mother, flourishes in the mythological interpretation of the universal life. . . . Earth, representing the whole of Nature, and to whom Dostoevsky offers a special worship, is drawn into the mystery of the Passion of the Son of Man.'[47] The first appearance of this mystical adoration is supposed to occur in *Crime and Punishment* with Sonya's curious advice to Raskolnikov to 'go to the cross-roads, bow down before the people, and kiss the earth' for the very reason that he had 'sinned before it'. The myth is clearer in *The Devils*, where Marya Timofeyevna has more than once been identified as the embodiment of the Earth Mother. A poor imbecile is chosen for this role, as here is contained the 'mystery of the Earth Mother'. Marya Timofeyevna, although the phrases she utters are no more than disconnected ramblings, is given a special voice, like Ophelia. Her scenes are transposed on to another plane, as with Pushkin's transfigured Tatiana in the closing scene of *Yevgeny Onegin*. She is a sorceress. Stavrogin's demented bride raves on: 'The Mother of God is the great Earth Mother, and she offers great joy to men. And every sorrow borne by the earth, and every tear she sheds, is a joy for us.' Ivanov detects an entire plan behind Marya Timofeyevna, but her role and actions must be interpreted symbolically. The mirror she holds is the symbol of 'the universal soul perpetually reflected in Nature'.[48] This is the prejudice of a symbolist poet, if you like, but Ivanov's deceptively glib explanations are deeply embedded in the Russian poetic tradition. 'Even her lameness is a sign of her secret guilt on account of her hostility towards God . . . an imperfect loyalty, a sign of her primordial resistance to the bridegroom who deserted her [Stavrogin].'

If Marya Timofeyevna symbolises the Earth Mother, then Stavrogin clearly represents the uprooted West. Stavrogin is bearing not a god, but a burden. His burden crushes him finally. The existence of God is for Stavrogin no intellectual or ethical problem, for his God is, like Nietzsche's, dead. The burden is all that remains, the void unfilled. The only thing left to do is to experiment, to go and seek. The emancipated 'liberal' finds himself on the open road with Stepan Trofimovich, the 'Russian liberal', chilled with dire forebodings; for 'it made no difference; even with the clearest recognition of all the horrors awaiting him he would have gone out on to the high road and walked along it'.

DOSTOEVSKY AT CLOSE QUARTERS

In the summer of 1862, less than two years after his return from exile in Siberia, Dostoevsky made his first trip abroad. His travels took him all over Europe. In his *Winter Reflections on Summer Impressions*, he writes: 'I have been in Berlin, Dresden, Wiesbaden, Baden-Baden, Cologne, Paris, London, Lucerne, Geneva, Genoa, Florence, Milan, Venice and Vienna, and there are some places I have visited twice, and all in exactly two and a half months.' This short visit left a deep impression on him. Not only was this his first direct contact with European civilisation about which he had, like every educated Russian, heard and read so much, but it was also the beginning of his disenchantment and disillusionment. Europe was, it seemed, no more than a cemetery, a vast reliquary. In London, at the Great Exhibition, he had come face to face with a symbol of dehumanisation, which was to haunt him for the rest of his life – the Crystal Palace.

Glancing back at the list of places Dostoevsky visited, one begins to notice that his selection was not entirely random: a number of these cities were famous for their casinos. Dostoevsky returned to Russia in the grip of a moral infection, against which he was powerless, and which he took many years to overcome. The pretext for his trips abroad during the next five years was always roulette. His acquired passion reached maniacal proportions during a prolonged and enforced sojourn abroad immediately after his second marriage in 1867. Even his attraction towards the young student Apollinaria Suslova, with whom he was having an illicit affair, was no match for the incipient stages of this obsession of his. We very soon find Dostoevsky turning to his friends and acquaintances, one after the other; to his publishers, to Turgenev, to his sister-in-law, and to various other acquaintances, for money. Even his young mistress did not escape: 'I am asking you to come to my rescue in case you have the chance of borrowing from anybody for me. I have almost no hope, Polya. But if you can, do this for me. . . .'[1] Another letter followed this the same day: '. . . Polya, my dear friend, come to my assistance, rescue me! Please get 150 gulden from somewhere, that is all I need. In ten days . . . I'll pay you back. I don't want to leave *you* in difficulties. . . . But, in any case, let me have an answer as soon as possible. . . . I just do not know what will become of me.'

Like the raw youth of his later novel, Dostoevsky during this period had visions of becoming a Rothschild. (It is however important to be quite clear about this; the dream was of *becoming* not of *being* very rich.) Buoyant after minor successes at the tables, the novelist looks detachedly, and, so he thinks, scientifically into the possibilities. In a letter to his sister-in-law, he writes:

> During these four days[2]. . . I watched the players closely. . . . Please don't think I'm complacent after winning, or that I'm wanting to show off, when I say that I have found the secret of how not to lose but to win. I really do know the secret, it is terribly silly and so simple. It consists in keeping one's head the whole time, whatever the state of play, and not getting excited. That is all. It puts losing simply out of the question and makes winning a certainty. But that is not the point; the real point is whether, having grasped the secret, a man knows how to make use of it and at the same time is capable of doing so. A man can be as wise as Solomon and an iron character, and still get carried away.[3]

In a letter three weeks later to his brother Mikhail, we read that events did not meet his expectations. Gambling had evidently got the better of him:

> You ask how anybody who was travelling with the woman he loved could gamble away everything. My dear Misha, in Wiesbaden I invented a system, used it in actual play, and immediately won 10,000 francs. The next morning I got excited, dropped the system and lost immediately. In the evening I returned to the system, observed it strictly, and

quickly and without difficulty won back 3,000 francs. Tell me, how could I help being tempted after that? How could I fail to be convinced that I had only to follow my system strictly and luck would be on my side. . . . I believed in my system. . . . Suddenly I began to lose, could no longer keep my head, lost every halfpenny. After I had sent you my letter from Baden, I took all the money I had left and went to the tables; with four napoleons I won thirty-five in half an hour. This extraordinary piece of luck tempted me; I risked the thirty-five and lost them all. . . . In Geneva I pawned my watch.[4]

The combination of roulette and a turbulent affair with Suslova did not make for a congenial atmosphere in which to write. Everything was going badly. The plan or broad outline of his story *The Gambler* belongs to this period, but it remained no more than a conception until it made its appearance some four years later.[5] Writing to N. N. Strakhov from Rome, Dostoevsky explains:

I would have begun to write before now, but it is quite impossible here. . . . The subject of the story is as follows: a typical Russian abroad. . . . I take a straightforward character, though a man of many parts, albeit still immature in every respect, one who has lost all faith but dare not disbelieve, rebelling against authority, but at the very same time afraid of it. . . . But the main thing is that all his vitality, his strength, his impetus, his courage have all gone into *roulette*. He is a gambler, but no more a mere gambler than Pushkin's Avaricious Knight is a mere miser. He is a poet in his own way, but ashamed of this poetry because he is profoundly conscious that it is unworthy, although the necessity of *risk* redeems him in his own eyes. . . .

It could be that in this last sentence we have the clue to Dostoevsky's gambling mania. The remainder of this sketch will not however be concerned with *The Gambler*–which readers will either be already familiar with or will be able to read for themselves, the writer's own comments being superfluous–but with Dostoevsky himself, in a period during which we find him under close objective scrutiny. The period in question began in Dresden but mainly belongs to Baden; the observer is Dostoevsky's second wife, Anna Grigoryevna. A few words of explanation only are needed.

Anna Grigoryevna's diary speaks for itself. She began it a short time after her marriage and kept it up for a few months only. Imagine a young woman in her early twenties, in Europe for the first time, pregnant, left to her own devices while her husband goes off to the other end of Germany to gorge his appetite for roulette. All the while, she finds herself poised between the extremes of affluence and penury, their fortunes tossed recklessly from one extreme to the other. She explains that keeping a diary was no luxury, but a very necessary part of her life in those months, a sort of therapeutic dialogue with herself.

> The idea of writing a diary occurred to me for a number of reasons. . . . My chief reason was different from all the rest: my husband was for me such a fascinating, such an enigmatic person, and it seemed to me that it would be much easier to get to the bottom of him if I wrote down his thoughts and remarks. Moreover, as a foreigner I was completely alone, I had no one to share my observations or any of the doubts which had begun to assail me, and the diary was the friend to whom I confided all my thoughts, hopes and fears.[6]

The diary itself is compact and laconic. This effect was not due to any conscious stylistic intention, but rather to the fact that she had already vested her own life in Dostoevsky's. Her diary is his mirror. Its directness contrasts markedly with the more widely known *Reminiscences* which she wrote many years after Dostoevsky's death expressly *for publication*. The latter, though not lacking in literary merit, are by comparison maudlin and sentimental, written for 'worshippers', appropriately trimmed, and dyed in the passage of time. The diary, on the other hand, was written with no public in view and was never intended for publication. The fact that the work is not easy of access, and that extracts from it are usually juxtaposed with the *Reminiscences* with their different quality and aim, are sufficient justification for devoting some space here to this portrait.

But first a word about Anna Grigoryevna, Dostoevsky's second wife. The circumstances in which Dostoevsky met his second wife-to-be are well known. He was at the time working on the drafts of *The Gambler*. There was a time limit, with barely a month left to go. In desperation he resolved to hire the services of a stenographer. Anna Grigoryevna, then a student of shorthand, aged twenty, was recommended to him by her instructor. She was well-read, already a great admirer of the novelist, and full of her recent reading of *Crime and Punishment*. When she arrived at his flat on 4 October 1866 the whole place, especially the staircase, reminded her of the description of the house in which Raskolnikov lived. (After their marriage, he showed his wife the spot where Raskolnikov had hidden the loot.) Dostoevsky himself seemed uncomfortably like his weird creations. 'His face is worn, sickly. . . . His eyes do not match. . . . This disparity gives his face a mysterious expression.'

It was fortunate for Dostoevsky that Anna Grigoryevna Snitkina (to give her her maiden name) was from a well-to-do family who were at all times eager to help her. In the first years of their marriage he did not hesitate to take advantage of this fact, frequently urging Anna to write home for money. She needed little prompting, so anxious was she to be able to assist him.

At first the dictation sessions went badly. It took Dostoevsky some time to adjust to the situation. The first session was a total failure, and Anna had to return home with a blank note-pad. When she returned the same evening to resume dictation, Dostoevsky found his style still cramped. The pauses were long, and he occasionally padded them out with remarks which both disconcerted and amused his eager and business-like young stenographer. He is relieved, he confesses, that his stenographer is a woman. 'You never know with a man; he is sure to get a bit tipsy. With you that won't be a problem.' Unperturbed, Anna Grigoryevna kept her appointments, turning up when requested, and at length dictation got under way:

> After he had been dictating to me for some time, he asked me to read out to him what I had written, and at the very first sentence he stopped me. 'From Roulettenburg? Did I say Roulettenburg?' he asked. 'You dictated just that,' I answered. 'Impossible!' 'But is there actually a city of that name?', I asked. 'The action takes place in a city where there is a casino,

which I must have called Roulettenburg,' he replied. 'If there is such a place, you must have dictated it, otherwise how could I have known it. This place is perfectly new to me,' I said. 'You are quite right,' Dostoevsky admitted. 'I must have muddled things up!'

It was not long before Dostoevsky proposed marriage. Anna accepted gladly. There were the familiar financial difficulties on his side, but several weeks later he writes: 'I am absolutely delighted, and we can now consider the matter closed. I shall announce our forthcoming marriage to my relatives. . . .' And again four days later: 'Now, my precious Anya, this is how things stand. Our fate is decided, we have enough money and we will get married as soon as possible. . . . Whatever happens, we shall be married. And thank God, thank God! I embrace you and kiss you a thousand times. . . .'

Anna was devoted to her husband, and seldom wavered in her devotion. She was not at all like him. Anna Grigoryevna was down-to-earth, the opposite of temperamental, downright; even her limitations turned out to be blessings. It is practically certain that without her Dostoevsky would never have completed his last four major novels,[7] for she not only rescued him from himself on numerous occasions, but acted as his secretary, stenographer, financial adviser, publisher, agent, and general manager, all rolled into one. Without her he would, likely as not, have succumbed to a debtor's fate, for it was just about the time he met her that his gambling obsession was tightening its grip on him. It is typical of her that after four agonising years she even found a way of turning his crazy passion to useful purposes. In her shrewd way she had come to see that roulette was the only way out of his gloom and general anxiety, which had become obstacles to his writing. When in his most dejected moods, she would even encourage him to go off to the tables. She calculated that, even if they were 100 thalers worse off as a result, the loss would in the long term be more than amply recouped in the form of royalties from as yet uncompleted works.[8]

But calm nerves have to be cultivated. It took a considerable time for her to acclimatise herself to the precarious day-to-day existence in which she suddenly found herself. Before they were married, and even before they became engaged, Dostoevsky had told her that he saw three choices before him: to go to Jerusalem or Constantinople, to re-marry, or to go abroad and turn gambler. It was through Anna Grigoryevna that he was enabled to combine two of these choices.

Our episode begins with a picture of Dostoevsky emerging from the direction of the railway station in Dresden. He has been away almost two weeks on a roulette expedition to Homburg. She has a letter for him.

> I had already lost hope of meeting Fedya to-day, when he suddenly appeared in the distance. For a minute I gazed fixedly, as if not believing my eyes. Then I rushed up to him. I was so glad, so happy! He has changed a little, probably as a result of the journey. He was a little flushed, yet our meeting was a happy one.[9]

He takes the letter and reads it. It is from his former mistress, Apollinaria Suslova.

> Either he really did not know whom the letter was from, or he pretended not to know; but he just ripped the envelope open, then glanced at the signature, and began reading. At the time he was reading that letter I watched his expression. He read and re-read the page for quite a long time, as if he could not make out what was written on it. Then, at last, he came to a stop, and blushed scarlet. His hands seemed to tremble. I pretended not to know whom the letter was from and instead asked what Sonechka[10] was writing about. He said the letter was not from Sonechka, and he gave me a bitter smile. I have never yet seen such a smile on his face. It was a smile either of pity or contempt. I know only that it was a pitiable lost smile. Afterwards he became terribly distraught, and could hardly make out what I was saying.

Dostoevsky's moods were alternating rapidly between extreme touchiness and irritability on the one hand and equally extreme gentleness on the other. He had lost a sizeable sum of money in Homburg, and his loss did not increase his self-respect.

> In half an hour Fedya came home. He was terribly gloomy. When he began drinking his tea he said that I had moved the

table just to spite him. I told him it was stupid to say that I wanted to spite him. Then he began getting at me. He said he had run out of money, but had to find some, and that in any case I ought to respect him. This offended me terribly. . . . Several times he screwed up his eyes and said: 'You are spiteful!' I said that perhaps I was, but never towards him. He stared at me very attentively, evidently trying to guess what was in my mind.[11]

A few days later[12] the Dostoevskys were on their way to Baden. Within four days of their arrival Anna Grigoryevna could see that the worst was still to come.

To-day we had twenty-five louis. Of these Fedya took five; and when he left, he asked me to be dressed by the time he returned. . . . After he left I felt very sad; I was sure he would lose that money as well, and would start tormenting himself again. I cried several times, and felt as though I was going out of my mind. But Fedya came back, and I asked him quite indifferently: 'Have you lost?' 'Yes, I have,' he replied in despair, and began accusing himself. Pathetically he explained that he could only reproach himself for his weakness for gambling, that he loved me, that I was his beautiful wife, and that he was unworthy of me. Then he asked me to let him have some more money. I said: 'I won't let you have any more to-day, but I might give you some tomorrow.' On no account would I let him have any, as he was bound to lose it all and torment himself again. But F. went on imploring me to give him just two louis, so that he could go to the tables and find relief. There was nothing for it – I gave him the two louis. F. was in a state of agitation. He begged me not to consider him a scoundrel who would take away my last penny in order to gamble it away. I implored him to be calm. . . .[13]

Two days later.

. . . F. returned home in a terrible state. He told me he had lost everything, and began begging me to let him have two more louis. He said he just had to go on playing, and that he had no choice in the matter. He fell on his knees imploring me to give him just two more louis. . . . At length he came back, and told me he had pawned his wedding ring and that he had lost every halfpenny he possessed. He asked me to let him have three more louis to redeem the ring in case it got lost.[14]

On the very few occasions Dostoevsky's fortunes rose–and rise they did, quite dramatically at moments–he would go on a shopping spree, returning home with all kinds of luxuries for Anna; brief intervals of great happiness for them both. But two days were sufficient to reduce a comparative fortune of the equivalent of many hundreds of pounds to a few shillings.

> . . . All we now have left is one louis. I walked up and down the Promenade for quite some time, waiting for him to come out; but there was no sign of him. At last he emerged, told me he had lost the money I had given him, and asked me to allow him to pawn a number of things. I got out my ear-rings and brooch, and looked at them for a long, long time. It seemed it would be the last time I would see them. I was so dreadfully upset. I loved those things so much, they were Fedya's presents to me. . . . F. kept on saying how ashamed he was to look me in the face, that he was robbing me of the things I loved–but what was he to do, we had surely known it would come to that. . . . F. dropped down on his knees, kissed my breast, kissed my hands, saying that I was good and kind . . . and that there was no one better in the whole world. . . .

A few hours later Dostoevsky returned with the announcement that he had lost even the money he had received for the few articles he had managed to pawn. He swore he would never play again, and broke into sobs. 'Yes, F. was crying. He said: "I've robbed you of your very last thing, and gambled everything away." I began to comfort him, but he would not stop crying.'[15]

Her loneliness and insecurity, combined with the usual effects of pregnancy, soon turned into brooding. '. . . It seems to me that F. will stop loving me when we get back. It is as though I were not sure of his love. . . . It seems to me that he has never loved, that he has only imagined that he has loved, that there has never been any real love on his part. . . . I even think that he is incapable of love. . . .'[16] On top of everything came the epileptic fits, and they were the most alarming aspect of this new life of hers. These fits were equally a risk, a different kind of gamble; a gamble with some inaccessible dimension of existence. Her husband was the strangest of strangers when recovering from this epileptic unconsciousness. Usually he had difficulty in recognising her; he could not make out for some considerable time what she was saying to him. For several hours afterwards, he was the victim of unaccountable whims and passing moods. '. . . At seven o'clock we went out for a walk, but F. was suddenly seized with the desire to kiss my hand in the street, and said that if I did not let him do it, he would cease to regard me as his wife. Of course I did what I could to dissuade him: in the middle of the street with people looking on–it would be terribly ridiculous.'[17]

His epileptic fits brought depression. His mood became petulant and irritable, even capricious. Anna Grigoryevna describes an occasion when she got up to let him in.

> He told me he had brought me only one thaler. I understood that he had won one thaler, and said I was very glad for if he brought a thaler every day, it would not be too bad at all. I immediately realised I had spoken harshly to him, and started to apologise. Then he showed me his purse. There were thirty thalers in it. F. gave me 25 and kept 5 for himself. As he produced the money, his tone of voice was decidedly caustic. He said he had supposed that, if he had lost the money, I would have assaulted him. . . . He was away quite some time, and came back in a rage; he had lost the five thalers. . . . Yes, there's no doubt about it, I have to guard F. not only against others, but against himself too. He has not the least bit of self-control. He will make promises, even give his word, but he will act quite differently. . . . He is a strange man, but how splendid he is![18]

'We are like gipsies–one day we have plenty, and the next day we are broke. Just a short time ago we were two independent people, now we have to run about pawning things.' In the meantime Dostoevsky has sold all his clothes to a second-hand dealer. He confesses to her that he is still not ready for the responsibilities of family life.

> . . . We lay down and discussed our unenviable situation. We said how in the future we would look back on this time; the terrible heat, the landlady's screaming children, the smithy

with its hammers hammering mercilessly all day, and without a penny, all our belongings at the pawn shop, with the prospect of never getting them back, stifling rooms, bells clanging, no books to read, and wondering where the next meal would come from.[19]

. . . He came back looking pale and anxious. I was simply astounded. I could not restrain myself and exclaimed: 'It's sheer stupidity.' I was not so much annoyed at what he had lost, as by the fact that he simply could not rid himself of the notion that he was going to get rich by gambling. It is this idea of his which makes me wild, for it has done us so much harm . . .

It turned out that F. had felt hurt by my going to bed early. He kept pacing the room, muttering to himself. He was in a violent state of agitation. I asked him what was the matter. He told me it was no business of mine. Then he explained that he had been going through agonies for the past seven hours, that I had deliberately refrained from talking to him, that I had been avoiding him—which I decidedly had not been doing. I asked him to calm down and stop making a noise with his boots. The landlady's bedroom was quite close, and she would be very cross if he woke the children. . . . Suddenly F. announced that if I was going to shout at him, he would jump out of the window. He was in a terrible state and kept screaming that there was only him to blame for the difficulties we were in. Suddenly and without any connection he told me he hated me. I was terribly upset and burst into tears. I went into the other room and told him it was just a lot of humbug to tell me one minute: 'You have made me so happy,' and the next to say: 'I hate you.'[20]

His epileptic seizures were often accompanied by a morbid fear of death. Two days later he had a crisis of just this kind, only worse than usual. He came round after one such attack and 'began saying he was afraid he would die very soon. He asked me to take a good look at him.' He prayed like a man about to die. 'He asked me to take care of our future child, and to come and see if he was still alive when I got up in the morning.'[21]

Anna realised very quickly that their only hope was to escape from Baden to a place where there was no casino. Such a place was Geneva. As soon as they had enough to pay their rent and buy the rail tickets, she was determined to get him there.

> We began reckoning how much we needed to redeem our things, and found it would take about 100 gulden, if we included the ring which F. had pawned that morning for 20 francs. It was distressing. I burst out crying, and when he got cross with me I too lost patience and told him he had lost because he did not take my advice. . . . F. replied that gambling was a passion, and that was why he could not take my advice; but in other matters he always did as I wished.

Coupled with his crazy dreams of winning millions was the genuine desire one day to be able to help all kinds of people. When he brought up the idea this time, Anna sarcastically hailed him 'benefactor of mankind'. Dostoevsky was deeply hurt.[22]

Eventually, their luck changed. Suddenly gains began to outstrip losses. But Anna knew their prosperity would be short-lived, and with a certain amount of swift and delicate manoeuvring, she managed to disengage her husband from the tables. On 11 August, some five days later, they found themselves on a train bound for Geneva, a town many miles from the nearest gambling centre. At this point the diary ends.

The worst was now over with the addiction at least curbed, if not altogether eliminated. It was not until four years later however that Dostoevsky renounced gambling for ever. It was on a visit to Wiesbaden, when he lost as much as 180 thalers and had to put up with a series of setbacks and humiliations, that he resolved never to enter a casino again. Anna was convinced that he never went back on this. He wrote to her from Wiesbaden:

> A great thing has happened to me; the filthy craze which has tormented me for ten years (or more precisely since the death of my brother, when I found myself suddenly crushed with debts) has vanished. I used perpetually to dream of winning. I dreamt seriously, passionately. Now all that is over and finished. This time was actually the *last*. Can you believe me, Anya, that now my hands are free again? Gambling was a chain round my neck, but from now on I shall have my mind only on my work and shall not be dreaming for nights on end of gambling, as I used to.[23]

AN EPILEPTIC MODE OF BEING

IT seems odd that a novel as popular and intriguing as *The Idiot* should have provoked so little controversy; indeed hardly any worth speaking of. None of Dostoevsky's novels contains quite so many contradictions, anomalies and conundrums; none anticipates so strikingly the metaphysical tenor of our own day; and, above all, none has concentrated so intensely on the epileptic personality, the common factor existing between Prince Myshkin and Dostoevsky himself.

The Idiot is not only the least debated of Dostoevsky's novels; it is also the least understood and the most frequently misrepresented. The usual suggestion is that Myshkin is a modern kind of saint, a latter-day Christ. One is sometimes informed that he is the perfect man, and that he has attained to sainthood and mystical beatitude precisely as a result of his epileptic 'supernatural' experiences. The following remark, taken from an introduction to one of the English translations, is characteristic: 'The Idiot, working with a clear motive in an apparently disordered record of men and women at odds, brings a character at peace with himself . . . to bear upon the fortunes, cares and misunderstandings of other people. . . . Dostoevsky projected his other self, his surer and stabler spirit into this remarkable character.'

A thorough review of the novel and the relevant documentary material seems to me long overdue. The notebooks alone are sufficient to compel anyone to think again, to revise any pre-conceptions they may hold. Fragments of personalities, ideas and world-views kaleidoscope there in bewildering sequence. As for the novel itself, a careful and objective reading is called for. It will soon be observed that Myshkin's charm and otherworldliness are fraught with cunning and ambiguity. In fact, the Myshkin we were led to expect is somewhat different from the character Dostoevsky intended; the 'legendary' Myshkin is largely the creation of a group of commentators writing in the 1880s, the chief and long-discredited culprit being De Vogüé, whose sensational and extravagant outpourings influenced generation after generation in every country of Europe.

I am not trying to say that Myshkin is entirely devoid of redeeming characteristics; merely that these are the comparatively unimportant characteristics. When they are singled out for special emphasis they are bound to distort an otherwise intricate and many-sided picture.

Fundamentally, Myshkin, as he appears in the notebooks, is not very different from the manifestly sinister Stavrogin of a later novel, *The Devils*. He has much in common with Raskolnikov too. Even if the less prepossessing features emerge in the actual novel shrouded in ambiguity, they show up starkly enough in the rough drafts.[1] Large stretches of seemingly disconnected jottings contain such remarks as: 'The idiot speaks, looks and feels like an overlord.'[2] Another fragment runs: 'The chief characteristics of the idiot. Self-possession resulting from pride (and not from any ethical motive) coupled with rabid self-licence in everything. . . . He could easily have become a monster, but love saves him from this.'[3] Nastasya, as she appears in the notebooks, ridicules the idiot's romantic overtures. At this moment we catch a glimpse of the fully-fledged Myshkin. He reacts to her mockery by declaring his determination to go on loving her, even if she does eventually marry someone else. This would be the Myshkin with whom we are familiar, were it not for the curious rider suddenly revealing the other side of the coin: 'It is all the same to me, because I love only for my own benefit really.'[4] There is more than a hint that our Myshkin-to-be is inclined towards homicidal mania, and a positive suggestion that he is not the sort of man to stop at murder.[5]

The skilled intriguer is already apparent. But the icy exterior conceals a venomous core. In the second of the rough drafts (Notebook No. 11) the final shape of the character of Prince Myshkin is even more transparent. He now seems overbearing, arrogant and godlike: 'his idea is power devoid of faith, power lacking any application'. He is the 'great playboy figure', a representative of the rising generation. 'He is so morbidly proud that he cannot see himself as a god, and is so lacking in self-respect that he cannot help but despise himself intensely, eternally, even to the point of dishonesty.'[6] His one unchanging desire is to rise above all men, and in consequence is hated by many. The 'fondness for children' theme, first introduced in this setting, appears at its most incongruous and with a suggestion of the unsavoury, perhaps yet another warning against taking Dostoevsky too readily at face value. Very gradually the superficially child-like innocent crystallises; the universal laughing-stock, scornfully but gladly putting up with insults and indignities.

True, notebooks are only notebooks. It will be observed, nevertheless, that even in the actual novel Prince Myshkin, far from passively accepting a slap on the face, glares at the culprit with 'a strange, wild and reproachful look in his eyes'. His lips quiver, and his mouth twists into an uncanny grin. We may also observe that Myshkin, although generally considered a simpleton, is actually very far from stupid. He finds it suits his purpose to play the idiot. Most people are taken in by him, and many of the characters in the novel find him amusing and captivating. But he does not fool everyone. Nastasya for one has detected the hollowness behind his professed sentiments. She finds his contrived attempts at wooing ridiculous. In Nastasya's view, the Prince is simply toying with his own and other people's feelings.

Myshkin in the meantime gives not the slightest indication of having noticed her rebuff. Instead he goes on feigning indifference. Beneath a cloak of simulated innocence he makes the most of his talent for scheming, playing off the various characters one against the other, and never failing to exploit his charm and ingenuousness to the full. The one character who can clearly see through this mask—and says so—is Aglaya Epanchina. In her eyes Myshkin is the glib poseur, and thick-skinned in the bargain. His anecdotes she finds insufferable. During the earlier part of the novel, Aglaya seems to be a kind of written-in commentary on the *real* Myshkin, as if all the while prodding *us* lest we too, like nearly everyone else in the book, should be taken in by this princely humbug. It is Aglaya who gets him to admit his craftiness: 'Don't suppose I am so candid out of pure simplicity of heart,' he confesses. 'It is possible that I have my own profound object in view.'

To give him his due though, Myshkin is very much outside the ordinary run of impostors. It would appear that even Dostoevsky could not quite make him out. Myshkin was an undertaking that almost proved too much even for him, and on a number of occasions Dostoevsky seemed on the point of abandoning the novel altogether. A closer look at the period during which *The Idiot* was taking shape makes it perfectly plain that right up to the very last chapter Dostoevsky had no more than the sketchiest idea as to what would be the final shape of the novel, and especially its central character Myshkin.

The Idiot was composed in Geneva, a place Dostoevsky never really liked. These were galling times. Over and above the usual financial difficulties, the growing doubts as to whether they would ever manage to extricate themselves again from Europe, came the realisation that Dostoevsky was now a chronic invalid. Epileptic seizures were becoming almost daily occurrences. He complained that a single scene in the novel had cost him two very severe attacks which had left him completely prostrate. During the same period, he wrote to his publisher:

> I ought to tell you I have had various thoughts ticking over in my mind the entire summer and autumn (and some of them are pretty ingenious), but having to live with them has forced me to have certain misgivings about them, especially about the ones that could so easily have looked contrived, phoney or implausible. In the end I settled on a single idea, and set to work. I managed to get quite a lot down on paper, and then on the 4 December I flung everything to the devil. I can promise you that it will probably turn out a second-rate novel. But it is absolutely sickening to think that it will be second-rate and not unreservedly good . . .'[7]

Dostoevsky's pristine inspirations were already thick with weeds.

Just what am I to do? . . . My head is in a whirl. It beats me I haven't gone out of my mind. Anyway, on 18 December, I sat down to write a new novel, starting completely afresh. . . . As far as I am capable of judging, what I have produced so far is neither very remarkable, nor the least bit effective. For quite some time now a single thought has been tormenting me. Yet I have not had the courage to shape it into a novel, simply because the idea is too difficult, and I am not yet ready for it, despite the fact that I am fascinated by it, and considerably enamoured with it. My idea was to portray the perfect man. It seems to me that nothing could be more difficult, especially in these times. . . . Only sheer desperation has impelled me to come to grips with an idea, which so far has defeated everyone. I have gambled as in roulette, hoping that everything would come out right on paper. I shall never forgive myself. . . .[7]

In a well-known letter to his niece Sonya, Dostoevsky is far more explicit:

The main purpose of the novel is to portray the man of real excellence and beauty. . . . All those writers – not only ours but European writers as well – who have grappled with the task . . . have simply succumbed in the attempt. It proved too much for them. Beauty is an ideal, but no conception of this ideal has yet been worked out, either by us or by the Europeans. There has only ever been one true embodiment of beauty, and that was Jesus Christ. For this very reason the appearance of such an incomparably beautiful person remains of course an unfathomable wonder. . . . But I've gone too far. Let me say only this: of all the noble and splendid figures in Christian literature the most perfect is Don Quixote. But he is so, precisely because he is at the same time a comic figure. Dickens's Pickwick is comic too. . . . There is sympathy for the clown who does not know the value of beauty, and needless to say this man strikes a sympathetic chord in his readers. . . . I have nothing of this kind to offer, nothing so decisive, and for this reason I am horribly afraid it will be a resounding fiasco. . . .'[8]

This letter to his niece and a few other sources have generally provided the cue for which the commentators were waiting. There seems nothing inexplicable in the fact that we had to wait for the very final draft of the novel for the sublime figure of Myshkin to be fully realised and revealed. It should however be quickly pointed out that an isolated letter such as the one quoted can suggest an entirely one-sided picture. The only sections of the notebooks in which Dostoevsky appears to be shaping the ideal described to Sonya (and earlier to his publisher) are parts II and IV of Notebook No. 10. The remark 'The prince is Christ' occurs twice. There is also a reference to Pickwick and Don Quixote, and the claim that these two figures win their readers' affection not only because they are comic but also because they embody *innocence*.[9] Such remarks and references are exceptional; they are hardly more than parentheses. The Prince (this is now his title) is still the familiar schemer, still morbidly proud, especially of his infirmity, although it has to be admitted that his 'measureless superiority' appears to have vanished. For all that, he remains a sphinx. We are left in no doubt that the author intends to try to induce the reader to conclude this for himself without having to resort to hints.

The Idiot is of course far from being a fiasco. Many regard it as Dostoevsky's greatest novel. Nevertheless, one does not have to look very closely to perceive that the novel consists of three quite separate and ill-fitting sections. There are also three distinct Myshkins, a different one in each section.

The first of these sections coincides exactly with Part I of the novel. It begins in the railway compartment in which Prince Myshkin is travelling, returning to St. Petersburg after a prolonged period of psychiatric treatment abroad. It ends in the climactic scene in which Nastasya burns the money Rogozhin has been attempting to buy her with. Nastasya has gradually become a super-presence, having undergone a kind of apotheosis. The narrative has become more and more confused, and motives are on the point of becoming totally inexplicable, when the section ends. I am tempted to label this section 'Nastasya's section'. At this stage the Prince definitely retains many of the sinister characteristics evident in the rough drafts. There is nothing especially redeeming about him. As for Aglaya, she is scarcely a character at all in this part of the novel. Yet, despite the relative insignificance of her role, there is something vast and uncircumscribed about her. She seems to recede into infinity, dimensionless and hardly more substantial than a *presence*; more like an inner voice than flesh and blood. It is as if, at this stage, her role is restricted to setting Myshkin in true perspective, sometimes merely serving as a foil. One of her sisters whispers: 'The Prince is a great humbug and by no means an idiot.' Aglaya chimes in with this opinion by accusing Myshkin of quietism, cowardice and indifference. The author seems to be at pains to underline her contemptuous attitude towards him. Myshkin though does not flinch before her taunts. Concluding his idyllic account of the poor Swiss girl, Marie, he admits the real possibility of hidden motives behind his heart-felt reactions and sympathy. His charm works on all the members of the Epanchin family *except* Aglaya. She warns her mother: 'Don't be in a hurry, the Prince says he has some motive behind his simplicity.'

The second section contains the whole of Parts II and III of the novel, together with the closing scene of Part IV, the famous scene in which Myshkin and Rogozhin enact a Kafka-like ritual in the presence of Nastasya's corpse. The dream sequence, which is the very fabric of this section, does not escape the present-day reader's notice. It is also worth noting that this section contains practically all the psychopathological ingredients of the novel.

It would be difficult to single out objective criteria by which dream sequences may be identified. Kafka provides some clues, when his secondary characters sometimes act without apparent motivation, and sometimes quite arbitrarily, as if prompted from outside the given world contained in the narrative; scenes with no centre, and inexplicable even causeless effects and events encountered at every turn and from every direction. Nowhere more than in this section of *The Idiot* are such features to be observed. Years ago Alexey Bem[10] drew attention to the dream quality of Dostoevsky's work, and carried out detailed studies. His thesis has failed to bear fruit, possibly as a result of its neglect of the subtle distinction existing between the many possible intermediate degrees and qualitative states falling between unmitigated surrealism at the one extreme and the merely dream-like at the other. (How is it for instance that in *Crime and Punishment*

Dostoevsky succeeds in weaving hallucination and literal nightmare into an artistic whole, whereas in *The Idiot* he seems to have failed or perhaps even not to have made the attempt?)

From the very earliest pages of this second section we may discern a number of significant changes. Nastasya has receded into the background. It is Aglaya's turn to come to the fore. She now seems more circumscribed, more distinctly characterised, more palpable than in the earlier section. She still makes fun of Myshkin but no longer holds herself aloof. It is as if Dostoevsky has begun a fresh novel with a completely new character. Her earlier cynicism and precocious penetration have gone, and she has suddenly become blindingly superhuman. Myshkin has shed much of his charm and simple candour. Overnight he has been transformed into an open sore, a paranoiac introvert. He is now the helpless victim of his own irrational contradictions, completely engrossed in an all-absorbing dream. Everyone attacks him. Lebedyev's nephew takes up Aglaya's earlier refrain: 'Why are you smiling, Prince? You look as if you disapproved of me.' Myshkin replies: 'I am not smiling, but I really think you are in the wrong to some extent.' Lebedyev turns on him: 'Don't shuffle! Say plainly what you think. I am absolutely in the wrong, without any "to some extent".' This attack strikes at the root of Myshkin's major flaw. He can only speak plainly when there is some ulterior motive, such as flattery. The young fellow continues: 'You don't know what life means!' Rogozhin laughs: 'You don't know what anger is either.' Keller, another minor character, ridicules Myshkin's ignorance of human nature; he tells him: 'Nobility of mind exists only in dreams.' The Prince, although as innocent as a 'knight of the Golden Age', is paradoxically gifted with the ability to see right through other people. Aglaya produces a riddle. Her sister is supposed to have sketched a portrait of the innocent knight from the lines of verse composed by Aglaya:

> From his face he never lifted
> That eternal mask of steel.

Aglaya is at pains to emphasise that she is not simply riddle-making but in earnest:

> In the poem the knight is described as a man capable of living up to an ideal all his life. That sort of thing, she holds, is not to be found every day among people in our day. In the poem it is not stated exactly what that ideal was, but it was evidently some vision, some revelation of pure Beauty, and the knight wore round his neck, instead of a scarf, a rosary. . . . Of course it's all an ideal, and in the 'poor knight' that spirit reached the utmost limit of asceticism. He is a Don Quixote; only serious, not comical. I used not to understand him, and laughed at him, but now I love the 'poor knight' and respect his actions.

Not everyone will have noticed the irony and *double-entendre* contained in this discussion of the riddle, but it will be evident to those familiar with the notebooks. Aglaya's riddle is not wasted on Myshkin: 'His smile was too mocking to leave any doubt on that score.' In some strange and scarcely discernible manner, Prince Myshkin and Aglaya Epanchina are like the complementary halves of some composite personality.

'Myshkin Number Two' displays considerable insight into his own predicament. 'He had begun to blame himself for two contradictory tendencies – on the one hand to extreme, almost senseless confidence in his fellows; on the other to a "vile, gloomy suspiciousness".' He is obsessed by double motives. He confesses his misgivings when Keller challenges his honesty: 'Double motives are most difficult things to fight against. I have tried, and I know. God knows whence they arise, these ideas you speak of as base. I fear these double motives more than ever just now. . . .' As he wanders about the strange Kafkaesque park, looking for the green bench where Aglaya had promised to meet him, he muses on his days in Switzerland, on the time he climbed the mountain-side one sunny morning, and the ineffable beauty of his surroundings.

> He remembered how he had stretched out his arms towards the beautiful boundless blue of the horizon, and wept. What had so tormented him was the notion that he was a stranger to all this, that he stood outside this glorious festival. . . . Everything

seemed to know its own path and loved it, went forth with a
song and returned with a song. It was only he that knew
nothing, understood nothing, neither men nor words, nor any
of nature's voices; he was a stranger and an outcast.

Like Raskolnikov and the Man from Underground, he too is
a 'type of the Petersburg period', a man sprung from a test-
tube, a flabby bundle of theories, an 'aesthetic louse'. He is
dazzled by his own vision of Perfection which, he has
persuaded himself, is the only state worthy of attainment.
He has short-circuited the normal paths of living. Like
Raskolnikov he shudders at ordinary human existence, at
the torturer's words: 'not to worry, life will carry you straight
on to the shore and put you on your feet again'. The mere
thought of such a 'shore' full of normal healthy individuals
is, like the Utopia of the Crystal Palace he rejects, intolerable.
Like Stavrogin, and permitted a few more years of sanity,
Myshkin too might have hanged himself, with a covering
note protesting his soundness of mind.

Now a few words about the third and last section of the
novel. This falls entirely within Part IV (the final part) of the
actual novel, and is an altogether patched-up affair, both
dramatically and technically not up to the standard of the
rest of the novel. My own guess is that Dostoevsky included
this section by way of compensation. Up to now we have seen
very little of the saint we were led to expect. At all events,
Dostoevsky in this section takes extravagant measures to
emphasise and exploit the more redeeming aspects of his
hero. Moreover, all this is clearly very much an after-thought,
for there is hardly any sign of this glamourised Myshkin in
the notebooks. Suddenly Myshkin is universally liked and
admired. Even Aglaya now hangs upon his every word. Long
tirades on Roman Catholicism, the Antichrist, 'simplicity of
heart' and other cant, jostle with each other, superimposed
upon an entirely unconvincing narrative. The novel is saved
from anticlimax only by the sudden irruption of the surrealism of the previous section into the midst of all this artificiality when we suddenly find ourselves again with the
fantastic Myshkin, and with Rogozhin, after the ritual
murder of Nastasya. Readers may observe for themselves

that this murder scene really follows without interruption from the end of Part III. The intervening ten chapters are enough to disrupt the dream sequence but insufficient in their impact to destroy it entirely.

And yet, when all is said and done, the total impression of Myshkin, despite the way the presentation of his character is fragmented, is a profound one. It is almost as though the Myshkin Dostoevsky had really intended to create is present none the less, despite the three different Myshkins of the novel. A unique and compelling personality shines un-mistakably through the disjointedness; a personality of such aspect that it lies almost beyond literature, like Heathcliff in *Wuthering Heights*.

I think the main reason for this lies in the resemblance between Myshkin and his creator. Both are epileptics, and Dostoevsky seems to have grasped—in certain respects perhaps even more firmly than the psychologists—the true nature and significance of epilepsy. Indeed, we would do better to regard Myshkin not as a saint, but as a special but deviant kind of human personality.

At this point a few remarks about Dostoevsky's own epileptic experiences will not be entirely out of place. Although reports are faulty and occasionally inconsistent, it has been definitely established[11] that Dostoevsky was an epi-leptic. His epilepsy appears to have been of the *grand mal* type; seizures taking the form of violent convulsions, foaming at the mouth, appalling screams, and so forth, followed by a period of unconsciousness. Dostoevsky's symptoms were accompanied by the legendary 'aura', or preliminary phase of enervation or nervous exaltation, which in earlier times attracted so much awe and veneration. Dostoevsky's own fits were probably complicated by schizoidal and psychomotor symptoms, although this is by no means certain. The most reliable account of a single occurrence of epilepsy is given by Nikolay Strakhov, in a description which bears a remarkably close resemblance to that of Myshkin's last major attack:

It was, I believe, in 1863, on the eve of Easter. Latish, about eleven o'clock, he dropped in to see me, and we got going on a very lively discussion. I cannot remember what we were discussing, but I do know that it was of some importance and of a highly abstract nature. Fyodor Mikhailovich [Dostoevsky] became animated and began to stride up and down the room while I remained seated at the table. He was trying to express some exalted and ecstatic sentiment. When I came to his support, he turned and faced me with an inspired look in his eyes, indicating that his animation had reached its zenith. He stopped for a moment as if searching for words to express what he wanted to say; his mouth was already wide open. I was looking at him with rapt attention anticipating that he was on the point of saying something extraordinary and that I was about to hear some strange revelation. Suddenly there came from his lips a strange, prolonged, inarticulate cry, and he fell unconscious on the floor in the centre of the room.[12]

In the past it has frequently been intimated that Dostoevsky was using his epileptic characters (Myshkin, Kirillov and Smerdyakov especially) for dramatic effect, even perhaps for the purpose of instilling superstitious terror into the reader. All Dostoevsky's main biographers and commentators, in so far as they have touched on the subject at all, have regarded Prince Myshkin's epileptic aurae as the sign of mystical ecstasy or the moment of supernatural revelation. As one of the foremost of them puts it: 'The Prince knows from experience what cosmic harmony is, having himself been inside the veins of Allah, in Paradise. Dostoevsky and his hero in their ecstasy had glimpsed the divine foundation of the world, that 'fire within things' which forever burns in the soul.'[13]

Interpretations of this kind are misleading. Partly because they are out of keeping with the modern medical view of epilepsy, but mainly because they prevent us from grasping the burden of Dostoevsky's study of what is in fact a startlingly original and unfamiliar kind of personality.

Firstly, let us make a clean sweep of the fables and misinterpretations. It has been established for well over a century[14] that epilepsy is not really a disease at all, but a disorder of a functional kind, a sort of cerebral diarrhoea. A violent emotion or a shock can transform the most ordinary nervous symptoms into serious epileptiform seizures. Even a common-or-garden sneeze has been described as a healthy form of epilepsy. It is also known that epileptic attacks can be pretty convincingly simulated, and even self-induced.[15] Recently developed techniques of electroencephalography (popularly known as brain wave recording techniques) have further helped to remove a great deal of the mumbo-jumbo.

The only thing medical science leaves out is the *subjective* experience of the epileptic. It seems to me that this is where Dostoevsky's importance lies, for his insights seem to be well ahead even of those of our own day. His descriptions of Myshkin's seizures leave no details untold. Like Dostoevsky, Prince Myshkin exhibits all the symptoms of *grand mal* epilepsy. He describes his aurae as moments in which 'his entire being was awakened to intensity and light'. All his nervous anxiety is swept away in the culminating ecstatic second (never longer) during which the attack begins. An 'inexpressible' second of time:

> these moments . . . brief as they are, when I feel *such extreme awareness of my own being*, and consequently *more alive than at other times*, are due solely to the disease–to the sudden rupture of normal conditions. . . . What matter, though, if it be only a disease, an abnormal tension of the brain, if when I recall and analyse the moment, it seems to have been one of harmony and beauty in the highest degree–an instant of deepest sensation, overflowing with boundless joy and rapture, ecstatic devotion and life at its fullest. [My italics]

These descriptions have taken their place in the literature of abnormal psychology. Unfortunately, those who have quoted them in a scientific context seem sometimes to have been unaware of the ambiguity of Myshkin's words.

The first clue to the meaning of these words came from the pragmatists, when they defined epilepsy as a *functional* disorder, not an organic disease. An epileptic seizure, whether 'major' or 'minor', may be described as an affective reflex of the organism, but *not* a disease of the organism. Epileptic fits may be thought of as sudden releases of tension. And one need not be an epileptic to experience epileptic fits. One becomes an epileptic by experiencing such attacks; and this is really the point. Modern techniques of investigation only lend support to the view that epilepsy may be viewed under

93

one aspect as a psychophysical function or mechanism permitting release of acute tension. It would of course be facile to suppose that epilepsy is *only* this, and it would equally be foolish to claim that there are not many other sides and complexities to this disorder; but this 'release of tension' aspect provides just the clue we seek. Before Myshkin's attacks go protracted preludes, a gradual and relentless accumulation of nervous tension, and abnormal anxiety, reaching an enraptured climax, followed by a sudden and dramatic release, a lightning switch from infinitude to nothingness. In Taoist terms, a state transformed into its opposite, inconceivably heightened consciousness suddenly converted into banality and oblivion.

If epilepsy can be said to be a release of tension, it becomes thereby a form of human limitation. If these moments were to endure for more than a second of time, the epileptic would be transformed into a god, or into a superhuman monster (Kirillov), or simply annihilated. An epileptic, then, is pre-eminently one who founders and miscarries, one who is compelled to stop short of a goal, which will remain unattainable for the very reason that his personality is (to use a currently fashionable term) 'structured' in a particular way. Epilepsy, subjectively viewed, is that which limits and holds in check. No wonder then that Dostoevsky failed in his attempt to bring Myshkin within the bounds of a novel, for he was attempting the impossible. Myshkin represents his own unattainable ideal. Myshkin's bewildering complexity is the pointer to this unattainability.

Limitation notwithstanding, Dostoevsky does succeed both in conveying the immediate experience of the epileptic, and in describing the epileptic syndrome from a subjective as well as physical point of view. Thanks to Dostoevsky's clearsightedness and powers of description, thanks to his meticulous and acute psychological observation, we are able to grasp the totality of the many different elements making up this syndrome: sensory, emotive, psychic, physical, moral and metaphysical.

The basic disorder, the fundamental of this totality, we gather, is of a *metaphysical* kind. Myshkin, we learn, is the victim of an *apparently* real world, a victim of *ideas*. Unhappily he has access only to *theories about life*, but *not to life itself*. Myshkin's world, like Schopenhauer's, is very much his own idea. We feel this for page after page. Even the other characters in the novel are, in a certain sense, his own projections, especially in the second 'section', where they seem to inhabit *his* nightmare.

This metaphysical malaise in turn sets up disturbances of an ethical nature: guilt and moral obsession. Myshkin admits that he is suffering from a peculiar obsession. He discovers double motives behind every intention and action. This he blames for his lack of sincerity. He is at loggerheads with the world and normality. And again, in turn, this produces in the psychic or cognitive domain hallucinatory obsession, associated with a vague anxiety; Kierkegaardian dread. The process culminates in an epileptic seizure. Dostoevsky's supreme achievement lies in his synthesis of all these elements; he weaves into his scheme the entire world, even a thunderstorm.

The thunderstorm suggests a particularly vivid physical analogy of the epileptic climax, and it seems natural that Dostoevsky should have chosen it as a symbol. But that is not all. Internal evidence compels the conclusion that Dostoevsky advancing far beyond mere analogy, was intent on sweeping the entire cosmos into Prince Myshkin's 'ontological' crisis.

Already in the sixteenth century, Paracelsus had drawn attention to the relationship between the onset of a thunderstorm and the inner tension of the epileptic, and to the fact that the two phenomena often coincided. Paracelsus explained the relationship in terms of the medieval microcosm-macrocosm dualism. The reader may have noted that only rarely does Dostoevsky provide a scenario, and when scenic description does occur, there is always a very special reason for it. Accompanying the most critical of Myshkin's epileptic crises is a detailed description of the prelude to a thunderstorm. Dostoevsky weaves the two into a counterpoint in the Paracelsan outer-inner sense.

> In early summer in Petersburg there are often magnificent days—bright, hot, and still. This happened to be such a day. . . . He was in a state of nervous excitement and perturbation; he

noticed nothing and no one; and he felt a craving for solitude, to be alone with his thoughts and emotions, and to give himself up to them passively. He loathed the idea of trying to answer the questions that would rise up somewhere inside him. 'I am not to blame for all this,' he thought to himself, half unconsciously. . . . A few minutes later, in the street, he recalled something that had bothered him that afternoon. He caught himself doing something rather strange. . . . He was looking about all around him for something, he did not know what. He had forgotten it for a while, half an hour or so, and now, without warning, the uneasy search had started again. But he had hardly become conscious of this curious phenomenon, when another recollection suddenly flitted through his brain, interesting him a great deal for the moment. He remembered that the last time he had been engaged in looking around him for the unknown something, he had been standing in front of a cutler's shop, where certain goods were displayed in the window. He was extremely anxious now to discover whether this shop and these goods really existed, or whether the whole thing had been an hallucination. Today he seemed to be in a very curious condition, a condition similar to that which had preceded his fits in years gone by. He recalled that at such times he had been particularly absent-minded and could not discriminate between objects and persons unless he concentrated hard upon them.

Myshkin begins to be haunted by a pair of eyes, Rogozhin's eyes. He stays a while in the Summer Garden turning over in his mind the possible significance of this recurrent condition, which gnaws at his very being.

He could not doubt, nor even admit the possibility of doubt, that there was beauty and harmony in these abnormal moments, that they really contained the highest synthesis of life. . . . These instants were characterised – to define it in a word – by an intense quickening of the sense of personality. . . . For the rest he could draw little comfort from the dialectical part of his argument, for he could see only too clearly that the result of these ecstatic moments was stupefaction, mental darkness, and idiocy.

The tension is piled up with great art. 'The stifling atmosphere augured a storm, and the Prince felt a certain charm in the contemplative mood which now possessed him. . . . All the time he was trying to forget something, to escape from some idea that haunted him. . . .' Startled by his own thoughts he gets up from the park bench. 'A minute later, he was still moving along, but without being aware of the fact. He could no longer think out his new *idea*. He tried to take an interest in everything around him; in the sky, in the Neva. He spoke to some children he met. He could feel his epileptic condition on the increase. The evening was very close. Thunder could be heard some way off.' The outer-inner storm was just about ready to break. 'Where was his *idea*? He was having to go along without it now. Yes, his malady was coming back, there was no mistaking it. All this gloom and heaviness, all these *ideas* were nothing more nor less than the onset of a fit.' He goes to see Nastasya, drawn to her irresistably. Again those dreadful eyes appear. They are following him. 'A great change had suddenly come over him. He went blindly forward; his knees were shaking; he was tormented by "ideas"; his lips were blue, and trembled with a feeble, inane smile. Once more his demon was upon him.' He dreads having to return to his hotel. 'The doorway was dark and gloomy at any time. But just at this moment it was rendered doubly so by the fact that the thunderstorm had just broken, and rain was coming down in torrents. And in the semi-darkness the Prince could make out the profile of a man standing close to the stairs, apparently waiting. . . . His heart froze. "In a moment or two I shall know all," he thought.' It is then that he is confronted with the vision of Rogozhin with a knife raised ready to strike. 'Next moment something appeared to burst open before him; a wonderful light illuminated his soul. This lasted perhaps half a second, and yet he could distinctly remember hearing the beginning of the wail, that strange, dreadful wail, which burst from his lips of its own accord. . . .'

It will be observed that Dostoevsky presents us with the entire ontological range of epileptic experience. The physical manifestations cannot be isolated from the non-physical. The experience is integral and indivisible. The physical phase is seen as the culmination of a prolonged piling up of dimly perceived happenings taking place within the very depths of Myshkin's being. Indeed, Myshkin's epileptic crisis is a disturbance of being, a 'being-quake', as it were.

We have already seen that the initial causation–if indeed this is the proper way of viewing the process–is meta-physical. The subject is in the first instance suffering not from physical symptoms, but from ideas. We are obliged then to try and discover the content and origin of these ideas.

Let us begin with Rogozhin. During the second 'section' of the novel Rogozhin sheds his flesh and blood, and becomes an hallucination, a wraith who haunts not only Myshkin, but in some undiscernible cross-connection, the sick youth Terentyev as well. As the latter lies in his bed tormented by forebodings of the ghastly insect waiting to devour him after death, Rogozhin silently enters the room, and sits down, still silent. Terentyev suspects that his visitor may be an appari-tion. But he shows no astonishment. To communicate verb-ally is unnecessary; 'though I had not actually told him what I was thinking, I could see that he had already understood'. Rogozhin is for Terentyev a haunting presence, a portent, not unlike the doppelgänger. For Myshkin, how-ever, Rogozhin is more of an entity to be reckoned with. Rogozhin explicitly embodies impulsive, uncontrolled emo-tion, life at its rawest, like the superhuman convicts Dostoev-sky knew intimately in Siberia. Unlike Myshkin, he is firmly carried along by the stream of existence. He is the personality *in whose direction Myshkin tends*. It was not for nothing that they 'exchanged crosses' as a sin of their deep identity. The symbol of the cross in Dostoevsky is an important one, although as yet unexplained. (Perhaps Jung's explanation that the cross is a sign of union between primeval animality and higher nature is of some help here.) Face to face with Rogozhin's terrible eyes, Myshkin finds his other self mirrored back at him. Another symbol is associated with the final apparition of these eyes – the symbol of the staircase. Myshkin would have been knifed to death, one supposes, had he not been saved by his epileptic fit, during which he slides the entire length of the spiral stairway. (The Freudian explanation of the stairs symbol fits badly.)[16] For an explanation, we return to the functional theory of epilepsy. In Myshkin's case the epileptic fit is both literally and figuratively an escape from an *alter ego*, an escape from a possible alternative self which would have been intolerable. In the light of this, Myshkin may be seen to be leading an unauthentic existence. He is neither willing nor physically able to take on *real* existence. His being will not permit it. Epilepsy will continue to prevent him from realising his 'idea', and likewise from turning into the potential monster that lurks within.

From a certain angle, the entire novel may be regarded as an allegory of Myshkin's ontological predicament. The central characters, indeed everything in the novel, can be taken to be the concrete mythical representation of a mode of being, of the epileptic mode of being. Myshkin has to be content with unauthentic existence and its consequences. Epilepsy will make it impossible for him to realise his monstrous potentiality. The epileptic mechanism is triggered off at the crucial instant, cutting him down like an axe.

At this point it is difficult to resist a short digression on the name Myshkin. Attempts have been made to link this name with a locality known as the Myshkinsy district,[17] where the heinous crime of the peasant murder, on which Dostoevsky based Rogozhin's account of a similar atrocity, is supposed to have taken place. It could of course be that, when Dostoevsky read about the crime in the newspapers, the name was suggested by association of ideas. It is much more likely, however, that the name Myshkin is derived from the Russian word *myshka* 'a little mouse' (as distinct from *myshonok* which would mean 'a young mouse'). In this case, Myshkin would be a fairly normal Russian surname derivative. It will be recalled that the Man from Underground contrasts the 'man of sensibility' with normal humanity, at the same time stressing that the former, for all his ideals, is 'sprung from a test-tube': 'This test-tube man sometimes capitulates to his antithesis to such an extent that for all his intense sensibility he frankly considers himself a mouse and not a man. I grant you that it is an intensely conscious mouse, but a mouse nevertheless. . . .' This mouse has much in common with Prince Myshkin. The creature is vengeful and spiteful (Myshkin of the notebooks, and the first 'section' of the novel); it has 'accumulated such a large number of insoluble questions round every question that it finds itself drowned in a sort of deadly brew, a stinking puddle made up of its doubts, its flurries of emotion, and the contempt with which plain men of action cover it from head to foot while they stand solemnly around as judges and dictators, and split their sides with laughter at it.' Raskolnikov, a later character who is ontologically more developed, finds a real confrontation with his real mouse-like nature in his inability to support the burden of guilt and his newly-acquired boundless Nietzschean freedom. Myshkin never actually refers to the overdeveloped mouse, but he has clearly much in common with the Man from Underground and the mouse there described. He is *physically* hindered from attaining superhumanity by the otherwise inexplicable phenomenon of epilepsy. The irony lies in the fact that the phenomenology of epilepsy contains both the intimation and promise of divinity, whilst at the same time punishing him for his Promethean rashness. Myshkin is aware that because of all his consciousness, sensibility and perfectionism he would make all the greater a monster, as great and wicked as Mahomet. Mahomet too was an epileptic, as Dostoevsky well knew. Like Pyotr Verkhovensky's Ivan the Tsarevich (*The Devils*) Myshkin would, as the monstrous saviour of mankind, have reached the depths of the hideous, and become transformed into the beast of the Apocalypse.

At the allegorical level, then, Rogozhin represents Myshkin's own demonic projection. Nastasya might be seen as representing or symbolising the common destiny of Myshkin and Rogozhin. Rogozhin is impelled, and Dostoevsky explicitly states this, to put her to death. The actual murder is bloodless, Rogozhin having perfected a technique of knifing without drawing blood. Myshkin marvels at this. Rogozhin has prepared a ritual for them both to enact: 'So let her lie close to us, close to you and me. . . .' 'Yes, yes,' agreed the Prince warmly. 'So we will not say anything about it, or let them take her away.' 'No, not for anything!

. . . No, no, no!' Rogozhin proceeds to make up beds on the floor.

> It was clear that he had devised these beds long before . . . he then approached the Prince, and gently helped him to rise, and led him towards the bed. But the Prince could now walk by himself, so that his fear must have passed. . . . The Prince stretched out a trembling hand and gently stroked Rogozhin's hair and cheeks – he could do nothing more. His legs trembled again and he seemed to have lost the use of them. A new sensation came over him, filling his heart and soul with infinite anguish. . . . His tears flowed on to Rogozhin's cheek. . . .

Rogozhin is still lying half-conscious on the floor in a state of high fever when people force their way into the flat and find the Prince mechanically stroking his companion's hair and cheeks – now an idiot in the true sense of the word. We learn that Myshkin is to be placed once more in the care of the Swiss doctor Schneider, and we are left to conclude that the dementia will be permanent.

Rogozhin has destroyed their common ideal and mainspring of their life, Nastasya. As a result Myshkin is left devoid of being, annihilated, a blithering idiot. Yet one need not mourn him, for his one real encounter with Rogozhin was the only truly authentic moment in his life. Myshkin for one brief moment savoured real existence, a Promethean sin for which he paid with his identity, a *mortal* sin if ever there was one. The epileptic mechanism had let him down on this one occasion, which was both his fulfilment and his undoing.

The Idiot, then, would seem to be a very different and more complex work than it is generally thought to be. It is my contention that this novel is primarily an exploration of the epileptic mode of being, which was also Dostoevsky's own. The existential riddle underlying *The Idiot* is so deep as to have remained beyond even Dostoevsky's conscious imagination. It is as though the entire range and significance of human existence lies coiled up within it like some prodigious and ghastly spring. For me *The Idiot* remains the most challenging and obscure of Dostoevsky's novels, and Prince Myshkin his most baffling and impenetrable creation.

STAVROGIN'S CONFESSION

IT took Dostoevsky almost exactly two years to complete his novel *The Devils*. He submitted it in instalments to his publisher Katkov and it appeared section by section in *The Russian Messenger*. When he came to submit what would have been Chapter IX of Part 2 of his novel, Katkov rejected it as pornographic. The three rejected sections or 'chapters' which make up this Chapter IX remained unpublished until 1922, following the release of documents by the Central Archive Department of the RSFSR (if we exclude the publication of part of the first section by his wife in the 1906 Jubilee Edition of his collected works)[1].

The contents of these unpublished chapters became known to Merezhkovsky, at the time when Anna Grigoryevna was trying to persuade him to edit the Jubilee Edition of her husband's works.[2] In Merezhkovsky's words 'it surpassed the bounds of the possible in its concentrated expression of horror'. From that moment the 'confession' became generally known, if only by hearsay, and rumour soon had it that Dostoevsky had secretly been a Marquis de Sade. 'The dark legend that Dostoevsky was a sensualist is based either on an obscure piece of fiction, or on coarse and thoughtless surmises as to what lay behind that troubled and overexacting conscience which was the hall mark of Dostoevsky's character.[3] Publication of the suppressed chapters in 1922 and 1923 scotched all but the hardest core of this legend.

The action of the three chapters takes place in a monastery. Stavrogin is brought face to face with Tikhon, a Russian Orthodox bishop living there in retirement. We do not meet this saintly recluse in the novel itself; we only hear of him through Shatov when he tells Stavrogin: 'Listen, go and see Tikhon. . . . Tikhon, the former Bishop, who on account of ill-health lives in retirement in this town. . . .'

The Tikhon of *The Devils* is based on an eighteenth-century ecclesiastic Tikhon Zadonsky. In a letter to Katkov Dostoevsky writes:

> I want to tackle for the first time in my life a type of character rarely found as yet in fiction. The ideal of this type I have taken to be Tikhon Zadonsky. My character is, like him, living in retirement in a monastery. I confront him with the main character in the novel, and bring them together for a time. I am somewhat apprehensive. I have never tried this kind of thing before. . . .[4]

The historical Tikhon Zadonsky[5] was elected Bishop of Novgorod at an unusually early age. A successful ecclesiastical career seemed assured, when he began to find the burden of administering his diocese excessive. He expressed a wish to resign, but his wish was refused. He appealed directly to the Empress Catherine, and he was allowed to retire officially in 1768. He eventually settled at the Monastery of Zadonsk (hence his surname: Zadonsky). The impression one receives is of a Russian Augustine with a distinct Jansenist streak. In his monastic retreat he shunned all visitors, except children, for whom he had a special fondness, and who delighted him more than anything or anybody. In contrast to the surroundings Dostoevsky's Tikhon lived in, his habitat was shabby and his furnishings a jumble of oddments. Books were few.

Our first glimpse of Dostoevsky's Tikhon is in *The Life of a Great Sinner*, where we find a distinct trace of what was later to become the unpublished chapters of *The Devils*. The Great Sinner encounters Tikhon, a figure who not only foreshadows the Tikhon of the 'Confession' but also the Russian Monk Zosima whom we meet in *The Brothers Karamazov*. A section of the rough drafts for *The Life* runs as follows:

> After the Monastery and Tikhon, the Great Sinner comes out into the world in order to become the *greatest of men*. He is convinced he will become the greatest of men. And in that way he behaves: he is the proudest of the proud, and behaves with supreme arrogance towards other people. . . . But he has (and this is of cardinal importance) *through Tikhon* got hold of the idea (conviction) that in order to conquer the whole world one

must conquer oneself only. Conquer thyself and thou shalt conquer the world. . . .[6]

In the notebooks we learn that the Great Sinner dies confessing a crime. We are not told what the crime was. Sophie Kovalevsky however in her *Reminiscences of Childhood*[7] recalls how Dostoevsky even as far back as 1866 (the time he was writing *Crime and Punishment*) had mentioned a plan he had for a novel in which the central character would be trying to recall something dreadful he had done. This character tries desperately hard, until one day he suddenly calls to mind, as if it had happened only yesterday, that one night some twenty years ago after an evening's debauchery and under provocation from his friends he had raped a little girl of ten. The character is Velchaninov (*The Eternal Husband*), but the crime is Stavrogin's.

In the actual 'confession'—the second of the unpublished chapters—the rape of the little girl is the central fact around which all else revolves. In the years 1922–23 two versions were published. In the first of these (sometimes referred to as the Moscow version[8]) the incident of the rape is ineffectively and only coyly suggested; in the second (the Petersburg version[9]) Dostoevsky employs a subterfuge: instead of going into detail, Stavrogin withholds the second of the printed sheets Tikhon is reading, and leaves it both to Tikhon's and the reader's imagination to infer the actuality. This second version also leaves open the possibility that Stavrogin was inventing a 'crime' which he perhaps did not actually commit, but which might have been suggested to him hypnotically by his apparition, which like Ivan Karamazov he sometimes took to be the Devil.

Komarovich[10] has discussed at length the question as to whether the unpublished chapters did in fact form an integral part of *The Devils* or whether it was rather a case of 'one of those fragments of Dostoevsky which, since they correspond to some earlier but subsequently altered scheme, have become detached from the finished novel . . . and are now preserved only in Dostoevsky's rough drafts as curious examples of the complex origins of his work'.[11] There has never been any doubt that Katkov did in fact refuse to publish the chapters in question. There is evidence also that Katkov's refusal caused Dostoevsky some distress. He even travelled to Moscow to have the matter out with him. In a letter to Sonya, his niece, he writes:

> When I left Moscow, I thought it would not be particularly difficult to revise the chapter in the manner demanded by the publisher. But when I got down to work, I found it impossible to modify it, and at most I was able to make only a few insignificant alterations. . . . In the end I scrubbed it, and started afresh; that is to say, *whilst retaining the essence of the thing*, I have modified the text in order to satisfy the publisher's qualms, and accordingly I am going to send them an ultimatum. If they do not accept it, I don't know what I shall do.

The revised version was again rejected.[12]

But Katkov's censorship was private and did not apply to later editions of Dostoevsky's novels. Why then did Dostoevsky make no attempt to include the unpublished sections in later editions of *The Devils*? The answer seems to be that Dostoevsky had changed his mind about it. An almost verbatim section of the 'Confession' appears in a later novel *The Raw Youth*, this time among Versilov's 'reminiscences' (Part III, Chapter VII (2).) Moreover, these particular chapters had been written at a time when *The Life of a Great Sinner* and *The Devils* had been closely wedded in Dostoevsky's mind. At that time

> he still meant to represent the Great Sinner, Stavrogin, in the light of Grace. But, as he worked on the last chapter of the novel and approached the catastrophe, Dostoevsky evidently realised it was impossible to achieve the religious and dramatic aims he had originally envisaged. Dostoevsky did not find himself possessed of the artistic powers needed to convert his Great Sinner, and everything that led up to the expected conversion was abandoned. Only an echo of his original intention remains – not in the novel even, but on the first page, in the quotation from the Gospel: the promise that the Sinner will find salvation only at the feet of Christ. The crimes committed by his leading character appeared to the writer at the end of his work suddenly and quite unexpectedly like a stronghold, enduring

and self-sufficient. . . . Stavrogin's Confession, in that it echoed Dostoevsky's more optimistic view, had inevitably to disappear. . . .[13]

What Komarovich does not suggest—and this seems a likely explanation—is that the organic development of *The Devils* was not entirely under Dostoevsky's conscious control, developing dynamics of its own. Once the permission to publish these chapters was finally refused it became equally clear that the novel would have to go its own way without them. Had they been incorporated the final shape of the novel would inevitably have been different. What is not always realised is that any section of a novel—especially one that is is being serialised—is a restriction upon any subsequent section. Antecedents determine the possibilities even if not the ultimate choice. A novel is like a life. Not only do opportunities realised shape the life, but the unrealised ones as well. Hence the discrepancy between the highly impassioned and disturbed Stavrogin of the Confession and the pale mask which stares at us from the pages of *The Devils*, indifferent to good or evil, life or death.

Of the two versions, I have chosen the 'Petersburg' one for my translation. (There exists a third version which is a hybrid of the two, and I have found that less suitable than either of the originals.[14]) My reasons are: firstly that it is dramatically the most convincing and probably the revised version he mentions in his letter to his niece; secondly it is based on Anna Grigoryevna's own draft, and she knew better than anyone Dostoevsky's intentions, since she helped him a great deal in preparing his manuscripts: from a mass of variants and corrections she could discern the version Dostoevsky would most favour. The main differences between the 'Moscow'[15] and the 'Petersburg' editions is in the Confession itself and in the closing section. In the 'Petersburg' edition the rape is no more than hinted at. In the former there is a suggestion that like Zosima's mysterious visitor who confessed a crime to him, Stavrogin was on the point of killing Tikhon.

As far as possible I have endeavoured to 'translate' the styles of the original (Dostoevsky is never other than a mosaic of contrasting styles). Tikhon's language tends towards the rhetorical and liturgical. Stavrogin's on the other hand, is 'familiar'; not chatty exactly, but always verging on the colloquial. The main feature of his style is that his Russian is 'Europeanised'. He had after all been living abroad for some time, and he had even adopted Swiss nationality. This is especially true of the 'Confession' itself, in which the language is deliberately clumsy and unpleasing. A more detailed discussion of Dostoevsky's stylistics is to be found in my essay 'Stylistics and Personality' (Chap. XI).

CHAPTER IX—A VISIT TO TIKHON

THAT night Stavrogin had remained awake,[16] just sitting there on the sofa, perpetually fixing his gaze on something over in the corner by the chest of drawers. His lamp had burnt the whole night long, and it was around seven the following morning before he finally dozed off. He had been roused in due course by his man-servant, Alexey Yegorovich, who from time immemorial had never missed bringing him his morning cup of coffee on the stroke of half-past nine. This startled Stavrogin; he had been annoyed at having slept so late. He had gulped down his coffee, got dressed, and left in a great hurry. Alexey Yegorovich had tentatively raised the subject of his duties for the day, but received no reply.

Stavrogin strode along, deep in thought, his eyes glued to the ground. Only now and again did he look up, and it was then that you could catch a glimpse of a vague but profound uneasiness. Not very far from the house, at a road intersection, he came upon a crowd of peasants, fifty or more of them, moving in single file across his path in an orderly and silent procession. As he was standing outside a shop to let them go by he was told that they were 'Shpigulin's men'.[17] This information did not seem to interest him particularly. At about half-past ten, he reached the gates of the Monastery of Our Lady Spaso-Yefimev, which was situated in the outskirts of the town, by the river. It was only now that he seemed to pull himself together. He fumbled hastily and anxiously in his side pocket and a smile stole over his lips. He went on through into the monastery enclosure and asked the first servant-boy he came across where he might find Bishop Tikhon, who was living in retirement in the monastery. The young fellow began bowing and without more ado led the way. Near a little flight of steps at the end of the long two-storied monastery buildings, a fat grey-haired monk promptly and authoritatively took over and ushered him along a narrow corridor. He too kept on bowing, though he was so fat that he could not bow very low, and instead kept on jerking his head up and down, all the time inviting him to follow. Stavrogin needed no inviting. The monk kept up a barrage of questions and wanted to talk about the Father Archimandrite.[18] When he did not get any reply he became more and more deferential. Stavrogin could not help noticing that he was no stranger there, even though, as far as he could remember, he had not been here since early childhood.

When they reached the door at the far end of the corridor the monk opened it without the least hesitation. A lay-brother came running to meet them, whereupon the monk enquired familiarly if they might enter. Without waiting for a reply the monk threw open the door, bowed as low as he could manage, and ushered him in with a sickly ingratiating smile. After receiving a tip he made off at the double. Stavrogin stepped inside a fairly tiny room, and almost at that very instant there appeared in the doorway of an adjoining room the tall slender figure of a man, aged about fifty-five, dressed in a simple cassock, looking rather ill, and smiling vaguely with a strange and somewhat diffident look in his eyes. This then was Tikhon, the Tikhon he had first heard of from Shatov[19] and about whom he had since picked up various scraps of information.

This information had been miscellaneous and contradictory, but one fact plainly emerged, namely that Tikhon's well-wishers and enemies alike were reluctant to speak their mind. Those who hated him probably behaved thus out of contempt; his supporters, on the other hand, even the most zealous of them, were probably inhibited by shyness. They seemed as if they had something to hide; perhaps some defect, perhaps even the symptoms of madness. Stavrogin had ascertained that Tikhon had been living in the monastery for about six years. He knew also that he was visited by the humblest as well as the most well-to-do people, that in places even as remote as Petersburg he had his admirers, although most of them were women. Again, from one portly old gentleman at the Club, a devout old fogey at that, he had gleaned the information that 'this fellow Tikhon is almost round the bend. At any rate he is a complete nonentity, and probably a toper in the bargain.' For my own part, I should add, even at the risk of running ahead rather, that this last statement is complete and utter rubbish. The only thing wrong with him is that he suffers from chronic rheumatism in the legs and occasionally from neuritis. Stavrogin had also found out that this Bishop, notwithstanding the fact that he had been living in retirement in the monastery, had not managed to inspire more than average respect in the monks there. This was either due to weakness of character or to his absentmindedness 'quite unforgivable and improper in a man of his rank'. It was also said that the Father Archimandrite, a stern man, conscientious in the discharge of his duties and a distinguished scholar in addition, harboured a certain hostility towards him and reproached him (not to his face, but in roundabout ways) for his lax mode of life, and all but accused him of heresy.[20] The monks too treated him not exactly in an off-hand manner, but with a sort of familiarity. The two rooms which Tikhon used as his cell were also rather peculiarly furnished. Side by side with heavy old pieces of furniture with shabby leather upholstery were three or four decidedly elegant pieces: a superb easy-chair, a large writing desk of excellent workmanship, a beautifully carved bookcase, miniature tables, book-stands, all of which had been given him as presents. There was an expensive Bokhara carpet, and a set of mats.[21] There were engravings but of a secular kind; their subject-matter was mythology. And right beside them in the corner was a large shrine glittering with gold and silver icons, one of which was very ancient and contained relics. His library likewise was said to be too varied and controversial. Side by side with the works of the Fathers of the Church and the bulwarks of Christendom there were collections of plays 'and perhaps even worse than that'.

After a preliminary exchange of greetings, not without evident awkwardness on both sides, judging by the way they were hurried and indistinctly muttered, Tikhon led his visitor into his study and offered him a seat on a divan with a table in front of it. He himself sat down on a wicker chair nearby.

Stavrogin was still in a highly distracted frame of mind, as though some inner anxiety was oppressing him. It seemed as if he had decided upon something unusual and incontrovertible, and yet could not bring himself to go ahead with it. For some moments he had been casting his eyes about the study, but evidently without being able to focus his attention on anything in particular. He was thinking hard but he could not have told you what he was thinking about. It was the silence that roused him from his reverie; and he had the sudden and distinct impression that Tikhon lowered his gaze as if out of shyness, and an uncalled for and ridiculous smile came over Stavrogin's face. This instantly filled him with disgust. His first reaction was to get up and leave, especially as it seemed to him obvious that Tikhon was tight. But the latter suddenly looked up, and gazed so steadfastly and thoughtfully into his eyes, with such a queer and unexpected expression on his face, that he could hardly prevent himself from shuddering. He had the uncanny suspicion that Tikhon already knew why he had come. He was already forewarned (despite the fact that there was no one who could have told him), and he was not going to be the first one to speak. It was as if he wanted to spare Stavrogin's feelings and to avoid humiliating him.

'Do you know who I am?' he suddenly blurted out. 'I don't know if I introduced myself properly when I came in. I am so absentminded. . . .'

'You did not introduce yourself, but I had the pleasure of meeting you on one occasion here in the monastery about four years ago . . . quite by chance.'

Tikhon spoke unhurriedly and smoothly; his voice was soft, and his enunciation clear and distinct.

'I didn't come here four years ago,' was Stavrogin's somewhat off-hand reply. 'I haven't been here since I was a child, and you weren't here then.'

'Well, perhaps you have forgotten,' Tikhon observed, guardedly and without insistence.

'No, I haven't forgotten. I'd be a fool if I couldn't remember so much,'[22] said Stavrogin rather overemphasising his point. 'Perhaps you have merely heard about me and formed some impression of what I am like. That would explain the mistake.'

Tikhon did not say anything. Stavrogin now noticed that a nervous tremor passed over his face at odd moments, a sure sign of chronic nervous exhaustion.

'I can see that you are not well today,' he said. 'I think it would be better if I went.'

He was even on the point of getting up from his seat. 'Yes, I have been having violent pains in my legs the whole of today and yesterday, and finding it difficult to sleep at night.'. . .

Tikhon broke off, for his visitor had again without warning fallen into his former vague reverie. The silence lasted a long time, about two minutes.

'Why were you watching me?' he asked suddenly with a tinge of anxiety and suspicion in his voice.

'When I was looking at you I was reminded of your mother's

face. Although your features have not much in common, there is a considerable inner, spiritual resemblance.'

'Pure imagination! As for spiritual resemblance there's *absolutely none*!' This outburst was uncalled for; he rather overdid his insistence, but without knowing why. 'You are just saying this . . . out of pity for me. You know it's rubbish,' he rapped out suddenly. 'Bah! And I suppose my mother comes and sees you.'

'Yes, she does.'

'I didn't know that. She's been keeping it quiet. Does she come often?'

'Nearly every month, and sometimes more often.'

'I have never heard a thing about it. Not a thing. And I suppose she has been telling you I'm insane,' he added unexpectedly.

'No, not exactly that. Nevertheless I have heard it suggested by others.'

'You must have a very good memory, if you can recall trifles of that kind. And I take it you have heard about the slap on the face too.'[23]

'I have heard something of the sort.'

'You mean you've heard the lot. You must have far too much time on your hands. And about the duel[24] too?'

'Yes, I have heard about that as well.'

'You seem to have heard quite a good deal. You don't need newspapers in this place. Was it Shatov who warned you against me? Eh?'

'No, it was not. I am acquainted with Mr. Shatov though, but it is a long time since I have seen him.'

'Hm. What's the map you've got there? Ugh! it's only a map of the last war. What do you want with a thing like that?'

'I wanted to refer to it in connection with this text. It's a most fascinating description.'

'Show me. . . . Yes, it isn't bad at all. But it's very strange reading matter for someone like you.'

He drew the book towards him and gave it a cursory inspection. It was a voluminous and weighty account of the circumstances of the last war; not so much a military history as a pure work of art. Having glanced through its pages, he put the book down abruptly and with obvious impatience.

'It beats me why I came here in the first place,' he muttered contemptuously, looking Tikhon straight in the eye, as if expecting some reply.

'You too must be unwell.'

'Yes, I am.'

And suddenly in the shortest and most abrupt manner possible, so as not to be misunderstood, he explained that he was subject to a certain kind of hallucination, especially at night. Sometimes he could see or at least sense the presence of a malevolent being, a mocking and 'rational' being. 'It takes on various forms and various characteristics but it's always the same one, and I'm always beside myself with rage.'[25]

These revelations were wild and confused, like those of a madman. And yet Stavrogin spoke with a peculiar frankness quite unknown for him, and with a simplicity that was totally unnatural; so much so that it seemed as if suddenly and without warning his former self had completely vanished. He was not in the least ashamed of betraying the dread with which he spoke of this apparition of his. But this lasted barely a moment and passed as suddenly as it had made its appearance.

'It's a lot of nonsense,' he murmured breathlessly and with ill-concealed irritation, retreating to his former position. 'I'm going to see a doctor.'

'Yes, I think you should,' agreed Tikhon.

'You speak with assurance. . . . Have you come across people like me before, who have hallucinations of this kind?'

'I have, but very seldom. Indeed I can only remember one such case. He was an army officer, who had lost his wife and nearly died of grief. The only other case was pure hearsay. Both of them found a cure abroad. . . . Have you been like this very long?'

'A year or so, but it's all nonsense. I'll go and see a doctor. It's nonsense, I tell you, the most fantastic nonsense. It's a projection of various aspects of myself, and nothing more. But even while I am saying this, you are probably still thinking that I'm still not quite sure, not quite convinced that it is I, and not the devil.'[25]

Tikhon gave him a questioning look.

'And . . . do you actually see him?' he asked, dismissing any question of its being an imaginary and morbid hallucination, 'Do you actually see a particular image?'

'It's queer that you should lay such stress on that, when I have already told you I really do see it.' Once again Stavrogin was becoming more and more distraught with every word he said. 'Of course I see it. I see it as plainly as I can see you . . . and sometimes I see it and I'm not sure whether I'm seeing it or imagining it; it's even difficult to know which is real: I or it . . . it's sheer nonsense. And is the possibility of it being the devil ruled out?' he added breaking into a laugh and promptly adopting a mocking turn of phrase. 'Surely that would be more in keeping with a profession such as yours.'

'It's more likely that you are ill, although . . .'

'Although what?'

'Devils certainly do exist, but people's ideas about them vary considerably.'

'I suppose that is why you have turned your eyes away again,' Stavrogin broke in with impetuous laughter, 'because you were ashamed of me for believing in the devil whereas I was trying to make out that I did not believe in him by cunningly asking you the question: does he or does he not really exist?'

Tikhon smiled wistfully.

'And you know what, it doesn't become a person like you to look away; it's unnatural, ridiculous, and affected. But to make up for my rudeness I will tell you in all seriousness and with utmost frankness that I do believe in the devil. I believe, as in the scriptures, in a personal devil, not an allegorical one; and I don't need anyone to tell me this. That's all I have to say. You should be absolutely delighted . . .' He laughed a strained and unnatural laugh. Tikhon eyed him curiously, but gently too and with a certain timidity.

'Do you believe in God?' Stavrogin blurted out suddenly.

'I do.'

'It is said that if you have faith and command a mountain to move, it will move . . . a lot of poppycock, though. But I am, even so, rather curious to know whether you could move a mountain.'

'If God wills it, then I shall,' Tikhon murmured quietly and reservedly, lowering his eyes.

'I am not interested in whether God himself could move one. What about you? It's you I'm asking, as a reward for your faith in God.'

'Perhaps I could move one.'

' "Perhaps" is a nice way of putting it. Why are you in doubt?'

'My faith is not quite perfect.'

'What? Do you mean to say that even *your* faith is imperfect?'

'Yes . . . perhaps. I believe, but not perfectly.'

'Well, at any rate, you do believe none the less that with God's help you could do it, and that is something, after all. Anyhow it probably amounts to more than the *très peu* of an Archbishop under threat of the sword. You are a Christian, I suppose?' mocked Stavrogin.

'Let me not be ashamed, Lord, of Thy Cross,' Tikhon almost whispered, with a kind of impassioned whisper, bowing his head still lower. The corners of his lips suddenly began twitching, rapidly and nervously.

'Is it really possible to believe in the Devil without believing in God?' laughed Stavrogin.

'It is very possible, and it happens quite often,' Tikhon raised his eyes and smiled.

'I'm quite convinced that you find belief of this kind more respectable than complete atheism. . . . You are all the same, you priests!' roared Stavrogin. Tikhon smiled once more.

'On the contrary, complete atheism is more respectable than worldly indifference,' Tikhon came back, gaily and good-humouredly.

'Come off it, that's no way of trying to get round it!'

'A complete atheist stands on the last rung but one before the attainment of the most perfect faith (but whether he will take the ultimate step is quite another question), whereas a person who is indifferent possesses no faith of any kind, only crass fear.'

'By the way. . . . Have you read the Apocalypse?'

'I have.'

'Do you remember the section which begins: "And to the angel of the Church in Laodicea write"? . . .'

'I remember those delightful words.'

'Delightful? That's a funny thing for a bishop to say. You *are* an extraordinary fellow. . . . Have you got a copy here?' said Stavrogin in a strangely anxious manner, trying to see if the book was anywhere on the table, 'I'd like to read to you . . . do you possess a Russian translation?'

'I know the passage very well,' Tikhon murmured.

'You know it by heart? Let's hear it then. . . .'

He promptly lowered his eyes, rested both hands on his knees, and impatiently prepared himself to listen. Tikhon began to recite the passage word for word:

'Write to the Angel of the Church in Laodicea: "The words of the Amen, the faithful and true witness, the beginning of God's creation. I know your works: you are neither cold nor hot. Would that you were cold or hot! So, because you are lukewarm, and neither cold nor hot, I will spew you out of my mouth. For you say, I am rich, I have prospered, and I need nothing; not knowing that you are wretched, pitiable, poor, blind, and naked.". . .'[26]

'That will do,' interrupted Stavrogin, 'this kind of thing is for those who sit on the fence, and for those who are indifferent, isn't it? You know what, I like you very much.'

'And I you,' Tikhon replied in a whisper.

Stavrogin lapsed into silence, and was soon immersed again in his own thoughts. These moods seemed to come over him in spasms; it was the third time it had happened. He was almost carried away when he admitted his fondness for Tikhon, and it certainly came as a surprise to himself. More than a minute passed.

'Do not be angry,' Tikhon whispered, touching his arm very lightly. He too appeared embarrassed. Stavrogin trembled, and glowered angrily.

'How did you know I was angry?' he spluttered. Tikhon was about to say something when for some reason Stavrogin became panic-stricken, and interrupted him: 'How could you have known that I would inevitably go off the deep end? I was angry all right. Dead right you were. And just because I'd said I liked you. You guessed right, but you are nothing but a crude cynic; you take a very condescending view of human nature. There would have been no spite, had it been anyone else but me. . . . But it isn't other people's reactions that we're talking about, but mine. When all's said and done, you are a crank and a nincompoop.'. . .

He became more and more exasperated, and, oddly, made no attempt to control his language:

'Listen, I don't like busybodies and psychologists, especially ones that try and pry into my inner workings. They can keep out. I have no need of their services. I can cope perfectly well on my own. I suppose you are thinking I'm afraid of you?' he raised his voice and looked up defiantly; 'you are quite convinced that I have come to confess some terrible secret to you, and you are relishing the prospect with all the monkish curiosity of which you are capable. Well, I'd better make it clear now that I've nothing to disclose, no secret; because I can perfectly well do without you. . . .'

Tikhon gave him a piercing look.

'It shook you that the Lamb prefers someone who is cold to one who is merely lukewarm,' he said, 'You don't want to be merely lukewarm. I sense that you are possessed by some extraordinary aim, perhaps not a pleasant one either. I implore you, stop tormenting yourself and tell me what you came to tell me.'

'And you of course knew that I had come with some express purpose.'

'I . . . I guessed it from your expression,' Tikhon replied in a whisper, lowering his eyes. Stavrogin was rather pale; his hands were shaking slightly. For several seconds he did not take his eyes off Tikhon, and seemed to be trying to come to a decision. At length he brought out of his side pocket a few printed sheets and put them on the table.

'These sheets were intended for distribution,' he said, his voice trembling. 'It only needs one person to read them, and I won't be able to keep them dark any longer; everyone will be reading them. It's settled then. I have no need of you, because everything's decided. Go on, read them. . . . While you are reading them, reserve your comment, but when you've finished, let's hear what you have to say. . . .'

'Should I read them?' Tikhon asked hesitantly.

'Yes, read them. I've long since resigned myself to the inevitable.'

'I shall not be able to without my glasses. The print is small, and not very Russian.'

'There are your glasses.' Stavrogin picked them up and handed them to him, and then leaned back on the divan. Tikhon quickly became absorbed in reading.

CHAPTER IX (SECTION II)

THE typography was in fact foreign. The document consisted of three loosely-bound sheets of typescript; ordinary octavo notepaper had been used. It must have been printed abroad on one of the secret Russian printing-presses, and at first sight looked very much like a political pamphlet. Its title read: 'From Stavrogin'.

The document is reproduced below entirely unabridged, although it must already be familiar to many of my readers. I have taken the liberty of correcting a number of spelling errors; they were rather numerous, surprising in view of the fact that the author was both well-educated and well-read (relatively speaking, of course). However I have left the style exactly as it was, despite its flaws (not to mention its vagueness). At any rate it is obvious that the author was by no stretch of the imagination a writer. I would however like to draw attention to one thing, even at the risk of anticipating.

This document is in my opinion the work of a diseased mentality, the work of some evil spirit that had taken hold of this fellow. It reminds one of a man suffering from acute pain tossing and turning in his bed, trying to find a position where he might be more comfortable even for a moment. Not even that perhaps, but of a patient finding relief from one kind of pain by substituting for it a different kind, if only for minute or so.[27] But we are not really concerned with the aesthetic quality or rationality of his position. The chief thing that impresses one about this document is its gruesome, undisguised craving for punishment, for public humiliation, for crucifixion. And yet this seeking after a cross seems incongruous in a man who does not believe in the Cross. On the other hand the entire document is a frantic and precarious piece of work from start to finish, despite the fact that it was obviously written with quite a different object in view. The author has stated that he could not help writing it, that he had no alternative but to do so; and this seems likely enough to me. Had he been able, he would gladly have let that cup pass from him. Instead, he merely seized on a convenient pretext for a fresh outburst. One is again inevitably reminded of the sick man tossing about in his bed, wishing only to exchange one kind of pain for another. In this instance a tussle with society suggests itself as the easiest position to adopt; and so, he duly hurls his challenge. In actual fact, the very existence of such a document foreshadows a new, unanticipated and irreverent act of defiance against society. The first likely candidate for this onslaught would do. . . .

And yet, who can tell? It is conceivable that this leaflet intended for publication is the same kind of thing as the incident in which he bit the Governor's ear, only this time in a different guise. But why such a thought should occur to me now when so much has been already explained, I simply cannot understand. Although I am not prepared to maintain that the document is a complete fabrication, I cannot prove anything one way or the other. Very likely it is not an entirely authentic record. . . . However, I have been running ahead somewhat, and I had better get back to the document in question. Here is what Tikhon read:[28]

'From Stavrogin.

'I, Nikolay Stavrogin, a retired officer, living in Petersburg in the year 186–, was addicted to vice, even though I derived no pleasure from it. For some months I had been keeping three apartments going. One of them was a private hotel suite where I lived with Marya Lebyadkin, now my wife. My other two apartments were at that time rented solely for my own private goings-on. In one of them I received a lady who was infatuated with me, and in the other her maid. For a time I was preoccupied with a scheme to bring this society lady and her chambermaid together on my premises. Knowing what they were like, both of them, I looked forward to the pleasure a stupid joke of this kind would give me. While I was making the necessary preparations for this encounter, I had to visit one of these apartments (in a large block of flats in Gorokhovaya Street) more often than usual, since this was where I arranged to see the maid. I had only one room there, on the fifth floor, which I rented from some tradespeople. Their room was right next to mine, but smaller; so small in fact that the door into their room was always open. This suited me admirably. The man of the house who wore a frock-coat and a beard, was a clerk of some kind and did not return home until late in the evening. His wife, a loutish woman of about forty, spent her time cutting up old clothes and making new ones out of them. From time to time she too went out to sell the things she made. I was left alone with their daughter, who was hardly more than a child. Her name was Matryosha. Her mother was fond of her, but thrashed her quite a lot, and shouted her head off at the slightest thing, like such people do. The little girl waited on me and tidied up my room. I am sorry to say I have forgotten the number of the house. I have been told though that it has been pulled down, and where there were once two or three houses a new block of flats has been built. I have even forgotten what these people were called; or perhaps I never knew. The woman's name was Stepanida, I can remember that much. But his I have completely forgotten. I have no idea what has become of them. I suppose if a search was started and various enquiries were made by the Petersburg police, they could be traced. The flat was in a courtyard, in one corner. The month was June. The house was painted a bright blue.

'One day a penknife of mine was missing. I did not need it, and it had simply been lying about on the table. I told the landlady about it, not thinking she would give her daughter a good thrashing. However the landlady had just been bawling at the little thing for losing some rag or other, accusing her of stealing it for her dolls, and had been pulling her hair. When the rag was eventually found under the tablecloth, the little girl did not utter a single word of protest, but just stared. I noticed that she did it deliberately and this stuck in my mind, because it was the first time I had taken a close look at her face. I had not really taken much notice of her before. She was fair-haired and freckled; her face was plain, but there was something childlike and gentle about it, extraordinarily so. Her mother resented the fact that she took her punishment in silence, and just at that moment the subject of the penknife turned up. The woman was furious that she had punished her unjustly the first time, stripped a handful of switches from a broom, and before my very eyes lashed her till the scars appeared on her body, even though the child was nearly twelve. Matryosha did not cry, probably because I was there, but made a peculiar whimpering sound at each blow. Afterwards she sobbed bitterly for an hour or more. The flogging was no sooner over, when I found my penknife again. It was among the blankets on my bed. I quietly slipped it in my waistcoat pocket, left the house, and when I had gone some distance threw it into the gutter so that no one would find it. I realised that what I had done was a rotten trick, although this did not prevent me from feeling a certain pleasure aroused by a burning inner sensation which began to absorb me. I should point out at this stage that I am frequently overcome by vile impulses which go to the extremes of foolhardiness or, rather, obstinacy, though never to the point where I lose my self-control. However fierce the sensation I could always control it, even bring myself to a halt at the very moment of climax. Yet I seldom felt like stopping. Let it be understood that I am not shrugging off responsibility for my crimes by ascribing them to environmental or abnormality factors.

'So I waited for two days. When she stopped crying the little girl was even more taciturn than before. However I am convinced that she bore me no grudge, although there was still a feeling of shame at having been thrashed like that in my presence. But, for this, she blamed no one but herself. In this way she was no different from any other child in her situation. I mention this because it is very important in what I am about to say. . . . After that I spent three days in my more permanent quarters in the private hotel. There were a good many rooms in the place all pervaded by the stale smell of cooking, and occupied by an assortment of people: unestablished civil-servants or petty officials, doctors who were just starting out, Poles of various kinds, all of them ready to ingratiate themselves with me. I can remember it all. In this Sodom I lived an isolated existence, in an inner sense that is, for the whole day long I was surrounded by a bevy of 'buddies', all of them were devoted to me and worshipped me almost. We did a lot of vile things, I suppose, and the other residents were even afraid of us. They went out of their way to be polite, even despite our pranks and practical jokes, some of them inexcusable. I repeat: I was not even averse to the possibility of being sent to Siberia. I was so bored, I really think I could have hanged myself. The reason I did not was that I had still something left to hope for. I remember I was preoccupied at that time with theology, deeply preoccupied in fact. I was rather fascinated by it for a time, and then I got more bored than ever. My political sentiments were confined to the possibility of planting dynamite beneath the whole set-up and blowing it sky high, if only I could have been bothered, that is. And without spite moreover; simply because I was terribly bored, and for no other reason. I am no socialist, and I can only suppose that I was suffering from some kind of disease. Doctor Dobrolyubov, who went bankrupt while he was living in the same hotel, could not see that I was pulling his leg when I asked him if there were any drops that could be administered to arouse political vitality, and he once told me: 'I am afraid not, but you will find that there are some perhaps for the criminal kind.' He let this pun pass, even though he was terribly hard up, saddled with a famished pregnant wife and two kinds. What is more, if people were not excessively satisfied with themselves, they would not want to go on living.

'After three days I returned to Gorokhovaya Street. The mother was just going out with a bundle under her arm. The man of the house was of course at work, and Matryosha was alone with me. The windows were open. The place was full of artisans, and all day long you could hear the din of hammering or singing on every floor. An hour or so passed, Matryosha sitting in her own room on a bench, with her back to me, sewing away. At length she began to sing, softly, very very softly. This was not unusual for her. I looked at my watch, it was two o'clock. My heart began to thump. I got up, and started to move towards her. On the window-sill were pots of geraniums, and the sunlight was very bright. I quietly sat down on the floor beside her. She shuddered, and seemed alarmed at first; she leapt to her feet. I took her hand and kissed it. I sat her down once more on the low bench, and began gazing into her eyes. The fact that I had kissed her hand made her laugh like a child, but only for a second or so, because she sprang to her feet a second time; this time in such panic that her face quivered violently. She stared at me, her eyes blank with terror, and her lips began to twitch as if she were about to cry. She did not cry however. I kissed her hand again, and took her on my knee. At that she turned away and smiled as if ashamed, but it was a very queer smile. Her face was red with shame. I kept whispering things to her and laughing. At last a very strange thing occurred quite suddenly. I shall never forget it; I was completely bowled over. The little creature flung her arms around my neck and suddenly began kissing me passionately. The expression on her face was completely ecstatic. I was so bewildered I almost got up; so distasteful was this to me coming from a small child, and so pitiful. . . .'[29]

He had reached the end of the page and the text broke off in mid-sentence. Then something occurred which should not escape mention.

There were five sheets in all. One of them was the page Tikhon had been reading; the remaining three were still with Stavrogin. Tikhon gave him a questioning look, but he had anticipated this moment and promptly handed him the next sheet.

'But there is something missing,' remarked Tikhon, peering at the print before his eyes.

'Yes, of course! That is the third page, the second is missing.'

'The third? I see – but what about the other one?'

'The second page is for the time being under censorship,' Stavrogin hastened to reply, smiling awkwardly. He sat on a corner of the divan motionless but in a state of agitation, watching Tikhon intently as he read.

'You will have it only when . . . you have merited it,' he added with a gesture of familiarity which he did not quite bring off. He laughed, but was a pathetic sight.

'No matter. Second or third page, it really makes no difference,' Tikhon was about to say, when he was forestalled by Stavrogin:

'What do you mean: makes no difference? It makes all the difference in the world. . . . Trust a monk to think that! Just like a monk to smell a rat at the first opportunity. A monk would make an excellent detective!'

Tikhon looked at him without saying a word.

'Well, just calm down. . . . It isn't my fault if the child was silly and unable to understand. . . . Nothing happened, I tell you, absolutely nothing.'

'Thank God for that!' Tikhon crossed himself.

'It would take much too long to explain. . . . It's . . . It's simply a psychological misunderstanding. . . .'[30]

He suddenly went red in the face. His expression was one of disgust, nausea, and despair. He did not seem to want to continue. For some time neither of them spoke, and more than a minute had elapsed before their eyes met again.

'Do you know what? I think you had better go on reading,' he said, mechanically wiping the clammy perspiration from his brow. 'And it would help matters if you didn't look at me. . . . It is as if I am dreaming. . . . And . . . whatever you do, don't overtax my patience,' he added in a whisper.

Tikhon quickly looked away, took the third sheet, and did not stop reading till he came to the end. There were no omissions in the three sheets Stavrogin had handed to him. But the third page began in the middle of a sentence. Here it is, without any alteration:

'It was a moment of real terror, although not very acute as yet. I was in high spirits that morning, frightfully amicably disposed, and my cronies were charmed. I did not stay, however, and went off to Gorokhovaya Street. I met her at the bottom of the stairs in the passage. She had been to the shops to fetch some chicory. When she caught sight of me she tore upstairs in utter panic. When I went in, her mother had already slapped her for bursting in like that; the real reason was not suspected. So for the time being there was no trouble. She kept out of my way and there was no further sign of her. I stayed for about an hour and then left.

'But towards evening the feeling of dread returned, only this time incomparably more intense. The real point is that I was afraid, and realised full well that I was afraid. There is nothing more absurd and horrible than this! It is the only time in my life when I really knew the meaning of fear, either before or since. But there was no hiding the fact; I was literally trembling with fear. To face up to the fact was humiliating. I would have killed myself, but I felt myself unworthy of death. Though it was not that that stopped me; I was too afraid to do it. Fear is responsible for suicides, but it is also responsible for keeping people alive. A man begins to lack the courage to kill himself, and suicide becomes unthinkable. Besides, that evening when I was back in my apartment, I began to hate her so much that I decided to kill her.

'At dawn I hurried off in the direction of Gorokhovaya Street. On the way I tried to imagine how I would kill her. The thing I hated most was her smile. I began to despise and loathe her for throwing her arms round my neck and for imagining things. But by the time I reached the Fountain, I was feeling queer. What is more, a horrible thought had entered my head, all the more horrible for being seen to be so. I went back to my apartment, and lay down on my bed in a cold sweat. I was in such extreme dread that I even stopped hating the little girl. I no longer felt like killing her. For the first time in my life I realised that intense fear drives away hatred and the desire for revenge completely.

'I awoke around midday. I now felt much better, and was surprised how violent and disturbed I had been the previous day. Nevertheless I was in low spirits and, although I dreaded the prospect, felt obliged to go to Gorokhovaya Street. I can remember the intense desire I suddenly had to pick a quarrel, a violent one at that, with the first person I came across. When I arrived there, I was astonished to find Nina Savelyevna, the maid I referred to earlier, waiting for me in my room. She had been there for an hour or more. There was something about her I always rather disliked, and she had come half afraid I would be angry with her for turning up uninvited. That was her way. But on this occasion I was heartily relieved to see her, and she was absolutely delighted. She was not at all bad-looking, but there was nothing particularly remarkable about her, and her demeanour was of the kind one finds only amongst tradespeople. This was the reason my land-lady had been recommending her to me so highly for such a long time. They were drinking coffee together when I arrived, and the landlady seemed thrilled with the refined conversation she thought she was being treated to. In the other room I could see Matryosha standing in a corner; she was eyeing her mother and the visitor, and keeping absolutely still. When I came in she did not run away and hide as before; I noticed this and was struck by the fact. I could see she was ailing and feverish. As for Nina I was especially nice to her and I could tell she felt her visit had been well worth while. We left the flat together, and for two days I did not set foot in Gorokhovaya Street.

'I was sick to death of everything. Things had now reached such a pitch that I decided finally to throw everything up and leave Petersburg. But when I called to give notice to my landlady I found her worried and distressed. Matryosha had been ill for three days and at night she was delirious. Naturally I made no bones about trying to find out what she had been saying in her delirium (we spoke in whispers in my room). I was told she had been ranting on about something that had horrified her: 'I have killed God', she kept saying. I offered to call a doctor at my own expense, but the landlady would not hear of it. She insisted she would get well without doctors if God wanted her to, and ex-plained that in any case she was not in bed the whole time, but had just been round to the shops. I made up my mind to see Matryosha, and as the landlady had let it be known she would be going into Petersburg at five, I decided to come back later that afternoon. But I'm blowed if I know the reason why.

'I had a meal in a pub. At a quarter past five precisely I made my way back. I always let myself in as I had my own key. Matryosha was on her own. She was behind the screen in her mother's bed. I saw her peep out, but pretended not to have noticed. The windows were wide open. It was hot and oppressive. I paced up and down the room, and then sat down on the sofa. I can remember everything down to the last detail. It gave me great pleasure to ignore Matryosha and to keep her on tenterhooks, though I cannot imagine why. I had been waiting for at least an hour when suddenly she sprang from behind the screen. I heard the light thud of her feet as she got out of bed and the sound of rapid footsteps crossing the room; then the next moment there she was, standing in the doorway. She just stood and looked, and said nothing. I had become such a blackguard that I was actually pleased it was she who had made the first move. I can't tell you how low I had stooped and what a cad I was in those days. It was some time since I had had the chance of taking a close look at her, and she really had grown thin. Her face had shrunk, and it was obvious she had a temperature. Her eyes were now big, and they stared at me in blank curiosity, or so it seemed at first. I kept still and did not get up. Just then the feeling of hatred returned. But I very soon noticed she was not in the least afraid of me, and I assumed she was delirious. But she was not at all delirious. She began nodding her head at me, as ill-bred and unsophisticated people do when they want to indicate their displeasure; and then she raised her tiny fist and began threatening me. For the first few moments her antics looked ridiculous, but soon I could stand it no longer; I got up and moved towards her in terror. I could not bear to see such despair on the face of such a little creature. She all the while kept on threatening me with her fist and nodding her head reproachfully. I started to say something, tentatively, in a whisper almost, sneakily trying to humour her; but I soon realised it was no good, and I became even more terrified. With an impulsive gesture she buried her face in her hands as she had done earlier, and then went over to the window and stood there with her back to me. I too turned away, and went and sat down by an open window.

'I cannot for the life in me understand why I did not leave at that moment. Instead I stayed where I was, as if I was actually waiting for something to happen. I could have got up and killed her if only to put an end to this agony. But then I heard footsteps again; she had gone out on to the wooden landing which led downstairs. I was just in time to see her disappearing into a tiny box-room, rather like a hen-house right next to the w.c. As I was sitting there a very curious idea shot through my mind. To this day I cannot make out why such an idea should have entered my head at all, but that is how it was. Of course, it was still impossible to take such an idea seriously, but one can never tell. . . . I can remember everything with terrifying clarity. My heart was beating violently. A minute later I looked at my watch and made a note of the time. Why I needed to I have no idea, but it was as though I wanted to pay attention to everything during those moments. The upshot is that I can recall and visually recapture everything as if it were happening now. There was a fly buzzing around and it kept settling on my face. I caught it, held it in my fingers, and put it out of the window. There was a loud noise as a cart trundled into the yard below. There was also plenty of noise coming from the other end of the yard, where a tailor was sitting by an open window singing at the top of his voice as he got on with his work. I could see him. But it crossed my mind that, since no one had seen me when I came in through the gate and made my way upstairs there was no reason why anyone would notice me on my way out, and so very carefully. . . . I moved my chair away from the window so that none of the residents would be able to see me. What a rotten thing to do! I opened a book, but put it down again, and began to inspect a tiny reddish spider on the leaf of a geranium, and promptly fell into a trance. I can remember every detail.

'Suddenly I looked at my watch. Twenty minutes had passed since she had gone out. But I decided to wait another fifteen minutes. It also occurred to me that she might have come in again, and that perhaps I had not heard her. But that would have been impossible; it was all so quiet, you could hear the humming of even the tiniest insect. My heart started pounding again suddenly. I took out my watch; there were three minutes to go. I sat them out, however, even though my heart beat as if it was going to burst. Then I got up, put on my hat, buttoned my jacket, and had a look round the room to see if I had left any sign that I had been there. I put the chair back beside the window where it had been before. At length I opened the door, locked it again, and made towards the box-room. The door was closed, but not locked. I knew it was not locked but I had no desire to open it, so I stood on tiptoe and looked through the chink above the door. At that precise instant, as I was standing there on tiptoe, I remembered that when I had been sitting by the window looking at the little red spider I had been imagining how I would stand on tiptoe and peer through this chink. I mention this detail, because I want to provide indubitable evidence that I was in full control of my mental faculties, that I could not have been out of my mind, and that I was fully responsible for my own actions. I peered through the chink for some considerable time, because it was dark in there, although not completely; there was just enough light for me to make out what I had been wanting to see. . . . I decided it was now possible for me to leave, and so I went down the stairs. I did not meet anybody, so there could be no witnesses. Three hours later we were in our shirt-sleeves back in my place drinking tea and playing cards. Lebyadkin was reciting poetry. Lots of stories were being told. As if by design they were good ones which made us laugh; not the usual stupid jokes. Kirillov was there too. No one was drinking, although there was a bottle of rum on the table; only Lebyadkin took an occasional swig. Prokhor Malov once remarked that 'when Nikolay Vsevolodovich is pleased and in a good mood everything goes well and the conversation is lively'. I remembered what he had said, for I must have been gay and in high spirits, and saying witty things. But I can remember being fully conscious that I was nothing but a mean and despicable coward. I was happy only because I had got away; I would never be anything but a blackguard. And there is something else; I suddenly thought of the Jewish proverb: 'One's own excretions do not smell.' Because, although I knew full well I was a scoundrel of the worst kind, I was not ashamed of the fact and did not lose much sleep over it. For the first time in my life, as I was sitting there drinking tea and chatting, I came to the startling realisation that I was not aware of the difference between good and evil. Not only had I lost all awareness, but it now seemed there was no difference, and that there was no such thing as good and evil (I found this reassuring). I have now only one conviction: the conviction that I shall never be free from convictions; and if I ever do become free from them, it will be the end of me. I arrived at this formula while I was sitting there drinking tea, joking and laughing about various things. And for that reason I shall never forget it. Commonplace ideas, ideas one has had before, often strike one as original. It happens to people even at fifty.

'This explains why I was expecting something to happen. I was not disappointed, for around eleven o'clock the janitor's little girl appeared. She had been sent by the landlady in Gorokhovaya Street to tell me that Matryosha had hanged herself. I went off with the little girl and when I got there discovered that the landlady herself did not know why she had sent for me. She was bawling and making a great to do, as people like her do in such circumstances. A crowd had gathered, and the police arrived. I stayed for a short while, and then left.

'They did not give me much trouble, although I was asked the usual questions. All I said was that the girl had been ill and delirious, and for that reason I had offered to call a doctor at my own expense. They also questioned me about the penknife. I explained that the landlady had thrashed her, but that was all. Not a soul knew about my having been there that evening. And there the matter ended.

'I did not go there for a whole week, and when I did go, it was only to give my notice. The landlady was still crying, although she was messing about with her rags again and sewing as usual. 'It was your penknife that made me do what I did,' she said, but she did not go out of her way to reproach me. I settled my account with her, explaining that I could not receive Nina Savelyevna any longer in a place like that. As I was leaving she again told me how wonderful Nina Savelyevna was. On my way out, I gave her five roubles over and above what I owed her.

'Generally speaking at that time I was sick of life to the point of dementia. I would completely have forgotten about the incident in Gorokhovaya Street, once the danger was over, had I not, for a certain length of time, been eaten up by the recollection of what a coward I had been. I vented my spleen on anyone I could find. Also at that time, and for no particular reason, I took it into my head to maim myself, only in the most revolting way possible. For the past year I had been thinking of doing myself in; but now I had a better idea. One day, as I was taking a look at the cripple Marya Timofeyevna (who at that time was a kind of charlady and not yet insane, simply a crazed woman, madly though secretly in love with me, as my companions had discovered) I suddenly decided I would marry her. The idea of Stavrogin marrying the last person you could possibly imagine had a powerful effect on my nerves. It was impossible to envisage anything more mon-strous. I will not here enter into the question as to whether I was influenced unconsciously (it could only have been unconsciously!) by a feeling of resentment at having been such a despicable

coward in my behaviour towards Matryosha. I do not think so.
But at any rate I did marry her, and not simply because of a bet I
made one day when I was drunk. The witnesses were Kirillov and
Pyotr Verkhovensky, who was at the time serving in Petersburg;
and two others, Lebyadkin himself and Prokhor Malov (he has
since died). No one else knew about it, and they promised not to
say a thing. This has always struck me as rather nasty, but the
secret has been kept to this day, even though I did have the
intention of making it public. So while I am about it, here goes.

'My marriage is hereby declared public.[31] After the wedding I
left for the provinces to stay with my mother. I went primarily to
recuperate, because life had been intolerable. In the town where
we lived I had left people with the impression that I had taken
leave of my senses, an impression which persists even now, and
certainly does me no credit, as I shall explain later. After that I
went abroad for four years.

'I spent some time in the East, at the monastery on Mount
Athos where I attended the eight-hour long services, then in
Egypt;[32] I lived in Switzerland and travelled in Iceland; I spent
a whole year at Göttingen University. In my last year I became
very friendly with a distinguished Russian family in Paris and
with two young Russian ladies in Switzerland. About two years
ago, in Frankfurt, as I was passing a stationers, I noticed among
the photographs for sale the picture of a little girl, elegantly
turned out, but very like Matryosha. I promptly bought the
picture and, when I got back to my hotel, displayed it on the
mantelpiece. I left it like that for a week, and did not once look at
it, and when I left Frankfurt, forgot to take it with me.

'I have included this detail just to demonstrate to what extent I
was capable of surmounting my past impressions and of becoming
indifferent to them. I dismissed the whole pack of them at one fell
swoop, and they did me the favour of vanishing, whenever I
wanted them to. It has always been tiresome for me to dredge up
the past, and I have never been able to reminisce as most other
people do. As for Matryosha, I even forgot to take her picture
from the mantelpiece. About a year ago, in the spring I was
travelling through Germany, when I absentmindedly overshot a
station where I should have changed, and found myself on the
wrong line.[33] I managed to get out at the next station: it was after
two in the afternoon, and a fine clear day. It was a tiny German
town. I was shown a hotel. I had a long wait ahead, because the
next train was not due until eleven that night. I was even pleased

with my adventure, since I was in no particular hurry. The hotel turned out to be a wretched little place, but it was surrounded by greenery and flower-beds. I was given a poky little room. I had a very good meal, and as I had been travelling the night before, I fell sound asleep after lunch, somewhere around four in the afternoon.

'I had the most unexpected dream; I have never known the like of it. In the art gallery in Dresden there is a picture by Claude Lorraine. In the catalogue it is given as 'Acis and Galatea', but I have always called it, although I do not know why, 'The Golden Age'. I had seen it before, but three days or so earlier, as I was passing through Dresden, I had caught another glimpse of it. It was this picture I dreamt of, but not as a picture, but as if it were real life. The scene is set in a corner of the Greek Archipelago; blue caressing waves, islands and rocks, verdant shores, a magical vista in the distance, an entrancing sunset – words cannot describe it. European man was returning to the scene of his origins. Here were the beginnings of mythology, his sylvan paradise . . . Wonderful people once lived here. They lived their days from morn to night in happiness and innocence. The groves rang with their gay singing; the great abundance of unspent vigour was poured into love and simple joy. The sun bathed these islands and the sea in beams, and rejoiced in its lovely children. What a marvellous dream, such a sublime illusion! This is the most improbable of all dreams, yet it is upon this dream that mankind has always lavished its powers; it is for this dream that they have made every kind of sacrifice, died on the Cross or as prophets; without it nations cannot live, but neither are they able to die. It was as if I lived through the whole of this in my dream. I cannot say exactly what I dreamt about, but it was as if I could still see the rocks and the sea, the slanting rays of the setting sun, when I awoke and opened my eyes, which for the first time in my life were literally wet with tears. A sensation of happiness, the like of which I had never known, permeated my entire being; it was even painful. It was now evening, and through the green leaves of the flowers on the window-sill a shaft of bright slanting rays from the setting sun entered the window of my tiny room and bathed me in light. I quickly closed my eyes again, as if my only desire was to recapture the vanished dream; then suddenly, amid this blinding light, I caught sight of some shape or other. It was then that I distinctly made out the figure of a tiny reddish spider. I at once remembered that I had seen it on the geranium leaf, also at the moment when the slanting rays of the setting sun were pouring in. It was as though something had plunged into me; I raised myself and sat on my bed (That is everything, exactly as it happened!) . . .

'I could see before me (No, not in the flesh. If only this vision had been real!); I could see Matryosha. Her eyes were burning with fever and she looked so thin, exactly as she was when she stood in the doorway, nodding her head at me and threatening me with her tiny fist. I have never known anything so agonising! The pathetic despair of a helpless ten-year old with as yet undeveloped powers of reasoning, threatening me (with what? What could she have done?) but naturally blaming only herself. I have never known anything like it. I sat there till it was dark and lost count of time. Is this what they call pangs of conscience and repentance? I do not know, and cannot tell even to this day. It is possible that even now the recollection of my doings is insufficiently abhorrent to me, and contains something to gratify my lusts. But no – I found this image standing there in the doorway with raised and threatening fist absolutely unbearable; just the way she looked then, at that precise moment, nodding her head; it was this, only this, I found intolerable. It is this I cannot endure, because ever since that time I have been haunted by it almost daily. It is not that it appears of its own accord; I summon it forth myself, and cannot help doing so, even though it threatens my very existence. Would that I had seen her in the flesh, even though it were an hallucination!

'I have some other hoary memories, perhaps even worse ones than this. There was one woman I treated even more abominably, and she died as a result. I killed two innocent men in a duel; they had done me no harm. Once I was mortally insulted, but refused to avenge myself.[34] Another time I poisoned somebody, deliberately too, and I got away with it.

'(I will confess everything, if I must.) Why is it then that none of my other remembered misdeeds troubles me like this one? They rouse only hatred, and were it not for my present state of mind I would not have brought them up; until now I have callously overlooked them and dismissed them from my mind.

'After that I spent almost the whole of the following year roaming from one place to another trying to keep myself busy. I know that even now I can dismiss the thought of the little girl whenever I want to. I am still completely in control of my will. The whole point is that I never wanted to do so; I do not want to and I never shall. And things will continue like this until I go out of my mind.

In Switzerland two months later I managed to get myself en-
tangled with a young woman or, to put it more accurately, I
was overcome by a fit of passion, one of those wild impulses I used
to have in the past. I felt a terrible temptation to commit yet
another crime, this time bigamy (because I was already married)
but acting on the advice of another girl, to whom I confided
almost everything, made my getaway. Moreover, a crime of this
kind would not have saved me from Matryosha.

'And so I decided to have these sheets printed, and three
hundred copies sent to Russia. In due course I shall send some to
the police and to the local authorities. Simultaneously I shall
circulate them to all the newspaper editors and to the majority of
my acquaintances in Petersburg and in Russia generally. Equally
they will appear abroad in translation. It could be that I shall not
be worried by the law, at any rate not to any large extent. I am
my own accuser, and no one is prosecuting me. Besides there is
no evidence, or rather, very little. Finally, the deeply ingrained
notion that I am mentally unbalanced and the efforts of my family,
who will naturally make use of this notion, will put paid to any
legal proceedings that might be instituted against me. Incidentally, I am telling you this simply to prove that I am sane and fully
aware how I stand. There will always be those who will know
everything; they will look at me, and I at them. The more the
merrier. As to whether this will be any consolation to me, I have
no idea. It may be my last resort. I repeat: if the Petersburg
Police make a thorough search, they might find something. Those
people could still be living in Petersburg. They will remember the
house all right; it was bright blue. As for me I shall not be going
anywhere, and for some time to come (a year or two) they will
always be able to find me at my mother's country house in
Skvoreshniki. I am ready to appear anywhere, if required to
do so.'

CHAPTER IX (SECTION III)

THE reading lasted for about an hour. Tikhon took his time, and
perhaps read certain passages twice over. Ever since the interruption during which the second sheet had been withheld
Stavrogin had been sitting silently and without once stirring,
huddled up on the divan in obvious expectation. Tikhon took off
his glasses, paused, and then looked hesitantly at Stavrogin, who
shuddered and heaved himself forward.

'I forgot to warn you,' he said sharply, 'that anything you say will be useless. I have no intention of going back on my decision; don't try to persuade me. I am going to publish it.' He blushed and said no more.

'You did not forget to warn me. You told me this only a short time ago, before I started reading.'

There was a note of pique in Tikhon's voice. The 'document' had evidently made a powerful impression. His Christian sensibility had been wounded, and he was not always capable of containing himself. I mention this only by the way, but it was not for nothing that he had acquired the reputation of being the kind of man who was, so it was said in the monastery, 'unable to control himself in public'. For all his Christianity, there was an unmistakable note of displeasure in his voice.

'It's all the same to me,' Stavrogin went on, somewhat abruptly, not noticing the change. 'However powerful your objections may be, I shall not abandon my plan. And please note that in saying this—whether you think I am being astute or inept, you are entitled to believe what you like—I'm not trying to get you to start arguing me round and going down on your bended knees,' Stavrogin sneered.

'Even if I wanted to try and dissuade you from your decision, I would not be able. Your idea is a great one. Christianity could find no more perfect expression than this. No penance could be more sublime than the one you have conceived, if only. . . .'

'If only what?'

'If in fact it were real repentance and a truly Christian intention.'

'Subtleties,' muttered Stavrogin, gloomily and almost without thinking. He got up, and began to stride about the room, but without realising he was doing so.

'You seem to want to make yourself out to be worse than you really are,' declared Tikhon, taking the offensive more and more.

'What do you mean exactly? I have not "been making myself out" to be anything, nor have I been giving myself airs. "Worse," what does it mean "worse"?' he blushed once again, and grew angry. 'I am fully aware that this thing,' he nodded indicating the sheets of paper, 'is pitiful, sneaky and nasty, but you must admit that vileness itself will only serve to aggravate . . .' he suddenly broke off, as though ashamed to go on, and at the same time considering it beneath him to get involved in explanations; nevertheless he was clearly distressed, although without realising it, at the prospect of being impelled willy-nilly to go through the whole business of unravelling. It is worth noting that no further reference was made to the reason given for withholding the second sheet; it was as if both of them had forgotten it. Meanwhile he had stopped walking about and was standing by the writing desk. He picked up a small crucifix made of ivory and began twisting it between his fingers, when suddenly it broke in two.[35] He came to with a shock, and looked at Tikhon in bewilderment. His upper lip started to quiver as if he had been insulted and was issuing a challenge.

'I thought you were actually going to tell me something. That's why I came,' he said in a hushed voice, as if doing his utmost to contain himself, and threw the fragments of the broken crucifix on to the desk.

Tikhon swiftly lowered his eyes.

'This document comes straight from the heart of one who has been mortally wounded. Am I not right in this?' he spoke with determination, and almost in a state of excitement. 'This is indeed repentance, and the natural urge to repentance has taken hold of you. The suffering brought about by the wound you have borne has compelled you to face the ultimate question of life and death. There is still hope. The way you have entered upon is great, unheard of, to do penance before the whole world, incurring the opprobrium you have deserved. You are appealing to the whole Church to judge you, even though you do not believe in the Church, if I understand you rightly. But you are already feeling contempt and scorn for anyone who happens to read what you have set out here, and you are defying them.'

'I am defying them?'

'If you are not ashamed to confess a crime, then why are you ashamed of repentance?'

'I – ashamed?'

'Yes, ashamed, and afraid too.'

'Afraid?' Stavrogin smiled awkwardly, and his upper lip started trembling again.

'Let them look at me, you say. Well, and how are you going to look at them? You are already anticipating their rage, in order only to pay them back in even greater measure. You have emphasised certain passages in your statement; it is as though you were revelling in your psychological analysis and clutching at every little detail simply for the purpose of shocking the reader with a callousness and shamelessness which is not really in you.

On the other hand vicious preoccupations and idle pursuits are all the while making you really thick-skinned and stupid.'

'Stupidity is no crime,' sneered Stavrogin, turning pale.

'It sometimes is,' Tikhon went on determinedly and heatedly. 'Although mortally wounded by the apparition in the doorway and tormented by it, you do not seem to see what your chief crime is and what these people you are wanting to judge you will find most disgraceful. It is your callous indifference to the rape you committed and your cowardliness they will notice. In one place you hasten to assure your reader that the threatening gesture made by the little girl did not seem "funny" to you, but terrible. Did it not seem "funny" to you even for a moment? It did; I know it did.'

Tikhon finished what he had to say. He had been talking as one who had no desire to control himself.

'Go on, please do,' Stavrogin urged. 'You are worked up and . . . you are being really scathing. I like this coming from a monk. But let me ask you just one thing. We have been talking for at least ten minutes since the time you finished reading and, although you are giving me a slating, I haven't noticed any sign of aversion or shame on your part. There is nothing squeamish about you, and you appear to treat me as an equal.'

The remark about 'treating him as an equal' was added in an undertone and as if unintentionally; very surprisingly for someone like him. Tikhon looked at him sharply.

'What you say surprises me,' he said after a moment's silence, 'for I can see that your words are genuine; in which case. . . . I too am at fault. Do you realise, I have been rude to you and have found your words not easy to stomach; but you in your frenzy of self-accusation did not even notice, although you were aware of my lack of forbearance and called it abuse. You consider yourself deserving of incomparably greater contempt, and your expression "treating as an equal" although unintentional is not altogether felicitous. I shall be frank with you. I was horrified at the immensity of this idle force, deliberately wasted on such trashy activity. It is evidently not for nothing that people acquire foreign citizenship.[36] But those who tear themselves away from their native soil are dogged by one particular penalty they have to pay: namely, boredom and a tendency towards idleness, even though they may be longing for something to do. Christianity recognises responsibility in all circumstances. The Lord has not done badly by you as regards intellect, and I ask you to judge for yourself, as soon as you are able to consider the question rationally: "Am I or am I not responsible for my actions?" The answer must be that you are responsible. "Temptations to sin are sure to come; but woe to him by whom they come!"[37] However as for the actual . . . crime itself, there are many people who sin like that, but live with their consciences in peace and tranquillity, even looking on youthful misdemeanours as inevitable. There are old men, with one foot already in the grave, who sin just like that, with relief even and sheer wantonness. The world is teeming with such horrors. But you have plumbed the depths to a degree which is extremely rare.'

'Could it be that you have come to respect me after seeing what I have written?' Stavrogin smiled wryly. 'And you . . . you, esteemed father Tikhon, so they tell me, are not fit to act as preceptor,' he added, still smiling, but his smile was becoming more forced and offensive. 'You are strongly criticised here. They say that the moment you see something sincere, some sign of humility in a sinner, you go off into raptures, saying how sorry you were, going all humble, and ingratiating yourself in front of the sinner. . . .'

'I am not going to answer that straightaway, but it is of course true that I am not good at dealing with people. I have always felt this to be one of my great faults,' Tikhon sighed, and with such candour that it brought a smile to Stavrogin's lips. 'But as for this,' he went on, motioning towards the sheets of paper, 'there certainly cannot be any greater and more terrible crime than the way you treated that little girl.'

'Let us stop measuring by the yard,' said Stavrogin after a moment's silence and with some annoyance. 'Perhaps I do not suffer quite as much as I have made out, and perhaps I have actually been telling a pack of lies about myself,' he concluded unexpectedly.

Tikhon did not say anything. Stavrogin hung his head forlornly and started to pace up and down the room.

'That young lady,' Tikhon suddenly asked, 'from whom you separated in Switzerland, she is . . . where, just at this moment?'

'Here.'

Again there was silence.

'Perhaps I did lie a great deal about myself,' Stavrogin suddenly insisted, 'I just do not know. . . . But what does it matter if I am trying to provoke people with the crudity of my confession, since you have already noticed this? It serves them right. They deserve what they get.'

'That is to say, hating them will make you feel much better than if you let them bestow compassion.'

'You are right. I am not accustomed to being candid, but if I did begin to . . . with you . . . you had better know that the more people there are like me, the more contempt I have for them, however many of them there are. Not one of them could be my judge. . . . I have written this rubbish simply because it entered my head, as an outrage. . . . It could be that I have simply been making it all up, exaggerating during a moment of fanaticism . . .' he broke off angrily and went red in face as he had done earlier, for having said more than he had intended. He turned away towards the desk with his back to Tikhon, and once more picked up one of the pieces of the broken crucifix.

'Answer me this question, in all sincerity, for me alone, just as you would for yourself in the hours of darkness,' Tikhon began, with a note of exaltation in his voice: 'If someone were to forgive you for this (he pointed at the printed pages), not one of the people you respect or fear, but a stranger, a man you would never know; if on reading this terrible confession of yours such a man were to forgive you in the privacy of his own heart, would you be relieved, or would it make no difference? But please, if you feel that to answer would present difficulties, then do not say anything; just think about it.'

'I would feel better,' replied Stavrogin quietly, 'if you forgave me; I should then feel much more relieved,' he added quickly and almost in a whisper, but without turning round.

'Provided that you forgive me too.'

'For what? I know; one of your monastic formulas. This is false humility. You know, all these antiquated monastic formulas of yours are not the least bit attractive. But you really think they are,' he snorted peevishly. 'I have no idea why I am here,' he added just then, looking round. 'Oh, and I've broken this. . . . A piece like this, I suppose, is worth about twenty-five roubles?'

'Don't worry about that.'

'Even fifty. Why shouldn't I worry? Why should I come and break your things, and you then go and forgive the damage I have done? Please take this; there are fifty roubles.' He brought out the money and put it on the desk. 'And if you don't want to keep it for yourself, give it to the poor, or to the Church. . . .' He became more and more tense. 'Listen, I'll tell you the whole truth. I want you to forgive me. And I would like one or two others to forgive me as well. But as for the rest, they are sure to hate me; but let them!'

'And if everyone were to forgive you and take pity on you, could you not bear it with equal humility?'

'No, I could not. I do not want everyone's pity, and in any case that kind of thing is impossible; it is an empty proposition. Listen, I don't want to keep on waiting; I am definitely going to publish. . . . It's no use your trying to get round me. . . . I cannot wait any longer, I simply cannot . . .' he added, beside himself with rage.

'I am afraid for you,' Tikhon said almost timidly.

'Afraid I shall not be able to bear it? Afraid I shall not be able to endure their hatred?'

'Not only their hatred.'

'Then what else?'

'Their . . . their laughter.' It was as if Tikhon wrenched out his words only with the greatest effort, and they were barely audible.

The poor man had not been able to restrain himself, and he shook his head knowing it would have been better to say nothing.

Stavrogin was taken aback; his expression was one of alarm.

'I foresaw this. I must have seemed to you a very comic figure when you were reading this "document" of mine. Don't upset yourself. I had been expecting as much.'

Tikhon certainly looked disconcerted. He began to make amends, but this of course only made matters worse.

'For undertakings of this order one needs to be at peace with oneself. Even in times of suffering a man has need of the utmost lucidity. . . . Nowhere today is any such inner composure to be found. Strife prevails everywhere. People have ceased to understand one another. . . .'

'All this is very boring; I have heard it all a thousand times already,' interrupted Stavrogin.

'You will not achieve your ends,' Tikhon proceeded. 'Legally you are practically invulnerable, and people will find this funny for a start. They will be puzzled. Who will be able to discern the real motives behind this confession? They will not even want to understand. People are afraid of prodigies of this kind, and regard them with trepidation. They react with hatred and revenge. The world likes its own kind of filth and does not want to be disturbed. And for this reason they will not be slow to make a joke out of it, because, for these people, poking fun at something is the quickest way of demolishing it.'

'Please be more precise; I would like to hear more.'

'To begin with they will of course give expression to their horror, but for the sake of appearances, it will be more a case of affectation than genuine response. I do not include those innocent souls who will be truly horrified and ready even to blame themselves; no one will take any notice of them, for they will keep their mouths shut. But the rest, those men of the world, who show anxiety only when their private interests are threatened; it is they who, after their initial bewilderment and conventional show of horror is over, will be the first to laugh. They will be curious about this madman, because they will undoubtedly take you for one. Nevertheless, in order to justify their derision, they will consider you not entirely lacking in responsibility for your own actions. Will you be able to stand this? Your heart will be eaten up with such fierce indignation that it is doubtful whether you could survive it. . . . That is what I am afraid of.'

'Well, and what about you? . . . I am amazed at the cynical view you take of people, how they disgust you,' Stavrogin said, showing clear signs of anger.

'Believe me, I was judging by myself, rather than people in general.'

'That's as may be. But there is something inside you that makes even a person like yourself find amusement in my misfortune.'

'Who knows, perhaps there is? That could well be!'

'Enough's enough. Come on, tell me then, where exactly do I make myself look ridiculous in this document of mine? I know perfectly well already of course, but I would like you to put your finger on it. Go on say it, with as much cynicism as you can muster, because you are a great big cynic. . . . You saintly types are dreadful cynics; you don't even seem to realise just how much you despise people. . . . Tell me with all the frankness of which you are capable. You really are a queer customer!'

'In the very form of this great penance of yours there is something ridiculous, something contrived one might say . . . but in general, it lacks firmness, and is confused, as though you were not able to sustain it as a result of the debilitating effect of dread. . . . Oh, you need not worry, you will get your victory!' he exclaimed, suddenly drawing in his horns, but in a state of rapture almost. 'Even the form it is in at present (he pointed at the printed pages) will win the day, if only you can submit sincerely to all the blows and the vilification . . . if you can bear it! It has always ended in the most ignominious cross becoming a very great triumph and supreme strength when the humility was sincere. But is there real humility here, that is what I would like to know? Is there going to be any? Oh, you need no challenge; only a very deep humility! It would have been better for you not to hold your judges in contempt, but to put your faith sincerely in them, as one would in the Universal Church. Only then could you win them over and make yourself an example for them, uniting yourself with them in love. . . . Oh, if only you could bring yourself to bear such a thing!'

'Go on then, tell me what is it you find most ridiculous in these pages?'

'Why, why all this preoccupation with seeming ridiculous, why are you so afraid of that kind of thing?' Tikhon exclaimed bitterly, shaking his head.

'That is my business. You just tell me what it is you find so comic. . . .'

'Ugliness kills,' Tikhon whispered, lowering his eyes.

'Ugliness? What ugliness?'

'The ugliness of crime. Crime is a truly ugly thing. Whatever the crime, the more bloody, the more terrible it is, the more picturesque and the more impressive it seems. But there are shameful and disgusting crimes, past all horror. . . .'

Tikhon did not finish what he had to say.

'You mean to say, you find me a highly ridiculous figure for kissing a little girl's hands and . . . and then turning coward . . . and . . . well, so on and so forth. . . . I understand you very well. And you are thinking that I shall not be able to bear it.'

Tikhon remained silent. Stavrogin's face turned white, and seemed to twitch.

'Now I know why you asked me about the young lady from Switzerland, whether she was here or not,' he muttered quietly as if to himself.

'You are ill-prepared, insufficiently hardened,' Tikhon added.

'Listen to me. I want forgiveness for myself; that is my chief purpose. My only purpose!' Stavrogin said suddenly with a gloomy look of exaltation in his eyes. 'That is the whole of my confession. It's the whole truth, and the rest is lies. Only then will the apparition disappear forever; I know it. That is why I am seeking immeasurable suffering. It is my own search. . . . Don't try and scare me, suggesting I will die of rage,' he added, as though he had not been able to stop himself. These words came as such a surprise to Tikhon that he got up from his chair in astonishment.

'If you believe you can forgive yourself, and attain such forgiveness through your own suffering alone, then you will believe anything!' he exclaimed ecstatically. 'How could you then say that you did not believe in God?'

Stavrogin made no reply.

'God will forgive you for your unbelief, for you revere the Holy Spirit, without knowing it.'

'There is no forgiveness for such as me,' Stavrogin said gloomily. 'It is said in your book that there is no greater crime than to commit an offence against innocent children.[38] It says just that!'

He pointed to the Bible.

'I have something to tell you which will gladden your heart,' Tikhon said tenderly: 'Christ will forgive you, if only you can bring yourself to forgive yourself. . . . Oh, please do not think I am blaming you. Even if you did not become reconciled to yourself and did not attain forgiveness. He would forgive you even so, because of your good intentions and your tremendous suffering. . . . In human language there are no words or concepts capable of expressing the many ways and reasons of the Lamb of God. He who embraces His immensity will be granted boundless understanding!'

The corners of his mouth quivered once again, and a scarcely noticeable tremor passed across his face. He had been trying to pluck up courage, but had not succeeded; he quickly lowered his gaze.

Stavrogin picked up his hat from the divan.

'I shall be coming again in due course,' he said, looking extremely weary. 'I . . . I am really most grateful for the pleasure of talking to you, for the honour you have done me . . . and also for your consideration. Believe me when I say that I can now understand why certain people have such great affection for you. I ask your prayers to Him whom you love so much. . . .'

'You are leaving already?' Tikhon made as if to get up; it seemed as if he had not expected to be bidding him goodbye quite so soon. 'I wanted . . .' he seemed to lose track of his thought, 'I was going to ask you something, but I do not know how . . . I am afraid to.'

'Please do me the honour.' Stavrogin promptly sat down, still holding his hat. Tikhon looked at this hat of his, at his posture;

the posture of a man who had suddenly become worldly again, but was also disturbed and half-insane; a man of the world who was giving him a further five minutes of his time. Tikhon became even more disconcerted.

'All I wanted to ask you was . . . but you are already well aware, Nikolay Vsevolodovich (that is your first name and patronymic, isn't it?) that if you publish what you have written, you will ruin yourself . . . from a career point of view, for instance, and . . . from the point of view of the rest of your life.'[39]

'Career?' Stavrogin frowned.

'Why spoil everything? Why this rigidity?' Tikhon exclaimed, almost pleadingly, and clearly aware of his own maladroitness. Stavrogin seemed pained.

'I have already asked you a favour, and I ask it again. I do not want your advice in this matter. . . .'

He deliberately turned away.

'You do not understand; please listen to what I am saying and have patience. You know what my opinion is: if this task you have set yourself were carried out with humility, it would be a very great Christian achievement, provided only that you were able to sustain it. Even if you failed, the Lord would all the same count it a sacrifice on your part. Everything would be taken into account: not a single word, not a single exertion of the spirit, not even a half-thought would escape His notice. I propose instead a different task, even greater than the one you envisaged.'

Stavrogin said nothing.

'You are eaten up with the desire for self-torture and sacrifice. Control this desire of yours, put aside your plan, and all will be well. Subdue this pride of yours and put to shame your demon! Victory will be yours in the end, and you will attain freedom.'

His eyes were burning. He brought his hands together beseechingly.

'How seriously you are taking all this, and how important you think it all is. . . . But do you think I don't know what is at the back of your mind?' Stavrogin said, not impolitely, but somewhat irritably. 'I have noticed that you have been wanting to trap me–doubtless with the best of intentions, and out of a desire for the well-being of your fellow-men. What you wanted was that I should settle down, stop my monkey-tricks, and, I dare say, get married and end my days a member of the local club, paying visits to your monastery at holiday times. Isn't that it? And what is more: being the psychologist and cynic you are, you have foreseen that things will undoubtedly turn out like this; that all I need now is a little coaxing, just for propriety's sake, since I have been wanting this so much, wanting only to be coaxed. That's the truth, isn't it? I'll bet you have got my mother's best interests at heart too.'[40]

VIII
TRANSMUTED DIALECTIC

VLADIMIR SOLOVIEV was perhaps the most remarkable
man Dostoevsky ever met. Soloviev was twenty-one at the
time, and already widely acclaimed as a brilliant and
original philosopher. He was a poet too, a major influence
on the symbolist poets of the next generation. His lectures
were immensely popular, and he could fill any of the larger
public halls in the capital. Everyone was enthralled; cranks,
critics, devotees, janitors and cloakroom attendants alike. He
had visions too, and made no secret of it. Today he would
inevitably have been subjected to psychiatric treatment; but
in the Russia of those days visions were still valid. The inspiration of his entire life was an overwhelming vision of the
Great Mother, Sophia, the Madonna of Near Eastern
Christianity in early times. The setting for the vision however was not a Byzantine basilica, but that most unlikely of
all places, the Reading Room of the British Museum. His
orders were to go to Egypt, and to Egypt he went, narrowly
escaping death at the hands of bedouins.

He became famous for his stand against the Tsar,[1]
demanding Christian forgiveness for his father's assassins.
In later life he struggled for ecumenism, but even his closest
Catholic supporter supposed he was speaking a different
language.[2] Towards the end of his life he retreated from
philosophy into his vision. Despite his craziness, people still
loved him. He had given away all his belongings, slept on an
assortment of crates, and lived on snacks at one of the station
buffets. It was in these circumstances that he produced one
of the most remarkable works in the whole of Russian
literature. Dostoevsky was long since dead, and the Revolution not many years away.

1 *A visit to a monastery*

Soloviev had been introduced to Dostoevsky in 1873, when still a mere youth. Anna Grigoryevna has put it on record that her husband was exceptionally impressed by this precocious young-old dialectician.[3] Their acquaintance was temporarily cut short by Soloviev's tour abroad. It was four years later in a public hall in Petersburg that the now rapidly ageing writer heard him delivering his lectures on 'Godmanhood'. The more Dostoevsky saw of Soloviev, the more he liked him. Here was a rare intellect indeed.

It was in the congenial atmosphere of the Countess Tolstaya's salon that their acquaintance grew into friendship. Dostoevsky did not make friends easily. It is true that he was fond of young people. But Soloviev's physical appearance belied his years. There was nothing in the least boyish about him. The attraction cannot have been Soloviev's ideas themselves, for Dostoevsky was never impressed by ideas as such. A more likely explanation is that Dostoevsky discovered he was in the presence of a man so possessed by ideas as to be entirely at their mercy. Soloviev was the real life counterpart of the character he was in the process of conceiving for his novel *The Brothers Karamazov*, the 'man of ideas', Ivan Karamazov.

During the time he was working on *The Brothers Karamazov* his little son Alyosha died. This came as a severe blow, from which he was never fully to recover. It was in the hope of regaining his mental equilibrium that he persuaded Soloviev to go with him for a few days to a monastery. The place they chose was known as the Optin Monastery, an institution famous for its *startsy*, or 'elders', spiritual guides and teachers in the oriental sense. The tradition is described in *The Brothers Karamazov*: a peculiarly Russian tradition interrupted only by the Mongol invasions that went back to the early Christian church in Sinai and Mount Athos. Father Ambrosius, whom Dostoevsky met there, was to become the model for his own character, Father Zosima.

The Optin Monastery is situated in Kaluga province near the township of Kozelsk, about a hundred and twenty miles south-west of Moscow. Dostoevsky and Soloviev went there in June 1878: 'Soloviev and I have decided to travel together to the Optin monastery on Friday. . . . He will come and see me at my hotel to-morrow at 5 p.m.'[4] And two days later: 'Tomorrow morning Soloviev and I are going to the Optin Monastery. On Tuesday (i.e. four days later) I shall be back in Moscow.'[5] And again in a letter to his wife a week later: 'I have just returned from the Optin Monastery. This is what happened. . . . We spent two days and nights there. . . . I will tell you about it when I return. . . .'[6] It is a pity that Dostoevsky followed his normal practice in correspondence of confining himself to trivialities. A great deal has to be surmised. We have to look to his last novel for the clues.

Those who have been fortunate enough to have been inside a Russian monastery will not quickly forget the experience. The atmosphere is totally unlike that of any English abbey, living or in ruins. Even on the calmest of days there is a pulsation in the air, everywhere. There are of course many pilgrims, trippers and others, but the strange agitation is not to be mistaken for bustle. Tyutchev, the poet, captured it in his Russian landscapes. Perhaps it is nothing more than the shimmer of palpitating birch leaves against an unrelieved expanse of indescribably remote and unrelieved blue sky. The total effect is more important than any single aspect; an effect that is experienced in the chorus of great and small bells that vibrate into one's very being. I cannot imagine that many go to Russian monasteries simply for a rest or recuperation. Participation cannot be avoided. The numinous is everywhere to be felt. We have simply to imagine the elation of the two visitors. Perhaps they too shared Alyosha Karamazov's vision:

> The vault of heaven, full of soft, shining stars, stretched vast and fathomless above. . . . The Milky Way ran in two pale streams from the zenith to the horizon. The fresh, motionless, still night enfolded the earth. The white towers and golden domes of the cathedral gleamed out against the sapphire sky. . . . The silence of earth seemed to melt into the silence of the heavens. The mystery of earth was one with the mystery of the stars. . . .

What we do know is that Dostoevsky mentioned his plans for a vast novel, the central idea of which would be 'the Church as a positive social ideal'.[7] *The Brothers Karamazov* was to be no more than the first part of the grandiose design. It is perhaps just as well that he never realised his aim. It is possible, though, that the project was never more than an idea, for he never even began to sketch it. There is also an account of a conversation between Soloviev and Father Ambrosius. It is more than likely that Dostoevsky made a fantasy out of this for the scene in the monastery, and that certain details of Zosima are borrowed from Ambrosius. It is certain that *The Brothers Karamazov* would have been a radically different novel had this episode at the Optin monastery never occurred.

2 *A conversation with monks*

There is a legend that Dostoevsky's paternal affection for Soloviev was somehow reproduced in his novel as the bond of affection between Zosima and young Alyosha Karamazov. The legend derives from Zosima's attachment to Alyosha, especially on account of his resemblance to his own brother, who had died before reaching manhood, and also from the fact that Dostoevsky likewise had found in Soloviev a resemblance to a certain Shidlovsky, whom he had known in his youth.[8] This legend has been accepted by many as it stands; one critic for example has written: 'In Dostoevsky's romance the name of the third brother is Alyosha, but his readers were well aware that his name stood for that of Soloviev.'[9]

But that is where the resemblance ends. Despite the vintage of this legend, there are considerably more grounds for supposing that the Karamazov brother who has most in common with Soloviev is not Alyosha, but Ivan. 'In actual fact, it is not the ingenuous and enthusiastic Alyosha, but the brilliant dialectician, Ivan, with his powerful formal logic and strictly rational ethic, with his brandishing of the socialist utopia and religious philosophy, who in external aspect reminds us of Soloviev.'[10] Anna Grigoryevna is inclined to support this view, and she has no small claim to authority.

Many of Dostoevsky's readers will have had difficulty in understanding why he should have chosen to bring in Ivan Karamazov's lengthy disquisition on ecclesiastical and civil jurisdiction in the middle of what is otherwise a lively and highly entertaining series of episodes. At first sight, its inclusion suggests that Dostoevsky was looking for a plausible means of spanning the short period during which Zosima had to be absent from the gathering. It is only when we take a closer look at Soloviev's early philosophical ideas that we begin to recognise the significance behind this otherwise relatively dreary passage.

In an early essay which he called *The Three Forces*, Soloviev developed in his own particular manner the Slavophil concept of the *Third World Idea*. Chaadaev, a contemporary of Pushkin, was the first to elaborate this Russian answer to the latent contradictions in European civilisation: 'I have a deep conviction that it is our mission to resolve many of the problems relating to the social order, to bring the greater part of those ideas engendered by earlier societies to their necessary conclusion, and to provide the answer to many important questions affecting mankind.'[11] Soloviev's 'first force' was represented by the depersonalised Moslem society in which the individual was submerged in total despotism both spiritual and temporal. The 'second force', although freeing the individual, had gone to the opposite extreme. Soloviev was convinced that the real trouble began with the separation of Church and State at the time of the Reformation, in the aftermath of which both State and Church have become divorced from their members, the community at large. These institutions have taken on a life of their own, and exist only for themselves. First Rousseau, then Hegel, Spencer, and finally the Welfare State, Technocracy, and uncontrolled political manipulation. Out of the social disorder crystallises a new order founded on science and technology, on the worship of facts and systems, on deference to the man in the white coat. The need for a 'third force', which would act as a synthesis of the earlier extreme positions, was already evident. And this third force was to be furnished by the Slavs, a 'nation which does not require any special advantages, any special powers or surface talents, since it acts not for itself. . . . Free from any limitation or one-sidedness this nation would be indifferent to this life of ours with all its petty interests.'[12]

This historical scheme outlined by Soloviev could have been overlooked as juvenilia were it not for its reappearance a few years later in his *Lectures on Godmanhood*. These were given as public lectures to an audience of more than a thousand, and attracted a great deal of attention. Dostoevsky was himself a member of the audience.

In these lectures, Soloviev laid much emphasis on the position of Christ: Christ as the synthesis of God and Nature—the God-man. All could participate in this synthesis through the Church which was neither more nor less than the mystical body of Christ.[13] Soloviev considered that there are two senses in which it is possible to be a Christian. Either one accepts Christ from within as a member (literal *and* metaphysical) of his body, or recognises the truth of Christ's divinity from the outside. The latter might be the view of an anthropologist or moralist, or a student of comparative religion. The danger, according to Soloviev, was that Christians who acknowledge Christ only in this external sense are easy prey to the kind of temptation with which Satan attempted to ensnare Christ.[14] A Church such as the Roman Catholic Church, which aims to bring the entire world under Christ's domination, will in reality have fallen for Satan's bait. Soloviev, like Dostoevsky, believed that the impressive edifice of Rome concealed a loss of religious belief, and accused the Jesuits of having nurtured this unbelief for their own cynical ends. Protestantism, a natural and inevitable reaction against Catholicism, had unfortunately petered out into arid rationalism, and had created an intellectual climate in which the human mind came to believe it was a law unto itself. The upshot is that in modern Europe life is lived with reference to mere formalities and empty systems: 'This principle is expressed in the form of a demand that all life, all political and social relations should be organised and directed exclusively according to principles fabricated by the individual human mind, regardless of tradition and contrary to all direct faith in God.'[15]

Only in the East was true Christianity preserved. Yet all was not well even with the Orthodox Churches. Their members were too ready to believe, and had never felt the need for the building of a Church. As a result the Church had not grown at the same pace as society, and had remained a stunted growth. The Eastern Church had been static from the outset, and had clung to the 'divine principle' exclusively at the expense of the 'human principle'.[16] Soloviev believed that those who had prophesied the Third Rome as Moscow, and the dawning of the 'third world-idea', had really meant that Godmanhood, the true union of God and Man, the true mystical body, would enter finally into human consciousness. The fertile soil of Russia would do the God-bearing.

True Christianity, or Godmanhood, would only be attained upon the historical emergency of a 'spiritual society' in which the ecclesiastical sphere would represent a synthesis (in the Hegelian sense) of the political and economic spheres.

> The Church will not interfere in political or economic affairs, but will endow both the State and regional governments with a higher goal and a positive norm of action. In other words, the central and regional governments remain completely free . . . provided that they make allowance for those higher needs by which a spiritual society may be defined.[17]

This brings us to Soloviev's much discussed principle of Free Theocracy. According to this, the 'spiritual society' is itself unmovable, even though it is a synthesis of the political and economic spheres, which move freely in their own orbits. In this historical process, the catalyst is Russia, in particular the Russian ordinary man. In the period before his *Lectures on Godmanhood* Soloviev showed no concern over the difficulty of reconciling a 'Church that will not interfere in political or economic matters' with an institution 're-sponsible as the prime mover for directing all else, yet re-maining itself unmovable'.[18] It may have been his discussions with Dostoevsky which led Soloviev to reformulate the problem. The crux of the matter was *control*. The Church would control the secular spheres not by institutional means, but by elevating them into itself, by hypostatisation. The body or non-spiritual element of the hypostasis is the sole means whereby the spiritual society becomes *actual*. A society lacking flesh is no society at all, but an abstraction. To make his point clearer Soloviev in a later work[19] borrows the analogy of the living organism. In a human organism there is no question of conflict between the arterial and nervous systems, although the latter clearly has greater autonomy.

For many Russians of Soloviev's day issues of this kind were live issues. It is scarcely credible that Soloviev attracted the general public in their thousands by what might appear to many of us a mass of long winded and arid sophistry. Ivan Karamazov's discussion with the monks should be read against this background. If a page-by-page comparison is made between this section and Soloviev's Lectures, it will be seen that Dostoevsky is subjecting Soloviev's ideas to the most radical criticism not however through the medium of the philosophical tract but through the real dialectic of the concrete situation.

A comparison of Ivan Karamazov's thesis and the second lecture of Soloviev's *Lectures in Godmanhood* reveals an interesting difference in emphasis. Their solutions to the problem of the union of Church and State diverge slightly. Both agree that Church should become State, but they hold conflicting views as to how this should be achieved. Ivan Karamazov rules out any possibility of the two powers ever mingling: 'the Church ought to include the whole State and not simply a corner of it, and if this is for some reason impossible at the moment, then it ought in reality to be made the direct and chief aim of the future development of Christian society!' Ivan reassures us that 'all this will not degrade it in any way or detract from its honour and glory as a great State . . . but will merely turn it from a false, still pagan, and mistaken path to the true and rightful path, which alone leads to the eternal goal'. How different from

Soloviev, who proposes that 'the spiritual society–the Church–should *subject* secular society to itself by raising it up to its own level, by spiritualising it, by making the worldly element its instrument and means, its body'.[20] Soloviev is clearly of the opinion that the two principles eventually become fused, if only in external appearance, and that external unity will appear of its own accord as a natural concomitant. A Church is to arise that 'must move everything, remaining itself unmovable'. The discussion with the monks does not really touch the root of the matter. The reader is left with Father Paissy's ineptly pious sentiment that 'the State should end by being worthy to become the Church alone and nothing else'. The logical solution, subjection, comes only from Soloviev. A subjection that will not necessarily preclude freedom, but may even encourage it.

Father Iosif goes on to ask how Christ's words 'My Kingdom is not of this earth' can be reconciled with this rational speculation about the future of Church and State. The latter seems to him no more than a 'most unworthy play upon words'. Father Paissy, less naïvely, allows that the Kingdom is in heaven, but that the way to this kingdom is through the Church alone. None of this, however, is consistent enough for Soloviev. For him the only possible answer was the final synthesis, the Free Theocracy, in which there is 'free subjection' of the secular element to the spiritual.

Comparison need not be taken any further. It is evident that the purposes of Dostoevsky and Soloviev are wide apart. As a philosopher the latter is obliged to tie up all loose ends; the former as a novelist must avoid wearying his readers with relentless dialectic. The schemes are nevertheless fundamentally the same, the main difference being that Dostoevsky will not have 'subjection' of any sort, eschewing the doublethink of 'free subjection'.

Dostoevsky might well have fallen in with those critics who accuse Soloviev of 'rationalising the mystical'. But, if anything, he was mystifying the rational. Soloviev ended his life a sceptic, bearing out the predictions of the ever-canny Dostoevsky. There remains the strange ironical parallel

between the lives of Soloviev and the fictional Ivan Karamazov. It took Soloviev, the philosopher of Antichrist,
another twenty-five years to see that he was caught inextricably in Dostoevsky's prediction.

The discussion in the monastery next turns to the punishment of criminals. Ivan Karamazov's thesis is that a man
can be rescued from criminality only when he is a true
member of the Church; the mechanical retribution exacted
at the present time merely poisons the heart. 'When the
Church replaces the State it will become difficult for the
criminal in opposition to the universal Church to commit
crime.' In consequence the Church will be 'forced to
renounce the existing almost pagan attitude, and to desist
from a mechanical severance of its tainted member simply
for the preservation of society'. Zosima cannot understand
why Karamazov is hoping for something that already exists.
Unless this was true, the criminal would have no sense of
sin: 'It is only against the Church, not against the State, that
the present-day criminal can recognise that he has sinned.'

Zosima is far from complacent. He inveighs against all
forms of corporal punishment. The attitude is that of our
own day: 'All these sentences to exile with hard labour, and
in former days with flogging as well, reform no one, and
what is more, deter hardly a single criminal, and the
number of crimes does not diminish but is continually on the
increase.' It is when the Church is weak, with hardly any
spiritual hold on its members, that the criminal's plight
becomes hopeless. In Europe, for instance, the criminal goes
unrepentant because he feels that his crime is no crime at all,
but only a reaction against an unjustly oppressive authority.
The prevailing social doctrines even encourage him in this
view. Humanitarianism is not enough:

> If anything does preserve society, even in our day and does
> regenerate and transform the criminal, it is only the law of
> Christ speaking in his conscience. It is solely by recognising his
> wrong-doing as a son of a Christian society – that is, of the
> Church – that he may recognise his sin against society. . . . So
> that it is against the Church alone, and not the State, that the
> criminal of today can be aware that he has sinned.[21]

Dostoevsky clearly marks out the positions of Zosima and Ivan Karamazov. For the latter, criminal law will be reformed only with the coming into being of Free Theocracy. Zosima, on the other hand, insists that there is no need for change or reform, for 'in reality it is so at this moment'. He feels it is presumption to hope to transform Church into State; no human being could ever be cut out for such a task:

> The Christian society at present is unprepared and rests upon some seven righteous men, but as these never fail in their task it will continue unshaken in the expectation of its complete transformation from a society almost heathen in character into a single, universal and all-powerful Church. . . . And there is no need to trouble ourselves about times and seasons, for the secret of the times and seasons lies in the wisdom of God, in His foresight, and in His love. . . .[22]

This betrays Ivan Karamazov's humanism. Any transformations he foresees will be the work of men. His Church is no more than a veneer, beneath which is visible a purely man-made institution, the theocratic State, the imposing mockery of the Grand Inquisitor.

It is tempting to interpret this opposition of Ivan Karamazov and Zosima as Dostoevsky's own way of countering Soloviev's perilous rationalism. There is no doubt whatever, though, that Ivan's article on civil and ecclesiastical powers is an undisguised exposition of Free Theocracy.

Soloviev's new preoccupation with crime and the criminal ostensibly stems from the novelist, who had scarcely had the matter away from his mind since the day *he* was condemned to death. The passion was infectious. In March 1881, Soloviev delivered two public lectures very shortly after the assassination of Alexander II. On the face of it the message was harmless and academic. The second of the two lectures happened to be on the theme of the Russian people's intuitive belief in the transcending personality of Christ, a topic that runs through Dostoevsky's *Diary of a Writer*. Soloviev's speech ended as follows:

> Evil has been wrought, a meaningless, terrible deed; the Tsar has been murdered. The criminals have been caught, their

names are known, and, in accordance with the existing law, death awaits them as retribution, as the fulfilment of a pagan command: an eye for an eye, a death for a death. But how should the true God's-anointed act, the highest bearer amongst us of the obligations of a Christian society towards those fallen into grave sin? He should give an example to the whole nation. . . . Our God's anointed need not excuse the crime; but all he has to do is to remove the assassins from society, to remove them without destroying them. . . .[23]

This public utterance, whether motivated by extreme courage, foolhardiness, or sheer folly, makes two things clear: first, that Soloviev was prepared to pursue his ideas relentlessly to their conclusion and to apply them in practice if necessary; and secondly that Dostoevsky was behind this new turn in his attitude. The influence was both benign and sinister. Perhaps he unconsciously desired to instil into the young academic the will to action at all costs that had fired him in his youth, in the company of Speshnev, Petrashevsky, Durov and the rest. In the long run Soloviev turned out to be least like Ivan Karamazov as far as the *action* of the novel goes.

Despite the divergent attitudes of Dostoevsky and Soloviev, there seems to be little doubt that Dostoevsky was not only impressed but influenced positively by his young philosopher friend. Readers of Dostoevsky are frequently irritated and sometimes dismayed by the chauvinism, verging on xenophobia, of his journalistic outbursts, and the many outrageous sections of his *Diary of a Writer*. It is easy, however, to miss an important break in Dostoevsky's natural development in the months preceding the well-known Pushkin speech, his last, telling utterance. A subtle transition has taken place from 'Orthodoxy at the service of mankind' to an 'all-European and universal significance of the Russian man'; a transition that seems at first sight continuous.

In the *Diary of a Writer* there was an unmistakable trace of Chaadaev; 'Meanwhile in the East there actually burst into flame and shone forth with unprecedented light a third world-idea . . . a new element, which had been lying passive and inert, and which in any case . . . cannot help but influence world destinies extremely violently and decisively.'[24]

But all this pure Chaadaev is mixed up with Panslavism. The third world-idea depends somehow on a 'union of the Slavs', on 'two terrible Russian forces worth more than all the rest of the world put together'. We may feel let down by the sectarianism, the one-sided manner in which Dostoevsky interprets the phrase 'every great people believes that in it alone resides the salvation of the world'. The only possible conclusion is either that Dostoevsky did not really understand Chaadaev, or that he had selected only those facets which squared with his own view of universalism. Despite the character in *The Raw Youth* who declares himself 'the only European in Europe', and Ivan Karamazov's lament over the graveyard of European civilisation: 'precious are the dead that lie there, every stone speaks of such burning life in the past, of such passionate faith in their work, their truth, their struggles and their science, that I know I shall fall on the ground and kiss those stones and weep over them'; despite this realisation of the purpose of the 'third force', all the while, explicitly or implicitly, Dostoevsky cannot shake off the jingoism of the worst of the slavophiles.

Yet the Pushkin speech reveals a completely new phase; Dostoevsky has taken over in its entirety Soloviev's view that the third world-idea will be incarnated in a people who are merely acting as go-betweens, 'not requiring any special advantages, powers or external gifts'. 'Surely, the significance of the Russian is indisputably all-European and universal. To become a true Russian, to become fully Russian, perhaps means no more than to become the brother of all peoples. . . .'[25] Apart from a curious reference to the superiority of the Aryan races, Dostoevsky has *almost* abandoned the worst sides of his nationalism. Whether Dostoevsky would have thanked Soloviev unreservedly for the new direction in his thinking is quite another matter. How essential this miscellaneous prejudice that makes parts of his *Diary* almost unreadable is we shall surely never know. Nietzsche at any rate had no illusions about its function!

3 *Antichrist*

A footnote to the last of Soloviev's *Lectures on Godmanhood*
runs as follows:

> Several years ago in Paris I heard a French Jesuit utter the
> following reasoning: 'Of course at present no one can believe
> the greater part of the Christian dogmas, for example, the
> Divinity of Christ. But you will agree that civilised human
> society cannot exist without a strong authority and a firmly
> organised hierarchy; only the Catholic Church possesses such
> authority and such a hierarchy'.[26]

This reminiscence appears at a point where Soloviev is
attempting to expose Jesuitism for what he really believed it
to be. Slavophile Russians will have rejoiced at this public
admission of what after all many of them had expected all
along. Soloviev came face to face with the atheism underlying Catholicism, which before had been only surmised, an
'imperceptible embryo' as he had been calling it. From now
on Jesuitism is denounced as merely another Machiavellian
organisation, ridden with a lust for power, and yet despite
everything 'the extreme, the most pure expression of the
Catholic principle'.[27]

It is difficult to resist the supposition that this incident in
Paris provided the inspiration for Dostoevsky's Grand Inquisitor. And some have accepted this without further examination.[28] The question is however rather more complicated. We have already seen that in many respects Soloviev's ideas are very close to those of Ivan Karamazov. But in
this case, it is Karamazov who condones the lust for power of
the Jesuits, whilst his brother Alyosha advocates the more
usual view. Ivan assures his brother that the autocracy of those
elect few who have 'also been in the wilderness' and 'have
lived on roots and locusts' is anything but the result of a
power lust: 'Do you really think that the Roman Catholic
tendency in recent centuries is actually nothing more than a
lust for power, or filthy earthly gain?' The anti-Jesuitism of
Soloviev is quite out of keeping with the theme of the extended
section of the novel entitled 'Pro and Contra', where it is

stressed that autocracy exists only through the aged cardinal's love and compassion for the feeble mass of mankind, and not through any desire for self-aggrandisement. In reality, the cardinal is a solitary, unhappy man, who has sacrificed everything for his fellow men – even his belief in God. Instead he has come to believe in Satan. It gives him no satisfaction to see people throwing themselves abjectly at his feet. He does not really enjoy his *autos-da-fé*, but he was forced to sacrifice the few to bring about the happiness of the vast majority.

Dostoevsky's Catholicism without Christ is, as it turns out, traceable to the preliminary draft of *The Devils*, to a time when he was an 'exile' from Russia, moving from one European city to another. The Franco-Prussian war had convinced him that the struggle from then onwards would take place between the European Antichrist and the Russian Christ.[29] The humanism of the Grand Inquisitor is already sketched for us in the *Diary of a Writer*: 'The sects of Europe are even now almost all inclined to go over to some kind of "humanism", or quite simply even to atheism.' Atheism is of course the cardinal's secret. The 'mystery' which his freemasonry is so sedulously guarding is no other than their pact with the dark spirit. Soloviev had yet to arrive at his own experiences of the underworld, and his acquaintance with Dostoevsky's work must already have convinced him that the satirist of *The Devils* was an unimaginable distance beyond him in his ability to discern the dark forces of evil.

There are, on the other hand, a number of details from the Grand Inquisitor which recur throughout Soloviev's work. Both writers foresaw the coming of 'the dreadful tower of Babel' which would be rebuilt for man's economic prosperity. The only difference is that, whereas the novelist keeps to the concrete and dynamic, the philosopher follows the path of abstract argument.

But that is not all. The theme as it appears in his last novel has taken on quite new dimensions. A 'striving towards a universal state'; a time when 'the only thing on earth that man wants is someone to worship, someone to keep his conscience, and some means of bringing together all men into a single unanimous and harmonious ant-heap'; a prophecy of times 'yet to come, of the confusion of free thinking, of their science and cannibalism'; here is something absolutely new in Dostoevsky. The total effect is altogether more convincing, more intricate, less flat, than his earlier notion of the Roman Church turning into a socialist democracy. Soloviev is without any doubt behind all this:

> The aims of life and science consist in the maximum possible satisfaction of material needs and the greatest possible knowledge of empirical facts. And, behold, indeed the dominion of rationalism in European politics and science is replaced by a preponderance of materialism and empiricism. . . . With their starting point as the material element of discord and chance, they (i.e. the leading minds of the West) wish to attain unity and integrity, to organise a right human society and a universal science. At the same time, the material aspect of existence, the cravings and passions of human nature, the facts of external experience, all these comprise only a general foundation of life and knowledge, the material of which they are formed; but in order that anything might be really created out of this material, a formative, uniting principle and form of this unity are necessary.[30]

We should not be misled by the ponderous style of such passages. Soloviev enthralled his listeners, Dostoevsky not excepted. It would be true to say that in some cases these abstract winding paragraphs have turned up in Ivan Karamazov's 'poem', decked out as Caesars, Popes, Temurs and Genghis Khans. It is also evident that, but for Vladimir Soloviev, this section of the novel would have assumed a very different shape, and might never have been written at all.

Many years later and towards the end of his life, Soloviev in one terrifying vision came face to face with what he recognised to be the Antichrist in person. This vision evoked the mood which pervades his last work *The Three Conversations*, a work which contains both the culmination and the shattering to smithereeens of his life's work. In the last of these 'conversations' Soloviev delivers his answer to Nietzsche this time, like Ivan Karamazov, in the form of an extended dramatic 'poem'. The Brave New World created by Soloviev's Antichrist can be seen as a development of the Grand Inquisitor's socialist utopia. Unlike the ambivalence of Dostoevsky's denouement, Soloviev's 'poem' ends in Apocalypse. His productive life began and ended in a vision of Sophia.

4 A new man

A basic premiss of the Legend of the Grand Inquisitor is that love of mankind cannot exist in separation from love of God. The aged cardinal embodies the central Christian virtues, and has sacrificed his own well-being for the sake of the wretched mass of humanity. But Christian virtue founded on humanism is doomed to decay. Zosima and the Inquisitor have much in common. They both take upon themselves the sins of others; but, whereas Zosima is acting on behalf of Christ, the Inquisitor has created a perversion of Christianity and has gone over to Antichrist.

The principle of Godmanhood is the opposite of mangodhood, and, in an important sense, *The Brothers Karamazov* can be said to be mainly a development of these two principles. Zosima is contrasted not only with the Inquisitor but also with the religious fanatic Ferapont; Dmitri and Alyosha Karamazov are contrasted with Rakitin; Ivan Karamazov with Smerdyakov, and so forth. In each case sincerity is contrasted with bad faith, and bad faith is always the mark of the opposite, 'mangodhood'. Dostoevsky had developed this duality in *The Devils*, and there is evidence that Soloviev borrowed the idea from this novel, which he had read shortly after its publication. In Soloviev the polar opposition of Godmanhood-mangodhood is worked out in metaphysical terms, though it is quite likely that the original impetus came from Kirillov's weird obsessions, and perhaps also from the confrontation of Stavrogin and Bishop Tikhon. It is equally likely that Dostoevsky, as a result of discussion with Soloviev, adopted a more dialectical approach to the problem. But, as we have seen, Dostoevsky did not see eye to eye with Soloviev on a number of fundamental issues. The superman motif of his earlier novels becomes associated with Soloviev's Free Theocracy—not Godmanhood, as Soloviev believed it to be, but a mockery of the Christian Church, Church turned State. The Grand Inquisitor's 'Church' is the concrete realisation of the potentially terrible Free Theocracy. (It took Soloviev many years to see this.) It is no surprise at all that Dostoevsky's projected novel was to have taken as its subject 'the Church as a positive social ideal'.

The difference between Godmanhood and mangodhood is that the latter represents the historical development of man's potentialities as such, whilst the former depends upon the Logos, which raises man to a new and positive relationship with God. In Soloviev's theology, Christ is only the *beginning* of christianity, the first actual God-man. Man as a whole, individual men, are able to become Christ through the Church. 'This body of Christ, which first appeared as a tiny embryo in the form of a not very numerous community of the early christians, is gradually growing and developing so as to embrace, at the end of time, all men and the whole of nature in a single universal organism of Godmanhood'.[31] Nothing will be effected until the 'human element' of the Western Church becomes synthesised with the divine element of the Eastern Orthodox Church; the human element 'will then be able to enter into a free union with the divine ground of christianity, which has been preserved in the Eastern Church—and, in consequence of that free union, to give birth to spiritual mankind'.[32] The world will then be ready for the true superman, the God-man as opposed to the man-god, a man bursting with the life of the Holy Spirit, and not the caricature who like Nietzsche will spend the last years of his life mentally deranged.

In reading Soloviev one must never allow oneself to forget that his prime aim all along was to give concrete form to his vision of Sophia. He attempted this through the medium of poetry, but discovered an even greater talent for metaphysics. The dialectical techniques he adopts are mere trappings compared with his central problem, which was to apply Schelling's epistemology to the working out of the *content*, the *meaning* of his vision. In Schelling's scheme the organs of sense enable subjective and objective to share a common boundary; the activity of the sense belongs to both subject and object, it is a function of both. For example, a rainbow can be seen only because there exists in the percipient's consciousness the representation of rainbow; the sense-impression is both interpreted object-matter and interpreting subject at one and the same time; the rainbow itself *transcends* both percipient and perceived. Soloviev compares the operation with the work of the poet. The words used by the poet are compared to 'a certain mental organism'; they are interrelated, but it is the poet who perceives their existence and clothes them in flesh for all to see.[33]

Awareness of God enters into Nature through man. Man is the cognitive union of subject and object. His feet planted in both worlds at once, he is a kind of intermediary. Religion arises as a real interaction between God and man, through the 'divine-human process' known as Godmanhood. God gradually permeates the world through man, as subject and object simultaneously. This follows directly from the Schelling-Soloviev theory of knowledge. Subjective apprehension of the Divine Presence and historical revelation are in step, because they are really two sides of a single process. In other words, there will be no Prophets, no Buddha, no Zoroaster, and no Christ until man's consciousness is sufficiently awakened.

In the beginning there were three unknit elements: Nature, or the given reality; the divine principle, or 'the sought end and content which are gradually being revealed'; the human personality itself, 'the subject of life and consciousness'. Then the divine principle enters into a union with Nature and, through the agency of man, transforms it into what it ought to be. The 'I am I' of the Hebrews is the first personal revelation of the Godhead. Man is the willing tool in the shaping and perfecting of the universe.

Nature is originally the 'representation of Chaos'. The natural world has fallen away from the divine unity, an agglomeration only of disjointed atomistic parts. When the world-process began, 'the soul of the world' had none of the organising force required for bringing it in the direction of

God. The Deity is 'stimulated to counteraction' by its opposite, the negative principle of non-integrated nature, and thus appears as an active force striving to embody itself in chaos.

The 'divine idea' becomes incarnate in the world by a 'union of the divine beginning with the world soul, in which the former is the active fertilising agent'. In this cosmic activity man is the necessary midwife: 'The actuality of God . . . presupposes a subject which is the organ of this action, presupposes man.'[34] Man is defined as 'a certain union of the Deity with material nature' which involves three constituent elements: the Divine, the material, and that which binds them—the properly human. The latter is further described in the *Critique of Abstract Principles* as 'that something which has an absolute . . . quality, through which it distinguishes itself as *this* subject from all other subjects'.

In one sense, Christ is the maturity of this human principle; the flower, the 'spiritual new man', or 'the eternal spiritual centre of the organism of universal mankind'. His key-position is that he is the first human soul prepared for total self-denial. To bring into being an actual bond between God and Nature, an actual living person is necessary in whom it might be forged. The whole idea of the spiritual man 'presupposes a single Godman personality uniting in itself two natures, and possessing two wills'. The three temptations are no other than the 'evil principle' trying to incline Christ's human will to self-assertion. The spiritual victory had to be accompanied by an ordeal of the flesh, for the very reason that He belonged to the natural material order as well as to the human; the final ordeal was the Passion and Crucifixion.

Finally, the Church: 'The due relationship between divinity and nature is mankind, which was attained in the person of Jesus Christ as the spiritual focus or head of mankind, has to be assimilated by all men as His body. Humanity reunited with its divine beginning through the mediation of Jesus Christ is the Church.'[35] The hypostatic union is not theory but reality. Each man may share in Christ's Godmanhood through the Church, which is an eternal extension of His divine and human person.

All this sheds some light on one outstanding enigma in Dostoevsky's novel. Dmitri, we remember, was in possession of a secret, not for secrecy's sake, but because he was overwhelmed at the mere effort of putting it into words: 'During the past two months a new man has arisen within me'. The newly attained state in which Dmitri Karamazov finds himself is the pure state of Godmanhood, the joy of the mystical union with Christ, the God-man personality. The greatest of Dmitri's fears is that 'this man risen again will leave him' or else that he will come to lose God in the end. We have now some inkling as to what Dmitri is attempting to express:

> Glory to God in the world
> Glory to God in me!

There is no more concise summary of Soloviev's God-man idea than these at first sight incoherent and haphazard words.

Dmitri Karamazov is Dostoevsky's supreme attempt to explore the living actuality of the Godman, beginning from where Soloviev left off. He was quick to learn about Soloviev's theory of knowledge, and saw how to turn it to account in his novel.

The possibility remains that Dmitri Karamazov might never have been conceived, had it not been for Dostoevsky's chance attendance at those crucial lectures.

THE TEMPTATION OF PHILOSOPHY

MANY theories have been squeezed and go on being squeezed from the pages of Dostoevsky. The temptation is great, perhaps overwhelming; but it has to be resisted. In Dostoevsky, all theories, all philosophical or religious ideas are traps. He sets traps not only for the reader, but even for the characters in his own novels. And not a few have fallen into them, on occasions disastrously.

Dostoevsky's purpose is best symbolised by Rakitin, the successful career intellectual, who is incidentally Dmitri Karamazov's thorn in the flesh. Rakitin is capable of dredging up a glib explanation for everything. Nothing defeats him. His name tells us all. 'Rakitin' as well as referring to the pliant and adaptable *rakita* 'a willow tree', contains two further nouns: *kit* 'a whale' and *rak* 'a crab', both signifying 'trap'.

I am not of course suggesting that Dostoevsky was deliberately playing practical jokes on his readers; only that he wished in a sense to make his novels the *measure* of his readers, and also incidentally of himself and his characters.

There are indications everywhere that, by the middle of the last century, rationalism had become bankrupt. Would-be system-builders had fallen upon hard times. The critique of European metaphysics, which had flourished with Hume and Kant, dislodged Reason from its place and left only a panoply of logical techniques and metaphysical possibilities which found their supreme virtuoso in Hegel. Voices advocating not merely doubt but a thorough-going rejection of systems were beginning to be heard with increasing frequency. These voices were more often poets than philosophers. A generation earlier than Kierkegaard, Keats had been advocating his 'negative capability'; a state of remaining 'in uncertainties, mysteries, doubts, without any irritable reaching after fact and reason'. But it was Kierkegaard himself who first formulated a method of *paradox*, in which paradox supersedes Reason.

'Paradox has made reason absurd.' This is one of the central themes of Kierkegaard's *Philosophical Fragments*. Paradox is an offence to consciousness. 'The offended consciousness holds aloof from the Paradox and keeps to the probable, since the Paradox is the most improbable of things.'[1] According to Kierkegaard, paradox was that which had sought out and discovered Reason. The discovery was bound to come. Since Kant's famous antinomies, the show-down had become inevitable. It did not matter that paradox had been treated patronisingly by Reason as a misguided wretch.

> When Reason takes pity on the Paradox, and wishes to help it to an explanation, the Paradox does not indeed acquiesce, but nevertheless finds it quite natural that Reason should do this. ... When Reason says that it cannot get the Paradox into its head, it was not Reason that made the discovery but the Paradox, which was so paradoxical as to declare Reason a blockhead and a dunce, capable at the most of saying yes and no to the same thing, which is not good divinity.[2]

In Kierkegaard's polemical *Attack on Christendom*, paradox becomes one of the main bulwarks in his interpretation of the New Testament. The categories of Plato and Aristotle dissolve at last before it: 'Either/or is the word before which the folding doors fly open and the ideals appear ... Either/or is the token which insures entrance into the unconditional.'[3] It was the very compromise of the 'to a certain degree' attitude which, in Kierkegaard's opinion, had transformed Christianity into 'twaddle'.

Kierkegaard was an obscure Danish philosopher and it is unlikely that his work was known to Dostoevsky. It is this that makes the coincidental development in their interpretation of experience and existence seem so remarkable. The technique of paradox is already present in *Notes from Underground*, and reaches its culmination nearly twenty years later in *The Brothers Karamazov*. The latter is an unbelievably complex system of counterpositions, either/or's. Sometimes the interplay is obvious, but more often it is hidden beneath the surface. I suspect that the entire novel may be broken down into paradoxical oppositions of the Kierkegaardian type. They range from novelistic technique–as in the chapter 'Ivan's Nightmare' where both the reader and Ivan Karamazov are left bewildered, not knowing whether the apparition is hallucination or really the Devil incarnate–to enigmatic parallels perhaps hardly fully clear to Dostoevsky himself, as for instance when the reader discovers that the Elder Zosima and the Grand Inquisitor stands in some ambiguous relationship to each other. The Grand Inquisitor has marked himself out as a saint, performing a service of untold value to the mass of mankind by saving them from their weak and undeveloped passions, by absolving them from the intolerable burden of freedom. We learn too that in the tradition of the Russian monasteries Zosima as an Elder was vested with the power of taking upon his own shoulders the burden of the guilt of others, who from then onwards remained mysteriously bound to him.

The three brothers Karamazov seem to present the reader with a triple choice. A reader who has not ventured beyond 'Pro and Contra' will be convinced that the novel is an embodiment of the ultimate atheistic argument, the most formidable argument ever put forward. Ivan finds God morally intolerable. The idea of the eventual universal harmony is noble and beautiful, but Ivan 'respectfully hands back his entrance ticket'. It is only if the reader proceeds to the next section, centred upon Father Zosima, Alyosha Karamazov and the monastery, that he finds himself in an entirely different world, in which the devastating thesis of Ivan Karamazov has no place. It is to this second 'choice' that Dostoevsky applies the whole force of his literary virtuosity to the vision of Cana in Galilee. Ivan's thesis is by no means 'refuted' by it, but made to seem (if only temporarily) irrelevant. The third of these 'choices', centred around Dmitri, will be treated in more detail later. Suffice it for the present simply to stress that Dostoevsky never intended the reader to select one or the other alternative. To make a choice is to fall into a trap. At least one commentator has assumed that Dostoevsky was inviting the reader to choose between Ivan Karamazov's 'solution' and what they assume to be Dostoevsky's own, namely the viewpoint represented by Alyosha Karamazov and his spiritual guide Zosima. Nothing could be further from the truth. Dostoevsky was inviting the reader to remain, like him, at the stage of either/or. If the reader surrenders to a 'solution', that is not the novelist's responsibility, for Dostoevsky is continually hinting that solutions are to be resisted at all costs. They are mere temptations; like Christ's temptations in the wilderness, so aptly described by Ivan Karamazov's Grand Inquisitor.

Solutions are traps. They are limiting, enslaving, and therefore evil.

In his *Concept of Dread* Kierkegaard attempted to show that evil or the 'demoniacal' arises from dread, dread of the Good. The demoniacal is *shut-upness*; 'shut-upness unfreely revealed'. In the world unfreedom becomes posited as freedom, and true freedom is consequently lost sight of. The Grand Inquisitor believes that true freedom is outside the ken of the average mortal, and sees it as a great burden which only a superhuman minority is capable of bearing. The entire episode, in which the Grand Inquisitor mutely kisses Christ wgose presence he so much dreads, is a reenactment of Kierkegaard's 'dread manifesting itself at once in the instant of contact with the good'.[4]

Kierkegaard develops the idea of the demoniac at great length, and in one place describes 'the countless multiplicity of nuances comprehended by the demoniacal ... some of them so infinitesimal that they are visible only to microscopic observation'. These nuances may be compared with the personality traits of the Man from Underground: 'an exaggerated sensibility, an exaggerated irritability, nervous affections, hysteria, hypochondria, etc.' (The demoniacal) 'shuns therefore every contact with the Good, whether this actually threatens it by wanting to help it to freedom, or merely touches it quite casually. . . . Hence one quite commonly hears from such a demoniac a rejoinder which contains in it all the horror of his state: "Let me be the miserable man I am".'[5]

Dread of the Good permeates *The Brothers Karamazov*. Ivan Karamazov becomes the slave and finally the victim of his own intellectual convictions, which exclude him from the possibility of freedom. Freedom will not confine itself to those of his categories which produce the *illusion* that he is really free, freer than the mass of humanity all around him. 'All is permitted' is the theme of *his* metaphysical rebellion. The illusion reinforces his pride; it precipitates his Promethean revolt. He has *talked* himself into rebellion. 'I would rather remain with my unavenged suffering and unsatisfied indignation, *even if I were wrong*.'

Yet, all the time, like the Fallen Angel, Ivan Karamazov can see the good clearly. He *understands* the intention of Christ in the wilderness when he rejected the three temptations, which would have made available to him the three powers of *miracle, mystery* and *authority*. 'There are three powers alone,' argued the Grand Inquisitor, 'three powers alone able to conquer and to hold captive for ever the conscience of these impotent rebels for their happiness. . . . Thou hast rejected all three and hast set the example for doing so.'

> Instead of taking men's freedom from them, Thou didst make it greater than ever! . . . Nothing is more seductive for man than his freedom of conscience, but nothing is a greater cause of suffering. . . . Thou didst choose all that is exceptional, vague, enigmatic; Thou didst choose what was utterly beyond the strength of men, acting as though Thou didst not love them at all—Thou who didst come to give Thy life for men! Instead of taking possession of men's freedom, Thou didst increase it, and burdened the spiritual Kingdom of mankind with its suffering forever.

Ivan Karamazov knows he is the slave of a paradox of his own creation, but makes the mistake of assuming that his own particular resolution of the paradox—metaphysical rebellion—is valid for the world in general. Dostoevsky avoids Ivan Karamazov's mistake, and leaves the reader free to accept or reject the Grand Inquisitor. Readers will always be for ever asking themselves whether the Inquisitor was sincere, whether Ivan Karamazov was really on the Inquisitor's side; for he allows Christ to go free in spite of an earlier intention of burning him alive along with the rest of the heretics. In Ivan Karamazov's 'poem' the Inquisitor and Christ are both heroes. The reader can make up his own mind, for its author (Ivan Karamazov) has long since made up his. This was his undoing, for we witness his downfall in a later section of the novel, where his own 'solutions' and 'theories' are mirrored back at him mockingly by the demon that may equally (and this is important) have been no more than a figment of his own imagination. With tragic irony his heroically entrenched world-position dissolves into a paradox of a very 'stupid' kind, one in which the subject has no reference points with the outside world, no supports, no susceptibility to logic and reason.

We now turn to the third brother Dmitri, who has until now received comparatively less attention than either of his brothers. He has much less appeal to the intellectually inclined than Ivan, and appears a rough diamond by comparison with either Ivan or Alyosha. Despite this, Dmitri has much more in common with modern Christian ideals than his more obviously devout younger brother Alyosha. It was once suggested that Alyosha stands for early Christianity and the Middle Ages, whereas Ivan represents the Reformation and the Age of Reason. I would add to this the corollary that Dmitri Karamazov in many ways symbolises the Christian Church of our own day.

Dmitri Karamazov is the only one of the three brothers who is portrayed in clear detail. His physical appearance is essential to him. Muscularity, considerable physical strength, and yet something unhealthy about his appearance. There is also something of the hippy about him. 'His rather large, prominent, dark eyes had an expression of firm determination, and yet there was a vague look in them, too. Even when he was excited and talking irritably, his eyes somehow did not follow his mood, but betrayed something else, sometimes quite incongruous with what was passing.' He could be light-hearted and gay, when at the same time his eyes expressed gloom. Capable of violent anger, his neighbours thought him reckless and unbalanced. Although

Dmitri combines many features of Shatov, something of Stavrogin, and unmistakable shades of Versilov, he stands out even so as something new in Dostoevsky. His precedents are not particularly significant.

Dmitri's discovery is that he is the 'new man'. His life has taken on a new lease only after he has reached the ultimate lower depths. It has more than once been pointed out that his name is connected with Demeter, the Earth-goddess. His poems are Dionysian, but their hero is the defeated Dionysius:

> Wild and fearful in his cavern
> Hid me naked troglodyte . . .
> Sunk in vilest degradation
> Man his loathsomeness displays.

Weeping he confides to his brother Alyosha: 'My dear, my dear, in degradation, in degradation now, too. There's a terrible amount of suffering for man on earth, a terrible lot of trouble. Don't think I'm only a brute in an officer's uniform, wallowing in dirt and drink. I hardly think of anything but of that degraded man–if only I'm not lying. I only hope I'm not lying and showing off. I think about that man because I am that man myself.' On reaching the pit of degradation he finds a new beginning. 'For when I do leap into the pit, I go head over heels, and am pleased to be falling in that degrading attitude, and pride myself upon it. And in the very depths of degradation I begin a hymn of praise.'

Dmitri has thus overcome dread. Like Kierkegaard's dread, Dmitri's too is like dizziness. 'Have you ever felt,' he asks Alyosha, 'have you ever dreamt of falling down a precipice into a pit? That's just how I'm falling, but not in a dream. And I'm not afraid, and don't you be afraid. At least, I am afraid, but I enjoy it. It's not enjoyment though, but ecstasy.' It is fairly obvious that Dmitri's enjoyment is lust and the pleasures of the flesh. But unlike many of his fellow-men he is unashamed, for he has plumbed the depths of sinfulness, in order to find the way through to his own regeneration.

Like Kierkegaard's God, Dmitri's is ambivalent, dangerous, enigmatic, a God who 'speaks only in riddles'. This God has somehow arranged things in such a way that what looks like a vision of God's throne to an angel seems like sensual lust when seen by an insect.

'I am insect, brother . . . sensual lust is a tempest, worse than a tempest! Beauty is a terrible and awful thing! It is terrible because it has not been fathomed and never can be fathomed. . . . Here the boundaries meet and all contradictions exist side by side. . . . It's terrible what mysteries there are! Too many riddles weigh men down on earth. . . . Beauty! I can't endure the thought that a man of lofty mind and heart begins with the ideal of the Madonna and ends with the ideal of Sodom. What's still more awful is that a man with the ideal of Sodom in his soul does not renounce the ideal of the Madonna, and his heart may be on fire with that ideal, genuinely on fire, just as in the days of youth and innocence. Yes, man is broad, too broad, indeed, I'd have him narrower. . . . The awful thing is that beauty is mysterious as well as terrible. God and the devil are fighting there and the battlefield is the heart of man. . . .'

Beauty contains the ultimate paradox, for man is never in a position to divide good from evil with confidence. The choice is not given. Freedom and unfreedom become identical. Dmitri has avoided becoming philosopher, not because he has no aptitude for ideas, for clearly he has, but because his ideal has effaced ethical and intellectual distinctions of every kind. For this reason he scoffs at ideas and theories. 'Ideas, ideas, that's all! Ethics! What is ethics? . . . Damn ethics, I'm done for.' He despises the Rakitins, scientists and theory fabricators. This does not prevent him though from being easily fascinated by the aesthetic, the *images* contained in ideas, which to him are more important than the ideas themselves.

Dmitri Karamazov's trial and cross-examination, the three 'ordeals', are the direct reverse of Raskolnikov's. In the latter we see a guilty man weighed down and ultimately crushed by his own guilt. In the case of Dmitri Karamazov there is no crime, no guilt, but the same confrontation with the 'common sense' of the normal man. Dmitri's indignation strikes the prosecution as pure cunning. The cross-examiner's cunning was appropriate for Raskolnikov; for Dmitri Karamazov it is shortsighted, stupid and a torment to the victim.

His brother, Alyosha, is aware that in matters of the spirit he is a beginner by comparison with Dmitri. 'The ladder's the same,' Alyosha tells him, 'I'm at the bottom step, and you're above, somewhere about the thirteenth.' This is not modesty, for Alyosha knows full well that to have stepped on the ladder at all would have been to court disaster:

> 'Then one ought not to step on at all?'
> 'Anyone who can help it had better not.'
> 'But can you?'
> 'I think not.'

Coming to terms with dread is, according to Kierkegaard, an adventure in store for every man. Without this opportunity a man would never recognise dread for what it is and would in ignorance succumb to it. 'He who has learned rightly to dread has learned the most important thing.'[6]

This brings us finally to Dmitri's double secret: on the one hand the discovery that he is the new man, yet on the other hand that he has lost God, or rather that he is about to lose God. 'A new man's arising—that I understand. . . . And yet I'm sorry to lose God.' Since Dostoevsky's time, and especially since Nietzsche, the idea of the death of God has taken on rather more than a purely intellectual significance for a number of theologians and religious thinkers. For many the loss of God, or the absence of God, has become a *sine qua non*. Dmitri Karamazov has intuitively become aware of this happening, and has prepared himself for the consequences: 'If they drive God from the world, we shall shelter Him underground.' His future as a convict in the wastes of Siberia is meant to symbolise the 'underground' period during which God is dead. 'Oh yes, we shall be in chains and there will be no freedom, but men, in our great sorrow, we shall rise again to joy, without which man cannot live nor God exist, for God gives joy.'

A 'thirst for existence and consciousness' has arisen together with the new man, and although Dmitri already sees himself in chains in some Siberian labour camp, he possesses true inner freedom, for he is not afraid, having overcome dread. . . . 'I seem to have such strength in me now, that I think I could stand anything, any suffering, only to be able to say and to repeat to myself every moment, "I exist". In thousands of agonies–I exist. I'm tormented on the rack–but I exist! Though I sit alone on a pillar–I exist!' However that may be, we sense the reality and dread behind his fear. Even his own precious awareness is at risk. There is always the danger he may be undermined by the Rakitins of this world. 'It's God that's worrying me.' He is afraid of scepticism setting in, and knows very well that to look for certainty is to lose his vital possession, Kierkegaard's 'inward-ness' or 'intuitive certitude'. Either a God with no explana-tion, or *no* God with proofs *ad nauseam*. Again: either/or.

Freedom then is not only a *theme* running through *The Brothers Karamazov*; it is the novel's very *raison d'être*. Dmitri, as we have seen, is in his life and outlook the nearest to the realisation of this idea. He represents a stage very much in advance of Ivan Karamazov's rationalistic enslavement, and one also considerably in advance of Alyosha's innocent Christianity, with its ideal of unconditional faith. Dmitri Karamazov belongs to our own day, the era in which God's absence and the recognition of the absurd have become a necessary premiss before honest living and thinking can again become possible. Dmitri is, like many of those of our own time, out over the 70,000 fathoms, unwilling to bow morally to scientific demonstration and proof; incapable of uncomplicated faith, because weighed down by the burden of scientific discovery. 'While dons and parsons drivel on about the millions of proofs of God's personality, the truth is that there are no longer the men living who could bear the pressure and weight of having a personal God.'[7]

The chief difference between Dmitri and his brothers is that he is not yet ready for truth. He stands dizzily in the realm of unknowing, the aesthetic realm, and declares only that he *exists*. 'I am tormented on the rack–but I exist!'

Dmitri's freedom is 'the irrational freedom in the very depths of the abyss' adumbrated by Berdyaev. 'Out of these depths pour the dark current of life. The abyss conceals all sorts of possibilities. This bottomless darkness of being, pre-existing before all good and evil, cannot be rationalised, fully and completely: it always hides the possibility of the outflow of new, unilluminated energies.'[8] Dmitri is the exuberant Dionysius, 'the primordial, irrational mystery', preceding all good and evil, all systematisation and all limitation, all choice and intellectual or moral enslavement.

RESURRECTION AND
APPLIED SCIENCE

You in others are yourself, your soul. This is what you are. This
is what your consciousness has breathed and lived on and
enjoyed throughout your life. . . . Your soul, your immortality,
your life in others. And what now? You have always been in
others and you will remain in others. And what does it matter
to you if later on it is called your memory? This will be you . . .
the you that enters the future and becomes a part of it.[1]

Yuri Zhivago is drawn into a state of exaltation by his
attempts to reassure Anna who is gravely ill with pneumonia.
His words are fashioned out of that Russian logic that will
find a resolution to problems however dismaying their immensity.

Like those many Soviet Russians, whether Marxists,
materialists, or Old Believers, who find their way irresistibly
and unsentimentally to known or forgotten graves, Yuri
Zhivago wants to abolish death. With St. John, he affirms:
'There will be no death. . . . There will be no death because
the past is over.' Yet death there is, and nothing whatever
can be done about it. There's the rub, the central tragedy of
human existence. To extricate themselves from this impasse
men need a new way of conceiving life and death. 'What we
need is something new, and that new thing is life eternal.'
For more than one Russian, this project has advanced beyond
wishful thinking.

In 1887, an obscure librarian by the name of Nikolay
Fyodorovich Fyodorov joined the staff of the Rumyantsevskaya Reading Room (now the Lenin Library) in Moscow.
He occupied his niche there for twenty-one years in all, with
an entirely unspectacular career leaving him hardly a bare
mention in the roll of honour compiled for the fiftieth anniversary of the library's foundation. Yet we have in Fyodorov

G   175

not only one of the resounding cranks of all time, but at the same time one of its most original minds, a man admired and befriended by the giants of the day: Tolstoy, Dostoevsky, Soloviev, Berdyaev, Aksakov, Shestov and doubtless others.

Dostoevsky first heard of Fyodorov very soon after his appointment, and was introduced to him by Fyodorov's close friend Peterson, who was later to edit his diffuse and variegated writings. Peterson's letter[2] came as a bolt out of the blue. Dostoevsky wrote to Peterson: 'Who is this thinker, whose ideas you have passed on to me? . . . I am more than curious. At least, can you give me further details about him? Please tell me all you can about him. I can say right now that essentially I am in complete agreement with these ideas. I read them as though they were my very own.'[3] Dostoevsky never received a reply to this letter. Peterson explained much later that Fyodorov certainly intended to reply, but wanted, before doing so, to be in a position to give a complete account of his 'project'. The reply grew and grew into a rambling series of articles, monographs and sketches which were still far from completion two decades after Dostoevsky's death. Fyodorov very likely never intended them for publication.

Fyodorov's 'project' itself is a preposterous pill to swallow. More will be said about it presently. Briefly, however, Fyodorov's scheme is made up of five stages: (1) a world-wide effort to gain control over natural and meteorological phenomena through the applied sciences and technology; followed by (2) a reconstruction of as much of the human past as possible, through archive work, through archaeology and eventually by retracing every particle of organic matter, whether human, animal or vegetable, to its source. This stage could not be undertaken without the universal participation of all men working in what Fyodorov considered to be real Christian co-operation under divine guidance; (3) to pursue research into restoring dead organs and organisms to life. Progress would begin with the resuscitation of someone recently dead, and later there would follow more ambitious successes on bodies already in the stages of decay, and so on, until a complete 'science' of resuscitation is attained; (4) each man would then be obliged to acquire this science and work towards bringing his own parents back to life; (5) the resuscitated parents in their turn would resuscitate the previous generation, and so on until the entire human race is resurrected. These five stages, Fyodorov believed, constituted the true meaning and significance of Christ's own Resurrection. The motif that runs from beginning to end is *cooperation*; nothing would be achieved without this.

It is a pity that Fyodorov's unique flavour and intriguing ambiguity is to some extent clouded by his disconnected, rambling style, his frequent repetitions and apparent contradictions; more than enough to exhaust the reader's patience. It is worth reminding ourselves that Fyodorov never set himself up as a writer. Moreover his friend Peterson could have been a less slavish and less faithful editor. Nevertheless, those who have persevered with *The Philosophy of the Common Cause* cannot possibly have remained unaffected by its moral persuasiveness, its obvious and fundamental appeal to an instinct for mourning the dead. Berdyaev found this quality alone sufficient to justify Fyodorov:

> I know of no more lofty moral consciousness in its attitude to death than that of Fyodorov. Fyodorov grieved over the death of every being and demanded that man should become a resuscitator. But grieving over death, since it has become active, is not the fear of death. . . . Fyodorov is right in saying that the fight against death is not only a personal matter, it is a 'public undertaking'. It is not only my death, but the death of all, which sets me a problem. Victory is not only over the fear of death, but over death itself, is the realisation of personality.[4]

Berdyaev never acknowledges his own indebtedness to Fyodorov; yet those conversant with his philosophy of Personalism will hardly fail to detect the cross-grain. It is significant that Berdyaev in one of his articles[5] records Fyodorov's anniversary alongside those of Tolstoy and Ibsen.

Although the product of an 'apocalyptic age', Fyodorov is himself really *anti*-Apocalypse. He was for avoiding the eschatological process and wanted instead a 'scientific' regeneration of man and the universe. His philosophy is decidedly opposed to gnosticism and theosophy in any form. He would have rejected Teilhard de Chardin's scheme not so much for its implausibility but primarily for its inhumanity. His vocabulary prefers the Russian active verbal noun 're-suscitation' to the passive 'resurrection'.* For his part, a paradise awarded gratis is worthless, as well as degrading the Deity himself. As Berdyaev put it, anything unworthy of man is equally unworthy of God.

Nearly all Fyodorov's admirers have gladly accepted the spirit of his writings, but have jibbed at the letter. Not surprisingly, since a standpoint such as Fyodorov's is totally alien to European thought-habits and presuppositions. His concepts seem to be neither mechanistic nor idealistic; his 'mysticism' purports to be empirical; even the capacious post-romantic framework will not accommodate such views as his. Fyodorov's readers willy-nilly are projected into a world in which matter and spirit are interchangeable, and not separate species. No physiologist later than the seventeenth century could fully comprehend Fyodorov's meaning of 'body'. His 'soul' does not even begin to have any connection with post-Cartesian dualism. His 'science' would have sent the pundits of nineteenth-century 'new humanism' off into howls of abuse. On every page, indeed in every paragraph, the reader finds at least one justification for rejecting Fyodorov outright. He is however in respectable company if he does so, for, as we shall see, Dostoevsky's loyalty to Fyodorov was also severely taxed.

Fyodorov the man is almost unknown. Not that he lived in obscurity. Quite the contrary; within limits he lived to be a myth, widely celebrated as 'the enigmatic thinker'. He appears not to have been the least bit flattered, dismayed amused, or irritated by the well-known fact that many of the trivial enquiries by some readers in the Rumyantsevskaya were simply a pretext for exchanging conversation with him. People were generally not so much interested in him personally, as in what he had to say.

Nikolai Fyodorovich (N. F. as he was affectionately known) was self-effacing and plain-living in an uncommonly uninteresting way. This is quite simply explained: in his scheme of world regeneration *individual* life is an inferior form

* Active *voskresheniye*–passive *voskreseniye*.

of existence, and he had already entered upon the first stages of his own project. Fyodorov therefore is clearly no biographer's meat.

From the fragments we can piece together, he appears to have been a man of extraordinary resilience and energy. He needed no more than two or three hours' sleep daily; even then, any bed other than the wooden chest he was used to, convex and full of ridges, with his coat rolled up for a pillow, seemed to him an unnecessary luxury.[6] Naturally such habits gained him the reputation of an ascetic. This irritated him, for in his eyes asceticism was suicide or, at best, exhibitionism.

'N. F.' died in a Moscow hospital on 15 October 1903, at the age of seventy. In spite of the poverty of biographical data, his personality pervades his work. Berdyaev describes him as 'the most Russian of all the Russians; it is possible through him to come to close quarters with the singularity of the Russian mind and Russian searchings'. He belongs inextricably to the fabric of Russian literature; there was about him something of Chekhov's country doctor, a streak of the Turgenev hero, the Russian country parson, a merest trace of the bureaucrat, and above all a close affinity (though not so much in ideas) with the grand-old-man of Russian letters, Tolstoy.

1 *The philosophy of the common cause*

In one place Fyodorov outlines his project with unaccustomed clarity:

> We believe it is possible for ourselves . . . as instruments of the God of our fathers, who breathes new life into us–possible and even necessary . . . to attain through all men . . . knowledge and control of all molecules and atoms in the external world with a view to gathering together what has been dispersed and putting together what has decomposed, that is, to put them together in the bodies which our fathers had at the time of their death; and again, we believe it possible and essential to attain to an inner control of the psycho-physiological process, to substitute our fathers and ancestors for the births of children like ourselves.[7]

There is no ambiguity here, and Fyodorov wishes to be understood literally and in no metaphorical sense. His 'resurrection' will come about not in some 'mysterious and dark' manner, but in the clear light of scientific enquiry and experiment.

He emphasises that any thought of resurrection for ourselves is futile unless we first of all restore our ancestors to life, beginning with our own parents. Magic is ruled out. Our own resurrection will presumably be the work of our descendants. Delay should be kept to a minimum and the project launched immediately.

A science of the universe in its totality must first of all be established; man must be able to understand completely and to *control* the 'macrocosm'.

Fyodorov warns that the discovery of the scientific laws of resuscitating the dead alone will not make the task any easier for generations to come. But the reasons he gives are totally unexpected, and non-scientific. The stumbling-block is of an *ethical* not a scientific kind, and each generation will have to grapple with different sets of insurmountable difficulties. Science and morals cannot be separated. We shall have to find a means of loving our parents intensely, of burying all our feelings of antipathy or rivalry; all this before anything constructive becomes possible. Every human being is 'a function of his mother's and father's organisms'.

The pervading ethical nature of Fyodorov's scheme is reminiscent of Confucius; but he is no Confucian, as the following extract demonstrates:

> A man, who looks deeply into himself with self-knowledge as his goal discovers . . . phenomena for which there is basis or cause in his own life; since out of his intention to know himself arises the knowledge of his constituent parts, as well as an awareness of what preceded him . . . that is, a consciousness of his own parents . . . The subtler the means of cognition, the more numerous the signs of heredity to be discovered, and the more clearly the image of the parents will be restored.[8]

Confucianism agrees to the extent of awareness of ancestral derivation but has nothing to say about 'restoration of parental images'. This psychological and spiritual restoration, a central theme in the *Philosophy of the Common Cause*, is in some ways more important than physical restoration.

Instead of producing more children, we have to learn ways of reversing the direction of the birth-cycle, in order to substitute our fathers and ancestors for children who at present are reproductions of ourselves. It is never quite clear what form this new 'birth' is to take; only one thing is certain, that no more children are to be born. In some mysterious way, we are to 'make ourselves unborn . . . to restore again from ourselves those who gave us birth, and to reshape our own beings so that everything is conscious and under the control of the will'.[9] The truth is that every birth is really a resurrection. In the words of Zhivago's uncle: 'You are anxious about whether you will rise from the dead or not, but you have risen already—you rose from the dead when you were born and you didn't notice it.'

Fyodorov often asserts that he is in the tradition of the Christian philosophers. In his view, Christ's Resurrection is inseparable from the universal Resurrection of the Dead, which will take place within the theological body of Christ. In Fyodorov's interpretation 'Christianity is the union of all the living for resuscitating the dead'. The Resurrection has to be seen as 'an activity as yet incomplete, and not as one that will take place only in the distant future'. If one is in any doubt as to what Christ meant when he commanded: 'Go ye, teach all nations', this paschal message can be rightly understood in the light of Christ's own subsequent resurrection.[10]

The rest of the 'project' follows from this, since universal resurrection can be attained only by all men working together as brothers in a 'common cause' and in the body of Christ. The substance of Fyodorov's project appears to fall into two quite disparate halves: The first contains much that would have held the interest and sympathy of the liberal humanitarians of his own day; for instance, the disturbingly rampant growth of industry and proletariat, the consequent lowering of social morale, or the festering preoccupation with money and luxury. The second half, however, would have been written off as blatantly outlandish. The disconcerting thing is that in Fyodorov no clear line can be drawn between these two halves. We are perplexed by his arbitrary but none the less integral mixture of the acceptable and the absurd. There is no indication whatever that he recognised any kind of dividing line of the sort necessary to modern Europeans. The result is a bizarre blend of spiritual intensity and bald matter-of-factness; something that is just beginning to captivate the logically more permissive outlook of our own day.

At the core of Fyodorov's philosophy is the striking interpretation of the Russian funeral banquet. His idea was that, originally, this custom had been connected with the Eucharist and especially the Last Supper. It was only in recent times, he believed, that these occasions had become 'epicurean, materialistic and atheistic'. In the popular mind, the Eucharist was still 'an active force for comforting the dead'.[11] The significance is that, whenever we eat, we are consuming organic matter, which in one form or another contains ancestral remains. The funeral banquet is at once a mystical symbol of regeneration, and a purely nutritive function. Current semantics, in either English or Russian, will not allow a unified explanation of Fyodorov's concept of the funeral custom. He would have been happier in the conceptual framework of the Upanishads, where food and sustenance are of prime metaphysical importance. Fyodorov sees the whole of history as one vast, unending funeral banquet.

The first practical step towards the realisation of his project is to gain absolute control over nature. He reminds those Christians who believe they should be content with their lot that God's explicit command to his first-created was to gain control over nature. Fyodorov's actual proposals have a flavour of Jules Verne, although essentially they are akin to the schemes of the more recent International Geophysical Year; the study of the earth's magnetic field, artificial rain production, and climatology are central to the plan. The complete control of nature would require everyone to be engaged in the service of science. The natural sciences in particular had become over-analytical. With Goethe he was unhappy with any science which did not enable us to use our 'hearts and wills'. Fyodorov had no respect for scientists who stand in the narrow empirical tradition. Among his published fragments is an interesting article treating of Renan's near-acceptance of actual resurrection from which he was in the end deterred by the arguments of a chemist. Chemistry, Fyodorov declared, is at present an unreal science, nothing more than 'a recreation or synthesis of substances similar to nature'.[12]

At this point the reader must either continue to meet Fyodorov at least half-way, or abandon him entirely. In Fyodorov's mode of scientific thinking, the organs of the human body are conscious, and thus capable of transforming themselves into quite unprecedented and more perfect instruments of consciousness. The traditional seat of the intelligence loses its pre-eminence; it is relegated to a status shared by the lungs and liver. In short, consciousness pervades the entire organism, and is not associated with any organ in particular.

In Fyodorov's terminology we keep coming across the phrase 'fully organic being'. According to one explanation this is the regenerated society of the future, the direct opposite of utopian socialism. By becoming 'individuals' men have lost their higher being or 'soul'. Society then has before it the task of turning itself into a single, all-comprising organism, devoid of all individualistic traits. If Fyodorov is right, the entire inorganic and organic worlds must become through man a single gigantic organism. Only then can the world be regarded as fully conscious. There would be 'a transformation by man of the elemental, cosmic substances into minerals, then into plant forms, and finally into living tissue'.[13] The earth would become one great, living creature. By this means alone could man be transformed into an instrument of God, in the complete knowledge of his own planet.

It is at this stage in Fyodorov's work that we have a foreshadowing of the recently fashionable theory of Teilhard de Chardin. The latter's 'point omega' is curiously similar to Fyodorov's organism of humanity. The essential difference lies in Fyodorov's compassion and intense concern for those of his fellow creatures who have been deprived of existence by death. Their resurrection depends on our love, however meagre and precarious.

Man will not become different from what he is now, but *more* himself than before: 'The wings of the soul will then become corporeal wings.' Fyodorov is a little vague about man's new capabilities. Is he to develop powers of levitation or ubiquitous materialisation? We are left with no clue. Nevertheless he clearly had in mind the kind of body that Christ appears to have possessed after the Resurrection. We are reminded of Steiner's 'consciousness soul'. Fyodorov's use of the adjective 'celestial' is worth noting. His space is essentially that of Plotinus, qualitative rather than quantitative. The earth itself is no mere chunk of solidified matter on a given trajectory through Newtonian space; it is a 'heavenly body' and not simply a planet. At present man is cut off from other worlds. The earth is, for the time being, to be regarded as a 'cemetery'. In this way men can 'direct the force emanating from other heavenly bodies . . . into the project of resurrection'. At present man is drawing his strength and sense of freedom only from the remains of his ancestors, carefully preserved in the earth.

Since paradise will not be given as a reward, it will have to be earned. Paradise cannot be 'some other' world. We need not become different beings in order to enter this state. Fyodorov emphasises that 'paradise, or the Kingdom of God, is not merely within us, in the imagination only, not spiritual merely, but *visible* and *palpable*, to be experienced universally by organs produced under psycho-physical control – organs to which not only vegetation but also the vibrations of molecules and atoms become accessible. The transformation will be the product of our initiative and not of some supernatural agency; we shall know the world through our own efforts and God's guidance.'[14] Paradise will be the reward only of man's own resurrection, and his re-creation of the whole universe.

Finally a word about Fyodorov's ethic, which he calls 'Supramoralism': a synthesis (in the metaphysical sense) of science, art and religion. It is a union 'with all and for all' in the joint action of raising the dead to life. This ethic is the fabric of Fyodorov's entire practical philosophy, and had such a profound influence on the later philosophy of Vladimir Solovyov, culminating in the latter's monumental treatise *Justification of the Good*. Sin, according to supramoralism, is nothing more than a failure to act. And guilt, which was hitherto individual, would henceforth be shared. There would be no more criminals, but 'each man would consider himself guilty in everything that is committed'. The meaning is literal. A crime committed by a criminal is really brought about by the will of the group, perhaps even the whole of society. The criminal is a scapegoat, the incarnation of others' common guilt. For Fyodorov, to will, to condone or even to *punish* a crime is to assume responsibility for it.

2 *Towards the true resurrection*

In his letter to Fyodorov's friend, Peterson, Dostoevsky quickly comes to the point. He wants to know explicitly whether this resurrection promised by Fyodorov is literal or figurative:

> In what way do you understand the Resurrection of the Dead, and in what form do you think it will come about? That is, do you understand it somehow spiritually or allegorically, like Renan, for instance, who saw it as nothing more than the enlightenment of human consciousness at the close of man's history . . . *or*, does your philosopher literally and directly believe, as religion intimates, that the Resurrection will be real, individual, and that the gulf separating us from the souls of our ancestors will be bridged . . . and that they will be resurrected not in our consciousness only, not allegorically, but actually, really, in the corporeal sense (N.B. not of course in their present bodies . . . there will be new bodies . . . like Christ's after the Resurrection . . .).[15]

Dostoevsky insists on knowing whether Fyodorov, notwithstanding his emphasis on the actuality of resurrection, *really* meant all this to be taken literally, or as a kind of parable: 'An answer to this question is essential, otherwise not everything will be cleared up. I can tell you now that we here, that is Soloviev and myself, at least believe in the Resurrection as a reality, as a literal fact . . . and that it will take place on earth.'

Renewal of life is a theme that occurs frequently in Dostoevsky's works. He knew well what was meant by it. In the 'house of the dead', the Siberian penal settlement, Dostoevsky had discovered a new life among the rag-tag and outcasts of society. He later idealised them as the real people of Russia. Equally, his second marriage had saved him from an existence 'beneath the floor-boards', and eventually led him to renounce his addiction to gambling. As he said at the time: 'It is as if I had been morally regenerated.' In the novels themselves regenerations are far more rare. In the Epilogue to *Crime and Punishment* life begins to hold new promise for Raskolnikov: 'there begins a new story, the story of the gradual renewal of a man, the story of his gradual regeneration, of his gradual transition from one world to another'. Also in the same novel there is the symbolical significance of the death of Marmeladov, followed by 'a germination of new life'.

Not one of these regenerations would have held the least interest for Fyodorov. Dostoevsky's 'resurrections' had been at best allegorical, not the real thing. At the time of his introduction to Fyodorov's thought, he was already disenchanted with mere allegories.

We find Svidrigaylov taunting Raskolnikov with the nightmare of a paradise of 'spiders or something of the sort', of 'a country bath-house ... with spiders in every corner'. All this adds up to considerably more than the twisted jest of a cynic. In *The Idiot* Terentyev, Dostoevsky's 'connoisseur of dying', poses the question: 'How can you overcome its laws, when even He, who conquered nature during his lifetime, could not overcome them?' If Christ himself was a failure, then what hope of surmounting death, which remains sole sovereign and ruler on earth.

Questions of after-life and resurrection were all one for Dostoevsky. One might even say that his obsession with resurrection in his later years amounted to a dread of annihilation or, worse, the fear of an eternity in a bath-house full of spiders. Physical resurrection became the only possible safeguard against such contingencies; the only way in which personal survival could be ensured. A letter he wrote to his niece Sonya brings this out quite plainly: 'Sweet Sonya, surely you believe in the continuation of life and, more important, in the progression and endlessness of consciousness, and also in the general reunion of all men. . . . Let us become worthy of better worlds, of resurrection, and not suffer death in lowly worlds. Have faith!'[16] Another Sonya, this time the fictitious Sonya Marmeladova, offers Raskolnikov an alternative to the eternity of spiders in the miraculous resurrection of Lazarus. She reads him passages from the Scriptures, judging him to be on the verge of belief. The scales fail to tip however, and Raskolnikov suddenly finds himself aghast at her foolish credulity.

If man is unsure of prolonged existence in a life beyond, the only worthwhile thing for him to do is to start investigations at the human end. Why wait for God? Even at the time he was writing *The Idiot* Dostoevsky had been occupied with this question. Yevgeny Pavlovich tells Myshkin: 'Paradise on earth will not be easily attained. But I see you are reckoning at least a little on paradise nevertheless; heaven, though, is a difficult thing, Prince, much more so than it seems to your fine heart!' The novelist already perceived that any transformation of man would not be brought about in any utopian sense, according to the lights of 'progress', but only in a radical-mystical sense. Dostoevsky appears to be absorbed by this problem from about the time he began work on his third major novel, *The Devils* (that is, after 1869). Golubov, a projected character in the preliminary draft of the novel, is of the opinion that perfection already exists, if only man will recognise it; unhappiness is merely a 'product of abnormality'.[17] In the final version of the novel this idea undergoes a transformation, and reappears in the strange other-worldliness of Kirillov, the man-god: 'Life there is, but death absolutely none'. 'You have begun to believe in a future eternal life then?' sneers Stavrogin. 'No,' he replies, 'not in an eternal life, but in the eternity of the present. There are moments when time suddenly stops still and will remain thus forever. . . . Man is unhappy because he does not know that he is happy; and for this reason only. That is all, everything! Whoever realises this will become happy in a flash.'

Kirillov goes on to name one very important condition: man will have to apply himself to the task of transforming himself: 'There will arise a new man, happy and proud. It will be a matter of indifference to him whether he lives or ceases to live; he will be the new man. Whoever conquers pain and fear, that person will be God.' Evolution, Kirillov claims, runs from the gorilla to the annihilation of God. This is to be no crude transmogrification, but a reshaping of the earth and its creatures until 'Man will be God and undergo a physical change. The world will be transformed, together with his actions, thoughts and all his feelings.'

Dostoevsky in his *The Diary of a Writer* tells us of a Christmas ball he attended. The Elysian enchantment of the children's festivities is ended; now it is the grown-ups' turn. What a sorry sight all this finery devoid of elegance, all this forced gaiety and downright gaucherie. Just then 'an utterly strange and fantastic thought' occurs to the author:

> If only all these nice, respectable guests were to take it into their heads, if only for a single moment, to become sincere and unaffected,–what would this stuffy room turn into then? . . . if each one of them suddenly were to realise how much they possessed in the way of straightforwardness, frankness, most sincerely cordial good-humour, purity, magnanimous feelings, good will, acuteness of mind. . . . Why, in this very place something would occur that even our sages had never dreamed of. . . . This power is within each one of you, but it is so deeply hidden that it has long seemed an improbability. Is it possible? Can it be that the golden age exists only on a few porcelain cups?[18]

A year later in the *Diary* comes the story *Dream of a Ridiculous Man*. This is a culmination and, to some extent, a synthesis of the different visions of resurrection already present in Dostoevsky's work: the Age of Gold, paradise on earth (Utopia), fantasy, and real transformation of the flesh. 'The earthly paradise is neither the socialist utopia, nor the humanist ant-hill, but the Second Coming of Christ.'[24] Dostoevsky describes the Age of Gold: 'This was a land unsoiled by sin, for in it lived people who had never fallen into sin, who lived in the very same paradise in which . . . our fallen first-parents had lived. . . .' The Ridiculous Man is greeted by uncomprehending smiles as he discourses on eternal life; these innocents were so convinced of the fact of life everlasting that it was axiomatic for them, and not in question at all. 'I have seen truth', exclaims the Ridiculous Man, 'and I now know that it is possible for people to be beautiful and happy, without losing their capacity to live on earth.'

Despite the paradoxical twist which occurs when the Ridiculous Man perverts the goodness he finds on this strange planet, the incident cannot be shrugged off as a mere dream: 'Even supposing that this is all a dream, is it not possible that things really could have been like this? Do you know, I'm going to tell you a secret: perhaps all this was anything but a dream!' 'What after all is a dream? Is not our entire life a dream?' Perhaps it is now easier to see why Dostoevsky so eagerly and impatiently awaited Fyodorov's reply to his letter, and why he was so insistent on knowing his *exact* thoughts on the matter.

The people in the Ridiculous Man's dream are in some profound and mysterious manner directly in touch with nature. 'Their knowledge was deeper and higher than our own science, for our science seeks to explain what life is . . . whereas they, without any science at all, knew how they should live.'[19] Like St. Francis, they were already familiar with the language of animals. They could speak uncannily about the stars, and the Ridiculous Man was convinced that 'they were somehow in contact with the stars in the heavens, not only in imagination, but in some living manner'.

This story is worthy of close attention. It provides a further clue towards our understanding of Dostoevsky. The narrative is not simply about a series of events with a superimposed allegorical register; it is rather a mirror of the narrator's kaleidoscoping consciousness. Dostoevsky has his precedents in Gogol, and in particular Pushkin, as far as this technique is concerned; a technique capitalized in our own age. The reader is beset with hazards, for, despite Dostoevsky's disarming sensibility and *earnestness*, the reader is in constant danger of *debunking himself*.

3 'The Joy of Resurrection'

When Dostoevsky first heard of Fyodorov (in 1878) he had already begun work on the preliminary drafts of the last of his novels *The Brothers Karamazov*. There are many passages, especially in the later rough drafts, which make it evident that the novelist intended to introduce certain of Fyodorov's themes without modification.

Originally the scene in Zosima's monastery was to have introduced the motif 'resurrection of ancestors'. There is a brief entry in the Notebooks: 'the resurrection of [our] ancestors depends on us'.[20] In the finished novel there is no trace of this idea. Another character sketched in the Note-books is Ilinsky, a prototype of Dmitri Karamazov, who according to Anna Grigoryevna is modelled upon the parricide in the *House of the Dead*, and is in some curious way linked with Fyodorov's philosophy: 'Ilinsky is against his parents,' says a landowner (who prefigures Fyodor Pavlovich, the Karamazov father); 'a man like him will not resurrect his parents'.[21] Revulsion against one's father is of the sort that Fyodorov inveighs so constantly against. Ivan Karamazov loathes his own father; Dmitri is ready to kill him.

But the fault lies not only with the children. The debauched father, the careless self-indulgent *roué* only vaguely aware of his family, is of course no uncommon figure in Dostoevsky. Fyodorov's 'problem of the generations' is inherent in Dostoevsky's two previous novels *The Devils* (Stepan and Pyotr Verkhovensky) and *The Raw Youth*. An entire section of the *Diary of a Writer* is devoted explicitly to the social disruption brought about by neglectful, shiftless parents: 'There never has been a time in our Russian life . . . like today. . . . The present-day Russian family becomes every day more and more the casual family.'[22] An outburst such as this, occasioned by a chance encounter in a railway carriage with a typical Russian *chef de famille*, goes only a little way perhaps towards explaining a family crisis such as that between the Karamazovs. The almost existential opposition of Ivan and Dmitri Karamazov to their father has only a little in common with the ruthless scorn of Verkhovensky

(*The Devils*) for his father, which goes no deeper than the level of social relations. *The Brothers Karamazov* is an ingenious counterpoint on the theme of parricide, and the uncanny *essential* identity of father and sons. The crime of parricide, responsibility for which falls on Smerdyakov, Ivan and Dmitri, 'becomes a symbol of the falling away of humanity from unity'.[23]

It would be idle to try to arrive at any conclusion as to why Dostoevsky omitted Fyodorov's theme of the resuscitation of parents from his final draft; one can only speculate. Could it be that, despite its fascination, Dostoevsky found himself unable to work with such an idea? Or could it be that the theme is implicitly present after all? How much less interesting the scene in Zosima's cell would have been, if the author had told us precisely *why* the 'elder' got down on his knees in front of Dmitri. Obscurity, after all, has a high literary value.

Berdyaev finds Zosima and Alyosha Karamazov 'not particularly successful characters from the artistic point of view'.[24] Ivan Karamazov seems to him far more convincingly drawn. Zosima, Berdyaev believed, is deliberately deprived of artistic form; Dostoevsky thought it more important for Zosima to be 'the bearer of the new soul', a spiritually naked figure 'already anticipating the joy of resurrection'. In Dostoevsky's chapter 'Cana of Galilee' Berdyaev finds the answer to Ivan's scepticism in 'the blinding white light of the religion of resurrection, which shone before him [Alyosha] after he had tasted the immeasurable bitterness of corruption and death triumphant'. Dostoevsky's 'joy of resurrection' distils the essence of Fyodorov's philosophy, but cannot rest content with a single simple form. Dostoevsky's joy is of many different kinds.

Dmitri in his 'Hymn to Joy' proclaims an earthy, Dionysian rapture. Markel, Zosima's brother, on the other hand has deluded himself into recognising paradise on earth. 'Mother. It's for joy, not for grief I'm crying . . . Am I not even now in paradise?' 'Do not weep, mother, life is heaven, and we are all in heaven.' Markel was convinced he had discovered the secret of paradise on earth: 'we do not wish to know it even, but if we did, we should have heaven on earth the very next day'. Dmitri Karamazov too has had a similar truth revealed to him, but he wishes to keep it secret. He experiences joy and bitterness in this truth, something bright as the sun, ineffable: 'I am here in secret, and I am guarding a secret. I'll explain later on, but knowing it's a secret I began whispering like a fool when there was no need. Let's go! Over there! Till then, be silent.' Ever since Grushenka confessed her love for him, Dmitri had been undergoing his (allegorical) resurrection. Only months later, in prison awaiting sentence, does he utter the promised secret: 'Brother, during the past two years I have felt a new man within myself, in me a new man has risen again! He was in me all the time, but had never appeared before. . . . An awesome thing!' Dmitri is afraid the new spirit will desert him before he has finished serving his sentence of hard labour: 'There is something else to be afraid of now: that the new man will leave me.' There is a whole allegory of Fyodorov's project in Dmitri's vision of life among the convicts, an underworld from which man is striving to rise again. 'We shall be in chains and there will be no freedom, but then, in our great sorrow, we shall rise again to joy, without which man cannot live nor God exist . . . and then we men underground will sing from the bowels of the earth a glorious hymn to God with Whom is joy.' The convicts are those aware of the 'common cause' who must eventually make it known to the rest of mankind.

A shorthand entry in the Notebooks in a section 'Confession of an Elder' says: 'Your flesh will be changed. . . . Life is paradise, the keys are with us.'[25] The simplicity of Fyodorov's idea becomes overlaid and obscured in the novel. It seems that Dostoevsky's 'transformation of the flesh' will take place only if preceded by a transformation of outlook and consciousness. The 'new man' will be resurrected spiritually before he is physically. In an article *Supramoralism in Opposition to Mysticism*, Fyodorov laments the novelist's complete misunderstanding of his whole conception of resurrection, and criticises him on several counts.

Fyodorov could see that Dostoevsky had failed to grasp the importance of applied science and its progressive and gradual development from one generation to the next. 'He evidently supposed that a fulfilment of this obligation was only possible in the very distant future, not earlier than 20,000 years hence, for example.'[26] Fyodorov and Dostoevsky were wide enough apart. The latter's perception of 'other worlds' was possible only through suffering, illness or mystical revelation: as Fyodorov said many years later: 'Dostoevsky . . . was a mystic and, in the manner of a mystic, was convinced that mankind is in opposition to other worlds and does not see them, and even does not live in them at all.'[27] The novelist's resurrection was 'one huge mystical hypothesis'. The 'new science' expounded by Fyodorov obviously never took root in Dostoevsky; that is not to say, however, that he was never attracted by it. In Dostoevsky's Notebooks there are passages which betray a specific influence. One such passage describes Fyodorov's cosmic organism: 'the family will be enlarged; even non-kindred will enter into it, and a new organism will have become woven together'.[28]

There is a curious section in Dostoevsky's novel, so far unexplained, but which may have some relevance to Fyodorov's 'new science' and his critique of empirical positivistic science. Dmitri Karamazov has an inkling that science has something to do with his 'new man'. Rakitin has been telling him things about the nervous system and the mechanism of perception, about chemistry. Dmitri is enthusiastic, although he is sad that Rakitin's science discloses nothing of God. He tells Alyosha about it: 'It's magnificent this science! A new man is arising–that much I understand. . . . And yet I am sorry to lose God. . . . It's chemistry, brother, chemistry! There's no help for it . . . you must make room for chemistry.' Dmitri knows nothing of the natural sciences, and his immediate reaction is that of the artist. 'The little tails of those nerves' are for him sheer poetry. It is the poetry of science, the creative science of Fyodorov, which overwhelms him. He is not so naive as to be taken in by the people who at present dabble in Rakitin's science: 'Claude Bernard. Who was he? Chemist or what? . . . A scoundrel of some sort, very likely. They are all scoundrels . . . Rakitin will get on anywhere; he is another Bernard.'

Zosima's corpse decays. A miracle is ruled out. 'Beware of miracles,' Zosima warned. Like Fyodorov, Zosima considered them an insult to man and God alike. Despite this, Zosima is resurrected. Not by any natural miracle, but by a reshaping of Alyosha's entire world and being, probably Dostoevsky's greatest literary feat. 'Cana of Galilee' bursts upon Alyosha (and the reader), a vision of endless dimension, more real than reality. The reader can see for himself the technique used; it would take a disproportionate amount of space to analyse it here. Much more important is the break-through by the imagination into a world of resurrected people which Dostoevsky was convinced existed, not in a crude 'spiritual-istic' sense, but in 'other worlds' normally hidden from human perception. Zosima's earthly body decays; no attempt is made to resurrect *it*.

In Alyosha's vision the basis of everything is memory. Memory must survive before it becomes possible to resurrect one's ancestors. Every single detail, however insignificant, must be retained in the memory, for it is these details which reconstitute the personality. Alyosha knew the truth of this. His young friends and he are heartbroken at the loss of Ilyushechka. At the graveside, Alyosha doles out not merely words of comfort but an entire philosophy of remembrance:

> You must know that there is nothing higher and stronger and more wholesome and good for life in the future than some worthwhile memory. . . . People talk to you a good deal about your education, but some good, sacred memory, preserved from childhood, is perhaps the best education of all. If a man carries many such memories with him into life, he is safe to the end of his days . . . and let us never forget one another! I say that again. I give you my word that, for my part, I will never forget a single one of you. . . . Well, and who has brought us together in this kind, good feeling which we shall remember and intend to remember all our lives? . . . May his memory live on in our hearts from this time forth! . . . Let us remember his face and his clothes and his tiny boots, his coffin. . . .

The point is that *all* the details have to be accurately remembered; dress and mannerisms, as well as character. It is this sentiment which lies behind Fyodorov's scheme for protecting the very graves and relics of the dead, where living memory of the dead is preserved alongside the remains. The process culminates in a perpetual 'funeral banquet' taking place in these cemeteries. Alyosha continues:

> Now let us finish talking and go along to his funeral banquet. Don't be put off at the pancakes—it's a very old custom, one that will last, and that is what is so good about it.

Alyosha believes in Resurrection 'real, personal, literal', about which Dostoevsky wanted reassurance:

> 'Karamazov', cried Kolya, 'can it be true what's taught us in church, that we shall all rise again from the dead and shall live and see each other again, and everyone else, even Ilyusha?'
> 'Of course we shall all rise again, certainly we shall see each other and tell each other with joy and gladness all that has happened!'

Alyosha is deceiving himself in his need to convince others. Zosima is not beguiled by visions of this sort. He shares the grief of the peasant woman for her dead child, and her loss. Her loss is so great that she all the time feels vividly the *presence* of her child, as though he were just hiding somewhere, just out of sight. The details she recalls are all of the most concrete kind. 'The artistic realism of Dostoevsky here reaches clairvoyance. Maternal love *resurrects* the image of her dead child; the concreteness of her vision verges on the miraculous.'[29] The Elder's efforts to console her with the thought of her child as an angel are of no use. He quickly sees that he must take her side and support her in rebelling against natural destiny, against the 'blind force': 'Refuse to be comforted, there is absolutely no reason why you should allow yourself any comfort.'

For the present the only consolation lies in rare momentary penetrations of the veil of appearances, through to 'other worlds'. 'If there are other worlds and if it is true that man is immortal, that he is from other worlds himself, then accordingly there is . . . a bond with other worlds.'[30] This piece of reasoning occurs quite casually in the rough drafts. In the finished novel it is this unseen 'bond' binding men with other worlds which Alyosha experiences in his tremendous vision.

Consciousness slips from one world to the other. Death then is not really death at all, but a transposition, a scene-shift, as it were. 'Dostoevsky acknowledges the fact of the mysterious transformation that turns man, while still on earth, into another and divine nature.'[31] The macrocosmic setting of Alyosha's ecstasy is more than a little reminiscent of Fyodorov's 'force emanating from other heavenly bodies':[32]

> From the zenith to the horizon, the Milky Way ran in two pale streams. . . . It was as if threads from all those numberless worlds of God came together linking his soul with them, and it was trembling 'in contact with other worlds' . . . but with every instant he felt clearly as though tangibly that something firm and unshakable as that vault of heaven had entered his soul . . . 'Someone visited my soul in that hour', he used to say afterwards with implicit faith in his words.

We are reminded of the biblical almighty Word leaping down from heaven 'while all things were in quiet silence and the night was in the midst of her course'. But in Alyosha's vision Earth figures more significantly even than Heaven. It is necessary to feel the soil, to fall upon it and 'water it with one's tears'. In this manner, Zosima believed, men may expect to penetrate these worlds beyond, which would then be revealed to them, as they were to Alyosha Karamazov. 'Much on earth is hidden from us, but in its stead we have been given a secret, mysterious sensation of our living bond with another world, a mountainous, lofty world. And even the roots of our thoughts and feelings are not here but in other worlds.' The earth-ecstasy is a means not only of discharging grief and despair, but also of effecting an actual shift into a world beyond, a world of resurrection.

4 *Action versus mysticism*

Dostoevsky's first thoughts on his last novel seem to have been chiefly taken up with the relationship between Alyosha Karamazov and Zosima. In the Notebooks there are some curious fragmentary sequences. For example:

'. . . why in a monastery?'
'Fanatic?–by no means.'

'Mystic?–never.'

'. . . he was something quite other than a fanatic. He turned up here a year ago, but how odd it was–with some strange end in view, which he made no attempt to hide . . . he came in order to save his mother's grave.'[33]

It is already clear that Alyosha was not to become a mystic or even a believer for belief's sake. His aim in returning to his home town was specific: it was consistent too with Fyodorov's project. In the final novel, the key word 'save' is nowhere to be found in this context, and there is no plan of any sort to go into hiding. For once Dostoevsky has culled the substance of Fyodorov and blinked the incidentals.

Alyosha, as he finally emerges in *The Brothers Karamazov*, is the youngest of the three brothers and the son of Fyodor Pavlovich's second wife, a pathetic crazed woman who died when Alyosha was barely four years old.

He had never forgotten her–her face, her caresses 'as though she stood living before me'. Such memories may persist, as everyone knows, from an even earlier age, even from two years old, but scarcely standing out through a whole lifetime like spots of light out of darkness, like a corner torn out of a huge picture, which has all faded and disappeared except that fragment. That is how it was with him. . . . It soon became apparent that he was looking for his mother's tomb. He practically acknowledged at the time that that was the only object of his visit. But it can hardly have been the whole reason of it. It is more probable that he himself did not understand and could not explain what had suddenly arisen in his soul, and drawn him irresistibly into a new, unknown, but inevitable path.

His mother's grave serves as a theme in counterpoint to the rapprochement of father and son, the self-lacerations of the former and the disarming candour of Alyosha; it also activates and explains both the psychology and the narrative development. Fyodor Pavlovich could not show him where the crazy woman's grave was; he had entirely forgotten where it was. It is then that we read of the prolonged debauch of the interim years, until Alyosha's arrival, when the young man 'seemed to affect his moral side, as though something had awakened in this prematurely decrepit man which had long been dead in his soul'. Alyosha reminds him of his half-witted wife whom, like Stavrogin, he had married probably as an experiment in sensuality. It is Grigory, a faithful old retainer, who takes Alyosha to his mother's grave, 'a cast-iron tombstone, cheap but decently kept, on which were inscribed the name and age of the deceased and the date of her death, and below a four-lined verse, such as are commonly used on old-fashioned middle-class tombs.' To Alyosha's amazement this tomb turned out to be Grigory's doing. He had put it up on the poor 'crazy woman's grave at his own expense, after Fyodor Pavlovich, whom he had often pestered about the grave, had gone off to Odessa, *abandoning the grave and all his memories*'. The narrator goes on to recall how 'this little episode' had a marked influence upon Fyodor Pavlovich, who, flushed with sentiment, takes a thousand roubles to the monastery to pay for masses for her soul. Either by a perverse twist or through sheer forgetfulness (we are not told which) the money is donated for masses to be said for his *first* wife, who used to thrash Alyosha.

So far, the dramatisation is coherent and convincing, the ribs of Fyodorov's project showing through hardly at all. Then the aesthetic limit is reached once more. There is no question of Alyosha 'making no attempt to hide' and declaring his intention of 'preserving' his mother's remains. Instead, at the graveside, 'he stood with bowed head and walked away without uttering a word'. It is consistent with the 'philosophy of resurrection' that he should have shown no emotion at the sight of the grave. As for the 'strange end in view', this has evaporated into a vague ideal: 'He was simply a precocious lover of humanity. If he took the monastic path, it was only because at that time it alone struck him and offered to him, as it were, the ideal of a way torn out of the darkness of the world of wickedness towards the light of love.' Such transpositions have naturally left slight blemishes on Dostoevsky's masterpiece. Some readers will have been left with a feeling of dissatisfaction, when the outline of Alyosha Karamazov's character and purpose given at the beginning of the novel does not match up fully with his subsequent role in the novel. It is impossible to see from the later stages of the novel alone why the author should have gone out of his way to sketch so deliberately the role he initially fulfils.

It is never easy to find Dostoevsky trafficking in others' ideas, or, for that matter, in his own either. Consider only the *Diary*, many parts of which have antagonised and incensed—as well as bored—readers who are otherwise admirers. And yet, many of the ideas found there reappear in *The Brothers Karamazov*, where they are clothed in such ambiguity that all might wonder and none take offence.

The side of Fyodorov that appears to have left the greatest impression on Dostoevsky's work is the theory of 'supra-moralism'. In the *Philosophy of the Common Cause* the latter has an obvious karmic colouring (where Fyodorov's concept of ethics is nearly the equivalent of the law of karma). Ethics rules not only all practical conduct, but all thought, creativity, science – everything human, in fact. Everything done, thought or achieved entails its own consequences, first on the metaphysical, then on the practical plane. Thus, each individual is responsible for the actions and fate of everyone else, in however minute a degree.

Markel, Zosima's brother 'resurrected in life', gives Fyodorov's premiss 'Everyone of us is guilty before all' an even more literal interpretation: 'No one will call anyone else a criminal but each will consider himself guilty in everything that is committed.' Dmitri is quite explicit: 'All are guilty for all.' In his ecstasy Alyosha 'felt as though he wanted to forgive all and for everything, and to ask forgiveness himself; not for oneself only, but for all, for everything and others will ask that he be forgiven'.

Ivan Karamazov is tormented by anxiety over the impossibility of forgiving the sufferings of innocent children and at last finds the answer to his problem, Alyosha's answer: 'No one man can forgive, but all in unison can.' Dostoevsky himself may well have been looking for such an answer. There is no evidence that Dostoevsky had any solution to Ivan's problem before 1878, if the *Diary* is anything to go by. In the latter, for instance, he quotes Christ as saying that 'He would cut short the times and seasons' for the sake of suffering children.[34] Christianity provides no ultimate solution to the problem of evil. At any rate, the solutions proposed do not satisfy Ivan Karamazov, who turns down the offered promise of universal harmony, and 'respectfully returns his ticket'. Alyosha, the vehicle of supramoralism, has yet to have his word. Ivan is of the past, Alyosha of the future.

The supramoralist ethic includes spiritual as well as physical murder. The novel makes it more than clear that Ivan, who consciously wishes the death of his father, is no less blameworthy than Smerdyakov the one who actually deals the blow. Dostoevsky's art compels us to sense this. Even Alyosha is guilty by neglect. Allegorically, the brothers represent the living generation; some neglectful, others actively vicious, and the rare few capable of parricide. Smerdyakov, a half-brother, an outsider, a reject of society, is the scape-goat, a murderer without a motive. Fyodor Pavlovich, a particularly vicious and hateful father, puts yet another barrier between fathers and sons. But supramoralism lays it down that he is as much deserving of love as the rest of his generation, for the theory is based neither on sentiment, justice, or even love, but offers instead the only practical route to universal harmony, where all are forgiven because everyone is responsible for everyone else's actions. Not only the St. Francis's, but the Caligulas will be among the resurrected.

STYLISTICS AND PERSONALITY

1 *Style and the structure of personal being*

I T was Bakhtin who first argued that Dostoevsky's originality lay in his ability to form 'an artistically objective conception of his characters and to project them as entirely independent entities, without having to resort to lyricism or to insert his own voice among theirs, and at the same time managing to avoid constricting them in a circumscribed psychological reality'.[1] Each character in Dostoevsky inhabits his own world, and not the author's. The interplay of these characters and their separate worlds is of a 'polyphonic' kind, more like an interweaving than a blend, an interweaving of an entirely unpredictable kind. Robbe-Grillet was right in claiming Dostoevsky as a landmark in the 'delyricisation' of the novel.

The extreme pluralism of Dostoevsky's world is ascribed to his own particular social milieu. Bakhtin was convinced that it was the age in which the novelist lived which engendered the 'polyphonic' novel:

> Dostoevsky was directly involved in the contradictions of the multiplanar existence of his own time. . . . This personal experience of his was profound, but Dostoevsky did not give it a direct monologic expression in his novels. On the contrary, this experience of his only helped him to arrive at a deeper understanding of the nature of coexistent and divergent conflicts, conflicts between real individuals rather than between ideas within a single consciousness. It was thus that the objective (social) conflicts of the period placed Dostoevsky's writings not on the plane of personal suffering, but on a plane in which he was able to observe them objectively as forces existing simultaneously but independently.[2]

The Russian society of Dostoevsky's time was severely fragmented and it was this, Bakhtin supposed, which suggested or rather *formed* his way of viewing personal identity and interrelationship.

Dostoevsky's characters fascinated Bakhtin on account of their separateness. The universe was no one's in particular, and existence was the realisation of each individual's possibility. It is still seldom realised that Dostoevsky never set out to become a philosopher, but instead used the material of philosophy and ideas to construct the mental and spiritual worlds of his characters. Like Nietzsche he could see perfectly that philosophy is 'a species of involuntary and unconscious autobiography'. As Bakhtin neatly put it: 'Two ideas in Dostoevsky means two people.'[3]

It is one of those curious coincidences that Bakhtin was working in the same direction as Heidegger. He could not have known of Heidegger, for *Time and Being* appeared only in 1926; yet many of his insights are strikingly similar to ones that emerge from Heidegger's investigation into the structure of personal being: 'It is enough for someone to appear on Dostoevsky's horizon, for him immediately to become an incarnated force in the process of realising its own possibility.'[4] Even Bakhtin's emphasis on the *word* reminds us of the importance ascribed to *logos* in Heidegger's scheme; the logos as 'discourse', as 'letting-something-be-seen', as 'something to which one addresses oneself'.[5] Although Bakhtin's *word* is the historically-derived Russian neoplatonic concept, and not the Aristotelean logos borrowed by Heidegger, it is this principle which occupies such an important place in Bakhtin's analysis: 'There is nothing but world-orientation, the word. And this word is dialogically contiguous with other words, a word about a word, oriented towards the word.'[6] According to Bakhtin, the failure of previous criticism to detect Dostoevsky's method was due to neglect of the actual fabric of the narrative and dialogue. 'The critics have interpreted Dostoevsky after their own fashion. All without exception have taken him to be a *single word*, a *single voice*, and a *single accent*. This is precisely where they have gone wrong. The supra-verbal, supra-vocal, supra-accentual unity of the polyphonic novel still remains to be explored.'[7]

Bakhtin never doubted that his concept 'polyphony' was a crude one, and he never intended it to be more than a beginning. The way ahead however seemed to him definite and unmistakable:

> The final *whole* that constituted the European and Russian novel before Dostoevsky, the monologic undivided world of the author's own fabrication, was to become in Dostoevsky's novels no more than a *part*, a mere *element* of the whole. Reality as previously conceived was only a partial aspect of a greater reality. The former technique of unifying the whole – the pragmatic plot line and the personal style and tone – has now become a subordinate factor. With Dostoevsky new principles of combining these elements and constructing the whole make their appearance. Metaphorically speaking, this is the beginning of novelistic counterpoint[8] [my italics].

Dostoevsky has found his way through to an art form in which the characters themselves literally take over from the author. The direction had already been indicated by Pushkin, although Pushkin was able to deal with no more than one world at a time. Dostoevsky too began with single worlds, and it is only from *The Idiot* onwards that his worlds begin to pluralise. In his last novel (*The Brothers Karamazov*) we are confronted with an immensely intricate interplay of 'monadic' worlds, reflecting and in turn reflected in other worlds.

In his exhaustive study *Dostoevsky's Style*[9] Leonid Grossman had argued that Dostoevsky was exploiting the detective story genre for its suspense value. Bakhtin could not entirely agree with this view. It seemed to him that Dostoevsky's purpose was more radical. Bakhtin insisted that Dostoevsky found the detective-story plot useful not so much on account of its suspense but mainly because of the boundless scope for allowing the personality to express itself:

> The adventure plot is clothing made to fit a particular character, clothing which can be changed as often as necessary. The adventure plot is based not upon the nature of a particular character nor upon his place in society. It is based upon what he is *not*, and upon what is, from the point of view of given actuality, not preordained and entirely unexpected. . . . The adventure situation is one in which any man, as a human being, might find himself. Moreover, this kind of plot never embodies a fixed social position as a final living form, but as a 'situation'

only. . . . The aristocrat of the thriller is a situation; a situation in which a particular man finds himself. The man assumes the mantle of an aristocrat, but remains the same man beneath. He shoots, commits crimes, dodges his enemies, overcomes obstacles, and so forth. In this sense the adventure plot is deeply human. All social and cultural institutions, all rules, strata, classes and family relationships are no more than *situations* in which the eternal human being, as a human being, finds himself. The needs dictated by his nature–self-preservation, thirst for conquest and success, sensual love–all these determine the form the adventure plot will take.[10]

Man enacts the roles he finds it necessary to enact. The more individual he is, the more likely he is to play a variety of parts and to precipitate action in a real-life plot. The more *conscious* he is of his own individuality, the greater the likelihood that he will either shut himself off (like the Man from Underground) or project himself as his own double. In either case he will find himself swept along in an adventure, totally unprepared for its unseen but inevitable consequences (as in the case of Raskolnikov, or the narrator in the *Gentle Creature*).

Dostoevsky's novels then are not psychological novels at all. Raskolnikov, Stavrogin or Ivan Karamazov are, if Bakhtin is correct, no more 'psychological' than the characters of P. G. Wodehouse.

According to another of Bakhtin's contemporaries,[11] Dostoevsky deliberately accentuated the *unexpected* in his characters' behaviour so that they should disrupt the lives of others around them. Each character is supplied with his own individual existential germ, which ripens in the dark and secret corners of the soul until one day it breaks through into actuality. Dostoevsky's characters are like creatures from different worlds. and the responses they strike in the world they find themselves sharing in common, the world into which they are 'thrown', turn out to be mere echoes. Whenever there is a conflict within a single individual, this conflict erupts as crime, actual or projected. It is characteristic of Dostoevsky that every crime occurs in circumstances in which one half of the personality overrides the other.

Raskolnikov was fully persuaded of the unfeasibility of his plan to murder the old hag of a usurer. In the end he commits the crime automatically as if his thoughts and actions were being guided by some power beyond his rational control. This interpretation of crime in Dostoevsky tallies with important sections of abnormal psychology and criminal pathology.

Bakhtin's most important discovery remains to be discussed. Dostoevsky's novels were fashioned out of what Bakhtin called 'contrapuntal inner dialogue'. This dialogue is discernible whenever there is any contact between characters. The speech of one character throws into relief the *covert* dialogue inherent in the speech of another. This 'speech' although it always verges on parody is poised between parody and sophistication or between suppressed and tense overt dialogue. The monologue of the Man from Underground can be seen to be a three-way communication of this kind. Two inner voices address each other, and in turn address themselves to the *reader*. It is possible to take any section of the monologue and to analyse it in this manner. At random, let us take the last paragraph of Chapter 2 of *Notes from Underground*. This paragraph may be transposed as follows:

Voice 1: Now, for instance, I'm very vain. I'm as suspicious and as quick to take offence as a hunchback or a dwarf.

Voice 2: But as a matter of fact there were moments in my life when, if someone had slapped my face, I should perhaps have been glad even of that.

Voice 1 (covert): (You can't be serious.)

Voice 2: I'm saying this perfectly seriously. I should certainly have found even there a sort of pleasure.

Voice 1 (covert): (Despair, I think you mean!)

Voice 2: The pleasure of despair, no doubt, but despair too has its moments of intense pleasure, intense delight, especially if you happen to be acutely conscious of the hopelessness of your position. And there, too, I mean after you'd had your face slapped, you'd be overwhelmed by the awareness of having been utterly humiliated and snubbed.

Voice 1 (covert): (And you didn't want to get your revenge?)

Voice 2: The trouble is, of course, that however much I tried to find some excuse for what had happened, the conclusion I would come to would always be that it was my own fault to begin with, and what hurt most of all was that though innocent I was guilty and, as it were, guilty according to the laws of nature.

Voice 1 (covert): (How on earth did you arrive at a conclusion like this, putting all the blame on yourself?)

Voice 2: I was guilty, first of all, because I was cleverer than all the people around me.

Reader (covert): (How preposterous and conceited!)

Voice 2: (No, I assure you) I have always considered myself cleverer than anyone else, and sometimes, I also assure you, I have been ashamed of it. . . .

etc., etc.

This kind of dialogue is not confined to the *Notes from Underground* but is the very fabric of Dostoevsky. There simply does not exist a single objective character about whom one can say: 'this is so-and-so', 'he is such-and-such'. All Dostoevsky's characters are 'open-ended'. 'All definitions and all points of view are converted into dialogue, and are woven into it as it develops. . . . The word "at a remove" adding up to the grand total of the personality forms no part of his design. That which is fixed, dead, finished, unable to respond, that which has uttered its final word simply does not exist in Dostoevsky's world.'[12] Dialogue and narrative action are likewise inseparable. Dostoevskyan man is revealed in dialogue.

It would have been surprising if such a radically new approach as Bakhtin's had not occasionally missed the mark. But his lapses are few, and among his more important achievements is a demonstration that in *The Devils* Kirillov, Shatov and Pyotr Verkhovensky are an integral part of Stavrogin's own dialogue. It is only when Stavrogin hears his own thoughts 'played back' to him by these characters that he is able to find them dead and 'monologised'. The life has gone from his ideas and they sound petrified when used by others. Stavrogin's reaction is one of amusement, bewilderment and pain. He talks of his 'burden'. What no one had realised is that the burden is nothing mystical or tragic, but a breakdown and subsequent loss of the dynamic in his own inner dialogue. In another of the novels *Crime and Punishment* the criminal investigator constantly teases the exposed nerve of Raskolnikov's suppressed second voice in order to force it into the open. The dynamics of Raskolnikov's inner dialogue was sufficient to undermine the carefully spun alibis. The legend of the Grand Inquisitor is the externalisation of the internal dialogue taking place between Ivan Karamazov and his other self; the ambiguity of its ending vividly signifies the duality of his nature.

The most patent example of Dostoevsky's use of inner dialogue is his early work *The Double*. The central character is a Gogolesque figure by the name of Golyadkin. Golyadkin's hallucination is that he has a double, and this double employs only those types of speech or tone adopted by Golyadkin himself. He is Golyadkin's stylistic mirror. When Golyadkin takes pity on his double and takes him into his house, the latter copies his mode of expression and behaviour. In the early stages of their acquaintance the double confines himself to that voice in Golyadkin's inner dialogue which betrays lack of confidence ('Will that be all right?' 'Is that convenient, are you quite sure?') It is only gradually that the real Golyadkin assumes his more confident second voice ('We shall live in clover', etc.). But it is just at the time when Golyadkin's second voice is becoming dominant, that their roles are suddenly reversed. The double begins to adopt the confident tone and this is the start of Golyadkin's undoing. From this time onwards the hallucinatory double begins to parody the real Golyadkin:

> This transference of words from the mouth of one character to another when, as far as the content is concerned, they remain identical, changing only their tone and ultimate meaning. This is what constitutes Dostoevsky's basic method. He compels his characters to recognise themselves, their own ideas, their own words, their aims, their mien even in someone quite different. Everything totally changes its significance, sounds entirely different, like a parody or a leg-pull. Nearly all Dostoevsky's major characters has his own partial double in some other character or even in several characters at once.[13]

The full development of this technique is reached in the scene where Ivan Karamazov is tormented by his devil-hallucination: 'Between the words of Ivan Karamazov and the devil's repartee there is no difference in content, only in tone or nuance. But it is precisely this which changes their ultimate meaning.'[14]

2 '*The Medium is the Message*'

It is often suggested that Dostoevsky is among the tiny handful of Russian writers who lose little or nothing in translation. After all, so the argument sometimes runs, his style possesses no particular merit; Russians often find it humdrum and even banal in places. The novels are anyhow, one is reminded, about *ideas* and are not so dependent on choice prose and poetic description as for instance Turgenev or Chekhov. I once shared this view, albeit with minor qualifications, until I was compelled to take a new and closer look and to make a reappraisal of Dostoevsky's stylistics. It now seems to me that Dostoevsky is one of the least translatable of all the nineteenth-century Russians.

An explanation of such a radical reversal is obviously called for. And this is not at all easy. To provide a convincing justification, an intimate knowledge of the Russian language would have to be taken for granted on the part of my readers. Let makeshift then suffice.

Dostoevsky's subtle use of style is not immediately transparent, and yet it is not veiled either. The trouble is that style in Dostoevsky lies so much at the surface that one does not think of looking there. It has nothing to do with idiosyncrasies of speech, mannerisms, such as one might find in Gogol, Dickens or Balzac; it has nothing to do with flights of rhetoric, special shades of prose, or pure skill either.

Each character in Dostoevsky has his own particular mode of discourse, his own individual speech. This stylistic structure extends beyond the dialogue and spills over into the surrounding narrative. Narrative provides the necessary backcloth to dialogue, and is determined largely by the dialogue, which is the most important element of all.

Grossman had noted the conflicting styles out of which Dostoevsky intentionally built his novels:

> Running counter to the age-old aesthetic traditions which demanded a correspondence between thematic material and its treatment, presupposing unity or, at any rate, homogeneity and affinity among the structural elements of a work of art, Dostoevsky sets about blending opposites. He openly defies the basic canon of aesthetic theory. His plan . . . was to create out of a diversity of material – materials with different values attached to them and extremely incompatible besides – a single and integrated work of art. It is for this reason the Book of Job, the Revelation of St. John, gospel texts, – everything on which he draws in the pages of his novels and which imparts various tones in different places – are here combined, in the manner peculiar to him, with newspaper journalese, with anecdote, parody, street scenes, grotesqueries or lampoons. He daringly tosses into his melting pot more and more new elements, knowing full well that the raw scraps of everyday reality, sensational material from cheap thrillers, and the pages of the Bible would blend and become fused into a new amalgam, bearing the unmistakable imprint of his own personal style and tone.[15]

Dostoevsky often shows a marked preference for the 'news-sheet' style, and seldom hesitates to introduce handfuls of trivia from everyday life. Bakhtin was inclined to place the whole of Dostoevsky's style squarely within the world of newsprint. 'His love for the newspaper, his penetrating and subtle understanding of the news-sheet, a living reflection of the contradictions of the contemporary social scene in the cross-section of a single day.'[16] Time in Dostoevsky is contemporaneous (although not instantaneous); the past appears only in flashbacks. It is as though the novels were vast newspapers with each character, as it were, adding his own contribution to the whole.

Only when forced to look closely at the *surface* of Dostoevsky's prose does one discover the diversity: an especially difficult task, as the author is persistently inviting us to consider other apparently more important things. *The Brothers Karamazov* is a huge patchwork of styles, of which little trace remains in translation. The idiom and syntax for a start; then allusion and choice of phrases and images; finally, the least tangible of all, colour, tone, and especially *taste*. Taste is probably the blanket term we are looking for, as all the rest follows from it. Ivan Karamazov and Rakitin share what might be called a 'neutral' style; this reflects their membership of the intelligentsia. Alyosha Karamazov and Zosima indirectly reflect the parable style of the New Testament, never homiletic (the European style) but simple, clean, rounded, limpid. Occasionally these styles are thrown into contrast, as when Ivan and Alyosha meet in the tavern (in the section 'Pro and Contra'). Nearly everything in this contrast is lost in the available English translations. The natural objection is: Does it matter? My answer is that these contrasts probably matter far more than is realised. Ivan Karamazov addresses his brother as if he were delivering a lecture, or composing a short memoir. The 'monographic' measure is almost entirely lost in translation. The phrases and sentences fall into familiar moulds; with the style of the Russian mid-nineteenth century intelligentsia – Herzen, Chernyshevsky and Belinsky – as the model. There are distortions too, and the occasional lapse into colloquial idiom. The corrections were omitted because he was not actually addressing his peers, nor was he committing his thoughts to writing. If Ivan Karamazov's style loses a little in translation, Alyosha's loses nearly everything. There is something *sec* about his turn of phrase, the faintest trace of a liturgical style, so slight that it could hardly attract attention to itself. Ivan sometimes takes up Alyosha's phrase in the manner of a refrain, and in so doing imparts to it quite a different tone and weight. The customary irony is Ivan's way of parrying the faintly insolent tone of his brother's style, insolent in a sly-subtle way. There is nothing to be singled out and made an issue of; it is simply a question of tone and manner. A perfectly innocent childlike-gay manner. Ivan is four years older than Alyosha, and not unconscious of his dignity (his success in academic circles has made him a shade pompous). Alyosha ruffles him by his candid assertion that Ivan is no different from other young men of his generation, with emphasis on the word 'young'. He employs the untranslatable Russian affectionate diminutive *molo-*

denkiy 'young-little'. Alyosha's style is the whitewashed monastery wall, the arrayed icons, the aroma of incense, the sound of chanted prayer; forbidding and congenial, superior and humble, admonishing and naïve. The delicate flavour evaporates in translation.

Fyodor Karamazov (the Karamazov father) and Smerdyakov share a style distinguished by its ugliness and disjointedness. Smerdyakov's speech is so anti-style, so Beckmesserish, as to be ludicrous. Again translation fails, for the problem is not simply linguistic but the impossibility of 'translating' an irreducible and unseemly chunk of Russian life, a sociological specimen. But if Smerdyakov is a cacophany of human expression, Dmitri Karamazov is sheer magnificence. Dmitri is the poet, and his language is Pushkin's language. It is never difficult to set out Dmitri's speech in free verse form, for it is the finest poetic diction. Dostoevsky nearly always throws him into contrast with some other character, who will become the distorting medium for Dmitri's words; sometimes his father, at other times Smerdyakov, or Rakitin, and finally that socially responsible and well-adjusted scoundrel, the criminal investigator.

Dostoevsky's reader is confronted with a gigantic canvas of ontological fragmentation, the diagnosis of a widespread disease for which there seemed to be no cure. Dostoevsky's characters do not communicate. They reflect and counter-reflect each other's discourse, and in turn the fragmented structures of their personalities. There is never any objective communication. The Socratic dialogue has been replaced by a new and deeply disturbing phenomenon; a network, a chaos of intersecting media. There is no longer a dialogic exchange. To borrow McLuhan's catchphrase: 'the medium *is* the message'[17]. 'Typographic man' is at the same time the disintegrated man of modern civilisation. The extension of man through typography, the rise of styles and their multiplicity has brought about an attendant fragmentation. The impossibility of intercourse between media is the new tragedy, as Dostoevsky seems to have been well aware. Style, if we read Dostoevsky aright, has been responsible for the

ontological disintegration and the uprooting of modern man.
It is perhaps high time for stylistics to join forces with
philosophy. Although Dostoevsky probably regarded philosophy as subordinate to the stylistics of discourse. European
Platonic dialogue was due for replacement by a completely
new form of dialogue, a kind of typography of Dasein.

3 *Stylistics and Stavrogin*

The famous confrontation between Tikhon and Stavrogin
reveals Dostoevsky at his most equivocal and ambiguous.
Tikhon is not merely a venerable sage at whose feet Stavrogin
has made the experiment of sitting. He is first and foremost a
human being with his own limitations, doubts, flaws, and
weakness. Stavrogin can easily get the better of him but only
momentarily.

> 'Do you believe in God?'–Stavrogin blurted out suddenly.
> 'I do.'
> 'It is said that if you have faith and command a mountain to
> move, it will move . . . arrant nonsense though. But I am even
> so rather curious to know whether you could move a mountain.'
> 'If God wills it, then I shall,' Tikhon murmured quietly and
> reservedly, lowering his eyes.
> 'I am not interested in whether God himself could move one.
> What about you? It's you I'm asking. If you can do it, I shall
> reward you by believing in God.'
> 'Perhaps I could move one.'
> ' "Perhaps" is a nice way of putting it. Why are you in doubt?'
> 'My faith is not quite perfect.'
> 'What? Do you mean to say that even *your* faith is imperfect?'
> 'Yes . . . perhaps: I believe, but not perfectly.'
> 'Well, at any rate, you do believe none the less that with
> God's help you could do it, and that is something, after all.
> Anyhow it probably amounts to more than the très peu of an
> Archbishop under threat of the sword. You are a Christian I
> suppose?' mocked Stavrogin.
> 'Let me not be ashamed, Lord, of Thy Cross,' Tikhon
> almost whispered, with a kind of impassioned whisper, bowing
> his head still lower. . . .[18]

Tikhon reels under Stavrogin's sarcasm. His advantage over
Stavrogin is however real, though based on something

entirely unexpected. Tikhon's superiority is an *aesthetic* superiority; it is through the *form* of his thinking, his psychology, his *style*, that he counteracts this corrosive power confronting him.

From the outset, Dostoevsky makes efforts to emphasise the contrast, the aesthetic contrast. Every detail is pressed into service. From the preliminary description of Tikhon's habitat we learn that he is surrounded by simple elegance and good taste.

> The two rooms which composed Tikhon's cell were also rather strangely furnished. Side by side with awkward old-fashioned furniture, covered with threadbare leather, were three or four elegant pieces; a superb easy-chair, a large writing-table of excellent workmanship, a tastefully carved book-case, little tables, shelves, all given to him as presents. There was an expensive Bokhara carpet, and also mats. There were engravings of a secular kind and classical reliefs, and along with these a large icon-case with dazzling gold and silver icons. . . . His library also was said to be a little too varied in character. Side by side with the works of the saints and the Christian Fathers there were works of modern fiction 'and possibly even worse than that'.

Tikhon is an artist, an artist in human and divine affairs alike. Stavrogin is taken aback when he discovers that Tikhon's first reaction to his favourite passage from the Scriptures is an aesthetic one.

> 'Have you read the Apocalypse?' asks Stavrogin.
> 'I have.'
> 'Do you remember the section which begins: "And to the angel of the Church in Laodicea write"?'
> 'I remember those delightful words.'
> 'Delightful? That's a funny thing for a bishop to say. . . .'[18]

Stavrogin is not only flabbergasted but bewildered too. Could this be a sign of dotage? It is only later that Stavrogin learns his painful lesson; the foolishness of his error in proclaiming that his 'Confession' is written in a bald, straightforward style, and that he is no writer.

To digress, it is perhaps worth comparing Tikhon with Semyon Yakovlevich, a minor character in *The Devils*. The appearance of this character is brief; hardly more than a caricature. The likeness is none the less real. It is even too close for comfort. For both Tikhon and this impostor, Semyon Yakovlevich, are reputed in various quarters to be cranks, drunkards and dotards. Both are surrounded by crowds of adulators. Many of Semyon Yakovlevich's visitors approach him with an attitude not at all unfamiliar to Tikhon:

> Everyone wanted to see him, especially visitors to the neighbourhood, to extract from him some crazy utterance, bowing down to him and leaving behind an offering. These offerings were sometimes considerable, and, if Semyon Yakovlevich did not himself assign them to some other purpose, they were piously sent to some church or more often to the Monastery of Our Lady. A monk from the monastery was always in waiting upon Semyon Yakovlevich with this object.

We learn that 'all were in expectation of great amusement'. In marked contrast with Tikhon's cell, Semyon Yakovlevich's quarters are the opposite of elegant. Like Tikhon he lived in two rooms; but these were formed by an ungainly partition of garden lattice running from wall to wall. The chairs were dilapidated, and he usually occupied a shabby arm-chair. 'He was a rather big, bloated-looking, yellow-faced man . . . with a bald head and scanty flaxen hair. He wore no beard; his right cheek was swollen, and his mouth seemed twisted awry. He had a large wart on the left side of his nose [a grotesquerie borrowed from Gogol?] narrow eyes, and a calm, stolid, sleepy expression.' Note the contrast with Tikhon's alert, nervous, fragile demeanour. The rest of Semyon Yakovlevich is as bizarre as Dostoevsky can make it. He lives on fish soup and potatoes boiled in their jackets, and gallons of tea. He goes on with his meals regardless of visitors waiting beyond the lattice partition. All is farce of the least diluted kind.[19] He capriciously hands out sugar loaves to bystanders, who detect in his actions some hidden prophecy. There are monks present for the purpose of interpreting the 'holy man's' extravagances. The scene ends with the old man uttering an obscenity at a lady visitor. The audience collapses in Homeric laughter. Stavrogin was present throughout, and one wonders to what extent the parallel between Tikhon and Semyon Yakovlevich attracted his attention. Resemblances must surely have suggested themselves when he was later confronted by Tikhon's own seemingly capricious turns of thought. Were they both chips off the same block? Hardly saints, more likely buffoons.

Stavrogin's 'confession', the second of the three suppressed chapters, is with the exception of a single passage an ugly document in every respect; composed deliberately nevertheless in the literary genre of the confession long since inaugurated by Rousseau. Dostoevsky takes care to preface it with the necessary contextual remarks:

> The printing was in fact foreign. Three little sheets of ordinary small-sized writing-paper printed and stitched together . . . at first glance it had very much the appearance of a political pamphlet. . . . I have allowed myself the liberty of correcting the spelling, for the mistakes are rather numerous and have surprised me a little, considering after all that the author was a man of education and well-read besides . . . . It is at any rate clear that the writer was not a man of letters.

From this point onwards the style is fashioned of crudity, slipshod expression and lack of taste. Dostoevsky has taken pains to strip the confession of any trace of literariness, turning it into a naked self-revelation, the naked admission of bestiality. It is written in the form of an *aide-mémoire*, with the appropriate officialese, mixed with conversational cliché, sprinkled with glaring inaccuracies. As Leonid Grossman put it: 'The impression made is of a damp rag of reality, drawn from the very dregs of human existence and thrown on to the pages of a novel in all its raw untrimmed state and repulsive unsightliness.'[20]

Dostoevsky grasped intuitively that the only attitude suited to Tikhon was the *aesthetic* one. The confrontation would in any other manner have been a fiasco. Tikhon suggests to Stavrogin that he is deliberately wanting to make himself out to be coarser than he really is. The whole scene is skilfully danced by Tikhon; for when Stavrogin asks forgiveness from him, his only possible rejoinder is: 'provided you forgive me too'. Stavrogin's sneer that this is false modesty (which in a way it is, and Tikhon possibly knows this) is of no avail, for at every juncture the tables are turned on him. The pit of shame is reached when he learns that the public reaction to his confession will be above all an *aesthetic* reaction. They will simply *laugh*. 'Stavrogin blushed; his face took on an expression of alarm. "I foresaw this. I must have appeared to you a very comic character after your reading of my document." ' Stavrogin rushes to his own defence: "Don't get upset. Don't look so disconcerted. I was expecting this." ' Instead of sparing him, Tikhon drives home the intolerable truth: "The horror will be universal and, of course, more false than sincere. . . . But the laughter will be universal." '

The portrayal of acts of lechery has always presented a formidable literary problem, even to the Marquis de Sade. Successful pornography is rare. Pornography must either be frankly comic as in Chaucer or Boccaccio, a sociological feature as in writers like Zola, abnormal and addictive as in a number of modern American writers, or sanctified as in D. H. Lawrence. Straightforward obscenity is unsuccessful. Like Stavrogin's attempt at obscenity it provokes mainly laughter. Dostoevsky is to be observed grappling with this problem. There are two versions of the central and crucial incident of the confession. In one of these versions the matter is coyly and rather ineffectually passed over. In the other the incident is missing altogether; the reason given was that the missing pages had been officially censored. The latter version is more successful. When asked what has become of the missing pages, Stavrogin explains that there was nothing especially important in them. What was written there now seems to him too ridiculous, too grotesque. By a reflex action he accuses Tikhon of 'monkish dastardliness' in suspecting the worst of him.[21]

Never a moment passes in which Tikhon does not have the upper hand. Stavrogin is pathetically on the defensive. He tries to find out what has made him look so ridiculous:

> 'Tell me then, where exactly do I make myself look ridiculous in this document of mine? I know perfectly well of course already, but I would like you to put your finger on it. Go on,

say it, with as much cynicism as you can muster. . . . Tell me
with all the frankness of which you are capable. . . .'

'In the very form of this great penance of yours there is
something ridiculous. . . .'

'So you find the form itself ridiculous?' insisted Stavrogin.

'The substance too. Ugliness kills,' Tikhon murmured in a
whisper, lowering his eyes.

'Ugliness? What ugliness?'

'The ugliness of crime.'

Suddenly we find ethic and aesthetic fused; they have become
the same thing. Exactly at the instant when Stavrogin has
resigned himself to Tikhon's apparently irrelevant remarks
on the style and literary effect of the confession, he learns to
his amazement that Tikhon is diverting attention from the
main point of the confession to the really evil aspect, summed
up in the phrase 'ugliness kills'. Tikhon goes on to explain:
'Crime is a truly ugly thing. Whatever the crime, the more
bloody, the more terrible it is, the more picturesque and the
more impressive it seems. But there are shameful and disgusting crimes, past all horror; they are, one is tempted to
say, almost too inelegant. . . .'

These posthumously published chapters of *The Devils* are
the supreme achievement of unity of content and style in
Dostoevsky–unity not according to the canons of classical
art, but as the new means of exploring the nature of human
reality and the structure of being. In order to achieve this
unity Dostoevsky had to wreck Russian prose. The 'Confession' is in Grossman's words:

> an outstanding stylistic experiment, in which the classical
> literary prose of the Russian novel has for the first time suffered
> a convulsion, been murdered, and displaced in the direction of
> some as yet undiscernible achievement. We have to examine
> the very foundations of modern European art to find criteria
> for evaluating all the precursory modes embedded in this
> deranged stylistic of Stavrogin.[22]

4 *Ontological fragmentation*

Viewed from a certain angle, many of Dostoevsky's characters seem to be the *reflections* of other characters. C. J. Jung

adopted the term *shadow*, the projection of one's personal unconscious. Dostoevsky's novels teem with such projections. Thus, for example, Svidrigaylov represents for the most part Raskolnikov's mocking *alter ego*. Similarly, in *The Idiot* Rogozhin is Prince Myshkin's projection and existential possibility. The process reaches a high degree of sophistication when in *The Brothers Karamazov* the shadow can be anything from a likely hallucination (Ivan's nightmare) to a flesh-and-blood character in his own right (e.g. Smerdyakov). The origin of Dostoevsky's double is neither psychological nor Hoffmanesque; it is purely stylistic. It can and has been traced back to the 'inner dialogue' implicit in his very first work, *Poor Folk*. Within a very short time this inner dialogue was to become incarnate and to produce its own human forms.[23] The projection or shadow became a stylistic necessity as soon as Dostoevsky discovered the need for the interplay and counterpoint of 'voices' which could not otherwise have been achieved.

His story *The Double* was first published in 1846 when Dostoevsky was still in his twenties. It reads on first acquaintance deceptively like Gogol, and in genre it certainly belongs with Gogol's three 'Petersburg' pieces: *The Nose*, *The Overcoat* and *The Nevsky Prospect*. The story is even subtitled 'a Petersburg poem'. This relatively minor work possessed a disproportionate significance for Dostoevsky, and he clearly identified himself at least for a time with his petty-official caricature Golyadkin. 'I've turned into a Golyadkin', he wrote to his brother. Dostoevsky was never satisfied with this youthful experiment of his, and brought out a revised version some nineteen years later. He was even contemplating rewriting the whole thing. 'If I had been working on this idea today,' he writes in the *Diary of a Writer*, 'I would have tackled it from a completely different angle.' It is only in the light of his breakthrough in dramatic conception – and his contemporaries knew nothing about it – that we can comprehend his inordinate concern for this early piece. He had clearly been mulling it over during his last years in Siberia. Writing from Tver he promises his brother: 'Towards the middle of December I'll be sending you (or I'll bring it to you

myself) the revised manuscript of *The Double*. Believe me,
this new edition, with a preface to go with it, is worth a
whole new novel. Then people will see just what a double
really is.' Nothing came of this 'project', for the revised work
was scarcely different from the original; but we shall see
that Dostoevsky's double turned up elsewhere, and more than
once, to enable us to see more than sufficiently 'what a double
really is'.

The Double itself is a work of undeniable virtuosity,
although it contains not even the promise of Dostoevsky's
post-Siberian development. There is only the occasional
meagre hint, significant only in the light of what was to come
later: for instance, the suggestion that Golyadkin's wraith
is a projection of his nastier side. His valet tells him: 'Good
folks never have doubles'; and a cabman informs him: 'We
cannot drive two gentlemen exactly alike, sir; a cabman
tries to live decently, your honour, and never had a double.'
The story takes on truly Dostoevskian dimensions only at the
very end when we suddenly find ourselves faced with the
concrete situation of Golyadkin's lapse into insanity.
Golyadkin has not yet grasped that his own doctor, Krestyan
Ivanovich, is taking him by cab to a lunatic asylum:

> When he came to, he realised that the horses were taking him
> along an unfamiliar road. . . . Suddenly he nearly fainted. Two
> fiery eyes were staring at him in the darkness, and these two
> eyes were glittering with malignant and hellish glee: 'That's
> not Krestyan Ivanovich! Then who is it? Or is it he? It is. It is
> Krestyan Ivanovich . . . not the old Krestyan Ivanovich, but a
> different one! It's a terrible Krestyan Ivanovich!'. . . 'Krestyan
> Ivanovich, I . . . I believe . . . I'm quite all right', our hero was
> timidly about to say. . . . 'You get free quarters, wood, with
> light and service, more than you deserve.' Krestyan Ivanovich's
> answer rang out stern and terrible like a judge's sentence.

The period during which *The Double* was written coincides
with Dostoevsky's well-known phase of hypochondria and
depression. 'Sometimes I get really depressed', he wrote his
brother Michael from Reval, 'I have such a wicked and repulsive character. . . . At times when I'm simply brimming
with love, you can't get a pleasant word out of me, my nerves

just don't obey me at such moments. I am foolish and wicked, and I am constantly suffering from the unjust opinion people have of me. They say I am dried-up and cold.' Petersburg itself was sheer nightmare:

> As the darkness increased, my room seemed to get bigger and to take on ever vaster proportions. . . . At that very instant something happened which left a lasting impression on me. I won't beat about the bush, but whether it was nervous depression, or the atmosphere of my new digs, or the melancholia I have been suffering from, gradually, imperceptibly, and as soon as night began to fall, I lapsed into a state . . . which I call *dread*. It is a cruel, unbearable fear in face of something indefinable, something inconceivable and quite outside the natural order of things, but which presents itself unmistakably at just the right moment to come and jeer at the arguments constructed by reason, and which comes and dogs me like some inescapable fate, terrible, hideous and implacable it is. This dread becomes stronger and stronger, despite all attempts to reason it away, so that in the end the mind is deprived of every means of fighting against sensations.

It is in a comparable state of dread that Raskolnikov is first confronted with his shadow, Svidrigaylov:

> 'Am I dreaming or not?' he wondered as he opened his eyelids imperceptibly to take a look; the stranger was standing in the same place as before, and was still watching him. . . . It was plain that he was quite prepared to wait for hours, if need be. . . . Ten minutes passed. It was still light, though it was getting late. There was complete silence in the room. Not a sound came from the stairs. Only a large fly kept buzzing as it kept knocking against the window-pane. At last it became unbearable. Raskolnikov suddenly raised himself and sat up on the sofa: 'Well, tell me what you want.' – 'I knew you weren't asleep, but merely pretending,' the stranger replied rather oddly, laughing quietly to himself.

It is now that Dostoevsky's readers find Golyadkin transposed into a very different key. This enigma, Svidrigaylov, becomes the dread at the pit of Raskolnikov's stomach; he has poured himself like a poisonous ink into his very being, and sickeningly anticipates Raskolnikov's most secret thoughts. He taunts his victim: 'Let me assure you on my

word of honour, my dear chap, that you interest me terribly.
I told you we'd become great friends, didn't I? I did warn
you. Well, and so we have. . . .'

Raskolnikov begins to find himself mysteriously drawn to
this character. At the climax of the cross-examination he
finds himself suddenly 'anxious to see Svidrigaylov as soon as
possible. Just what he could hope to get from this man, he did
not even know, but the man seemed to have some power
over him. . . . In his heart of hearts he could not help
admitting to himself that he had long been needing him for
something.' Like all Dostoevsky's doubles and projections,
Svidrigaylov seems to be ubiquitous. He represents the
materialisation of Raskolnikov's indefinable dread. Note the
resemblance to Dostoevsky's depressive moods: 'There was
another thought haunting Raskolnikov at that time, and it
worried him terribly, though he had tried very hard to drive
it away, so very painful was it to him. . . . He could not help
thinking sometimes that Svidrigaylov was following him
around, and that Svidrigaylov had discovered his secret. . . .'
Raskolnikov sets out to look for Svidrigaylov, and unexpectedly (but as the reader anticipates, inevitably) stumbles
upon him. Raskolnikov had absentmindedly turned into a
side street when he suddenly caught sight of Svidrigaylov
sitting drinking tea at the open window of a rather shabby
restaurant. The scene is pure Kafka. Raskolnikov:

> was terribly surprised, almost shocked by the coincidence.
> Svidrigaylov was watching him, in silence, and Raskolnikov
> could not help being struck by the fact that Svidrigaylov
> seemed about to get up so as to steal away unnoticed. . . . Yes,
> he was right; Svidrigaylov was evidently anxious not to be
> seen. . . . What now happened between them resembled the
> scene of their first meeting in Raskolnikov's room, while
> Raskolnikov was asleep. A sly smile appeared on Svidrigaylov's
> face and grew bigger and bigger. Each of them knew that the
> other had spotted him and was watching him. At length
> Svidrigaylov burst out laughing loudly, 'Well, come in if you
> want to – I'm here!' he shouted from the window.

Svidrigaylov as always is already ahead of Raskolnikov's
thoughts. He admits he finds it strange that Svidrigaylov

should be sitting where he was: 'The moment I turned the corner, I caught sight of you. It's all very odd!'–'Why not admit frankly–it's a miracle?'–'Because it's probably pure coincidence.' But Raskolnikov is already beginning to suspect something uncanny, when his hallucinatory projection turns the tables on him and wryly reassures him there was no miracle. Like Ivan Karamazov's hallucination, Svidrigaylov hastens to trick his victim into believing that all was as it should be, and by so doing, plunges him into even more treacherous doubts. . . . 'Miracles be damned, I can only say that you seem to have been asleep for the last two or three days. I told you about this restaurant myself, and there's nothing miraculous about your coming here. I even gave you directions how to get here, told you all about the place, where it was and what time you would find me here.' The rock bottom of Raskolnikov's being is thrown into question as Svidrigaylov's handsome-repulsive, mask-like face leers at him, constantly shifting its expression, at one moment enigmatic, the next moment inane and debauched. The hallucinatory Svidrigaylov does eventually turn into a character in his own right; but, as a full-blown character, he is not one of Dostoevsky's most successful, and we have to wait for his metamorphosis in a later novel as Stavrogin before the suicide motive in such a character becomes plausible.

The device of the shadow or projection is used repeatedly in Dostoevsky's later works. The supreme masterpiece is his minor novel *The Eternal Husband*. Completed in 1869, at the height of his most creative years, this work has more than once been hailed as Dostoevsky's technically most perfect creation. *The Eternal Husband* owes its success to its predecessor *The Double* in which most of the problems of technical composition had already been overcome. It is the ultimate in the exploration of the dual interaction of personality, a brilliant 'two-part invention'. As one critic has put it: 'In this work Dostoevsky has discovered the previously unknown laws of the psychological realm. Human personalities are joined by mysterious bonds: one consciousness, like the pole of a magnet, serves to attract the other, which stands in complementary opposition to it.'[24] Not only is virtuosity complete, but the double of *The Eternal Husband* stands also as a character in his own right. In a manner that defies comprehension, Dostoevsky has managed to produce hallucination and flesh and blood in the same figure. To cap this, the novel is, existentially speaking, probably Dostoevsky's most profound.

The foremost character of the two is Velchaninov, who is also the narrator. Like Verkhovensky and Versilov, the first syllable of his name contains a hint of superiority. The other character, who is also Velchaninov's projection, emerges in the first place from the latter's depressive moods and restless dreams. He is called Trusotsky, a name containing the element *trus* 'a coward'. Technically Trusotsky resembles Golyadkin's double, but the true kinship is with Svidrigaylov whom he resembles down to the smallest detail. Except for one deliberate difference: Trusotsky is a *shut*, 'a clown', which Svidrigaylov is not.

The novel begins with one of those blends of mood and narrative we frequently find in Dostoevsky. Velchaninov, an ageing Don Juan, happens to be in the grips of one of those depressions with no identifiable cause. The change that has taken place within him of late appears to be 'rather from within than from without'. Unlike the rest of Petersburg who have all taken themselves off to the country away from the oppressive dust and heat of summer, Velchaninov has decided to stay put on account of an unsettled law-suit. This 'worn-out man of doubtful morals' who only a couple of years before was fond of the social round, a gay dog, a *bon viveur*, has now taken to solitude for preference, finding himself in growing perplexity before the cancerous change taking place within.

As far as he is capable of judging at this stage, Velchaninov suspects that he is 'worrying about some sort of *lofty* ideas of which he would never have thought twice in his younger days'. On account of this flirtation with ideas he has become 'excessively sensitive about everything, trifles as well as things that really matter. . . .' The symptoms are probably recognisable enough medically. He is worried by the fact that he now possesses two completely distinct sets of thoughts and sensations, and discovers that convictions built up over a lifetime are being surreptitiously undermined. He is pathologically depressed. Sometimes he managed to shrug it all off resentfully: 'I'm ill; that's all that's wrong with me; all these "lofty ideas" are a mere illness, and nothing more.'

Suddenly, to his great relief and surprise, Velchaninov discovers what he believes to be the root cause of his depression: an insignificant little man who has been attracting his attention of late. It was this creature's hat especially that had been irritating him, a ridiculous mourning hat covered with black crape. But how could a nonentity like him have disconcerted him to such an extent, Velchaninov wonders? Velchaninov is about to dismiss the whole thing as a stupid lapse, when he remembers vaguely that he had once, many years ago, been associated with this caricature of a human being.

All the narrative skill of *The Double* is packed into the introduction of *The Eternal Husband* and Chapter III can be said to begin at the point where *The Double* leaves off. In this scene, Velchaninov is dreaming of a strange person, once an intimate friend, who pays him a visit but sits absolutely mute throughout. Velchaninov strikes him for refusing to speak, and is about to beat him to death, when a crowd that has gathered to watch the incident shrieks and turns to the door as though expecting something, when at that very instant the door-bell rings violently three times. Velchaninov is startled out of his sleep, but cannot tell whether the ring at the door is real or dreamt. He opens the door, but the staircase is empty. Finding his bearings again,

> he went mechanically to the window, meaning to open it for a breath of night air, and—he suddenly shuddered all over. It seemed to him that something incredible and inexplicable was taking place before his eyes. He had not got as far as opening the window when he made haste to slip behind the corner of the window and hid himself. On the deserted pavement opposite he had that moment seen the man with the crape on his hat looking his way.

The mysterious figure behaves exactly as Velchaninov predicts. He has entered the block, climbed the stairs, and is standing there behind the door exactly at the moment when Velchaninov flings it open and confronts him.

The rest of the novel is nightmare transposed into actuality. Trusotsky preys upon his host, fastens upon him for support, takes advantage of his generosity and patience. Like Svidrigaylov he is insolent, and sniggers slily whenever their conversation takes a serious or candid turn. He is unable or unwilling to speak in a straightforward manner. Velchaninov yells: 'You're taking advantage of a man who is nervous and ill . . . you're fastening upon him in order to extort some monstrous confession from him in his delirium!' Velchaninov's boast that they have nothing in common, that they belong to different planets, is vain. He is hypnotised by this visitor who, as the incarnation of his conscience, slowly and gloatingly unlocks Velchaninov's past. Within minutes of wanting to be rid of him forever, he is trying to cling to him. 'You are trying to give me the slip', Velchaninov shouts after him as he makes off down the stairs.

Trusotsky is among Dostoevsky's grisliest creations: he abandons the step-daughter after a long period of ill-treatment and lets her die uncared for by him, indulges his lascivious attraction towards a schoolgirl over whom he strikes a marriage bargain with her parents, and finally attempts to cut Velchaninov's throat while he is sleeping. These abominations only serve to enhance his uncanny fascination for Velchaninov.

> He woke up next morning with another headache, but with a quite *novel* and quite unexpected terror in his heart. . . . This new terror came from the positive conviction, which suddenly gripped him, that he, Velchaninov, would finish up that day by going of his own free will to see Trusotsky. Why? What for? He didn't know, and didn't want to know. All that he knew was that, for some reason, he would go to him.

It was Trusotsky's attempt to murder him which resolved the tensions that had been building up in Velchaninov, tensions which had found their outlet in those lofty ideas: 'A feeling of immense, extraordinary relief took possession of him; something was over with, settled; an awful weight of depression had vanished and was gone forever.' It was not just the relief at having narrowly escaped death, but the whole incident touched off resonances at a deeper and more real level. The important lesson for Velchaninov was that he should never have entertained those ideas of his. Lofty ideas are no part of nature. 'Nature dislikes monstrosities', Velchaninov discovered; words echoed in our own time by Bonhoeffer: 'Whoever does injury or violence to the natural will suffer for it. . . . The natural is the safeguarding of life against the unnatural.'[25] Nearly all Dostoevsky's major characters, and many of the minor ones, are guilty of this sin against the natural. And the guilt produced by sin generates its own punishment: the gemination or splitting of the personality, the coming face to face with one's shadow. 'Yes, indeed. Nature abhors monstrosities', Velchaninov warns Trusotsky, 'and destroys them with natural solutions. The most monstrous monster is the monster with noble feelings. I know that from personal experience! Nature is not a tender mother, but stepmother to the monster. Nature gives birth to the deformed, but instead of pitying him, she punishes him, and with good reason. Even decent people have to pay for embraces and tears of forgiveness, nowadays, to say nothing of men like you and me!'

5 *O Word, Thou art Sick*

'Even embraces and tears of forgiveness have to be paid for nowadays. . . .'

In our time we have grown accustomed to every kind of revolution; as familiar now in the humanities, the sciences and fine arts as in politics. One of the most startling of these is the revolution that has occurred in theology. Especially so, as the major impetus seems to have arisen from without. Since Nietzsche and Kierkegaard, dramatists, novelists, poets, psychologists have to an increasing extent become deeply concerned with 'theological' questions, and in a few cases have become 'secular' theologians. Scarcely a single traditional concept or attitude has been left unturned. Tillich has characterised our time as the 'shaking of foundations'; the concentration camps have cut off all escape routes to the past. Camus has insisted that all contemporary action leads to murder directly or indirectly.[26] Consciousness of the absurd has swept the ethical slate clean: 'Ideology, a contemporary phenomenon, limits itself to repudiating others; they alone are the cheats. This leads to murder. Every dawn masked assassins slip into some cell; murder is the question of the day.'[27] Man has only himself to look to. Reason alone is valid; the rest is absurd. 'We are living in an unsacrosanct age.' Since Kafka's *Trial* a new kind of sin, the unidentifiable sin, has become familiar. The Law is inaccessible, and the available interpretations ambiguous. In the parable told by the priest in the empty cathedral, Josef K. learns that, although the door-keeper of the door leading to the Law has no inside knowledge of the Law, he remains despite everything firmly devoted to it. It is the Law that has placed him at his post; and to doubt this devoted man's integrity is to doubt the Law itself. K. finds he cannot agree: 'for if one accepts it, one must accept as true everything the door-keeper says'. The priest tries to reassure him: 'It is not necessary to accept everything as true, one must only accept it as necessary.' K. is far from reassured: 'A melancholy conclusion. It turns lying into a universal principle.'[28] The priest is not being cynical, but *traditional*. His theology consists of what to K. are opaque truths from the fossil remains of the past. The messages are still being handed round, but the Authority who issued them is long since dead. Even the Categorical Imperative is fit only for archaeological investigation. The machinery of the Law is fast mouldering, for although Josef K. is found guilty, he cannot ascertain the charge, and although condemned to death, remains ignorant even of his judges.

Dostoevsky was alive to these nowadays commonplace dilemmas; indeed he throve on them. His métier was writing; hence the medium he chose was discourse. In Dostoevsky, discourse holds in latent or potential state the wide extent of good and evil. His work maps the entire metaphysic of morals. Ethic and aesthetic, human conduct and stylistics merge in a mosaic of discourse.

There is not a single thought, idea, view or sentiment in Dostoevsky which is not embedded in and intimately bound up with discourse. Discourse is a relationship of stylistic keys and harmony. The same thought in two different harmonic settings becomes two different thoughts. It is not the thought which ultimately counts, but its mode of expression, its utterance. Truth depends not on what is said, but on who says it, how it is said, and in what circumstances. To find support for an approach of this kind we have to turn to writers of our own days. In the closing pages of his *Ethics* Bonhoeffer discusses the implications of 'telling the truth'. He begins with what might be called a relativity principle: 'Telling the truth means something different according to the particular situation in which one stands. . . . The truthful word is not in itself constant; it is as much alive as life itself. If it is detached from life and from its reference to the concrete other man, if "the truth is told" without taking into account to whom it is addressed, then this truth has only the appearance of truth, but lacks its essential character.'[28] The word, a living utterance, can never become a philosophical specimen. 'Each word must have its own place and keep it.' A word has its roots in discourse. Uproot it and you will kill it. 'It is a consequence of the wide diffusion of the public word through the newspapers and the wireless that the essential character and the limits of the various different words are no longer clearly felt and that, for example, the quality of the personal word is almost entirely destroyed. Genuine utterances are replaced by idle chatter. . . . There is too much talk.'[29]

During the 'unfortunate gathering' in the monastery, Zosima deftly handles the mock entreaties of the old buffoon Fyodor Karamazov. 'What should I do to gain eternal life?' asks Karamazov. 'You have known for a long time what you must do. You have sense enough: don't give way to drunkenness and incontinence of speech; don't give way to sensual lust. . . . And above all – *don't lie*.' Lying is old Karamazov's basic vice, a most insidiously undermining vice, for it has taken away from him all possibility of seriousness or sincerity. He is a buffoon with no control over his buffoonery. '. . . Above all, don't lie to yourself', Zosima tells him. 'The man who lies to himself and listens to his own lies comes to such a pass that he cannot distinguish the truth within him, or around him, and so loses all respect for himself and for others.' This is followed by Karamazov's wry rejoinder: 'I shall take note of that. But I have been lying positively my whole life long, every day and hour of it. Of a truth, I am a lie, indeed the father of lies.' A master stroke this. The deep integrity of Zosima momentarily sounds priggish in this particular context. Our sympathies switch to the old *roué* who for an instant overtops the saint.

'One might say that the man who stands behind the utterance makes that utterance a lie or a truth.'[30] Dmitri Karamazov detests his father mainly for his knack of concealing falsehood behind what is outwardly true. The lie is the malignant disease of discourse, and disrupts the entire man and his environment. It is the perversion of innocence which, said Kierkegaard, in turn begets Dread. But Dread only flourishes in the man of heightened sensibility and moral awareness. The Karamazovs, all four, are excellent breeding grounds. Their very name signifies 'black beetle', symbolising the sensual lust which they share. 'The more dread, the more sensuousness.'[31] Dread contains innumerable traps; and as we have just seen, Fyodor Karamazov has fallen into one of his own making. The great peril is to become responsible even for the death of Trusotsky's little girl who, he learns, is his own illegitimate daughter. Trusotsky's malice is the reverse side of the coin of Velchaninov's effortless superiority. Discourse was ruptured when years ago they both said and did certain things and left other things unsaid and undone. The entire novel *The Eternal Husband* is concerned with the culmination or resolution of the dread engendered. To take a related case, Versilov in *The Raw Youth* appears to be waging an internal war against his own particular burden of dread which takes the acute and highly malignant form of hollowness. He is capable of uttering profound and moving truths, but only with some spurious end in view. We find him tormenting his son with them and using them to corrupt the boy's nature, and in a strange way to punish him for his (Versilov's) sin. Versilov is outwardly an aristocrat, with all the concomitant snobbish habits. 'To hear him, one would suppose he was speaking quite seriously, and all the while he was posing to himself, or laughing.' Even the bond of mutual dishonesty between master and servant is among his foibles: 'My dear boy, we must always let a man lie a great deal. In the first place, it will show our delicacy, and secondly, people will let us lie in return–two immense advantages at once.' Versilov's insincerity, as he is aware, takes two forms: firstly, intellectual insincerity: 'if it happens that I try to explain an idea I believe in, it almost always happens that I cease to believe in what I have been explaining'. The second is more serious still; it is a blend of aesthetic and ethical insincerity which Makar Ivanovich (the pilgrim foster-father of the raw youth) calls 'unseemliness'. On his death-bed he describes these unseemly men of the world he has met in the course of his life:

> They read and argue day in day out, filling themselves with the sweetness of books, while they remain in perplexity and can come to no conclusion. Some quite let themselves go, and give up taking notice of themselves. Some grow harder than stone and their hearts are full of wandering dreams; others become heartless and frivolous, and all they can do is to mock and jeer. . . . And then again there is a great deal of dreariness. . . . Some have been all through the sciences, and are guilty in a state of dread.

It is this peril which befalls Ivan Karamazov; 'he who becomes guilty in dread becomes as ambiguously guilty as it is possible to be'.[32] Only Dmitri Karamazov has 'learnt rightly to be in dread'. Kierkegaard was nevertheless convinced that, despite its dangers, Dread 'is an adventure which every man has to confront if he would not go to perdition either by not having known Dread or by sinking under it.'[33] There is no character of any importance in Dostoevsky that is not assailed by Dread: Raskolnikov face to face with his cross-examiner or with Svidrigaylov; Myshkin's anxiety taking the form of Rogozhin; Ivan Karamazov caught between his ideas, his half-brother and his half-hallucination.

> No Grand Inquisitor has in readiness such terrible tortures as has Dread, and no spy knows how to attack more artfully the

man he suspects, choosing the instant when he is weakest, nor
knows how to lay traps where he will be caught and ensnared,
as Dread knows how, and no sharp-witted attorney knows how
to interrogate, to examine the accused, as Dread does, which
never lets him escape. . . .[34]

These words of Kierkegaard would make a fitting super-
scription for any of Dostoevsky's major novels.

Since everything in Dostoevsky is mediated through discourse, and since Dread *is* discourse undergoing lesions, we
have to look to the internal structure of the discourse for the
healing mechanisms. Delay in recognising and utilising
them leaves the character in a state of increasingly uncon-
trollable dread. In the years immediately following the
publication of *The Devils* this motif recurs constantly. For
example, Velchaninov in *The Eternal Husband* only discovers
the dread which has been building up when it is almost too
late. Trusotsky is a visitation from his past, from the time
when he was Velchaninov's victim. He is however structurally
bound to be his victim in all circumstances involving social
action, and Velchaninov finds no difficulty in getting the
better of this pathetic 'eternal husband' in amorous matters.
It is the law of spider and fly. He becomes indirectly still more
depressed, 'and I fancy the more intellect a man has, the
greater his dreariness. . . . And another thing I must tell you:
they have no seemliness; they have no use for it at all; all are
ruined, but they boast of their own destruction. . . . It's
impossible to be human and not bow down to something;
such a man could not bear the burden of himself, nor could
such a man go on existing. . . .'

In his *Diary of a Writer* published in the years preceding
the publication of *The Brothers Karamazov*, Dostoevsky
includes two stories both of which are manifestations to the
highest degree of diseased discourse, although in entirely
opposite ways. The first of these *The Gentle Creature*[35] is a
sort of allegory of the discourse structure of power. The
narrator of the monologue is trying to overcome the shock of
finding that his wife has committed suicide by jumping out
of the window. The fact that he is a pawnbroker symbolises
his power for good or evil in a highly ambiguous mutual

relationship. His victim (and future wife) is a girl of sixteen who is driven in desperation to submit to his designs. She is proud, and he is set on dominating her. He succeeds, but his success is also her suicide. His basic plan is to react to all her 'raptures and transports' in cold silence:

> Benevolent silence, no doubt, but all the same she soon realised that we were different and that I was an enigma. And it was the enigma that was my trump card! . . . To put the whole thing in a nutshell, though I was eminently pleased at the time, I managed to create an entire system. Oh, it came naturally enough, without the slightest effort on my part. Besides, it couldn't have been otherwise. I had to create that system owing to one unavoidable circumstance—why indeed should I be slandering myself! The system was perfect. A real system.

The pawnbroker's technique turns out to be wordless discourse, speaking without using words, the most vicious discourse of all:

> I am an old hand at speaking without using words. I have spent all my life speaking wordlessly. I have lived through whole tragedies without uttering a single word. . . . Yes, I went on being silent especially, especially with her—until yesterday. Why was I silent? Well, because I am a proud man. I meant her to find out for herself, without my help, and not from tales told by all sorts of scoundrels. I wanted her to discover *by herself* this man and understand his ways![36]

The technique produces the anticipated result. All the girl's entreaties and arguments are met with a blank wall of silence, and she in turn is forced to reciprocate. Her smiles become bitter and sardonic. She had been prepared to find a way of loving him, but he would not let her. Her youthful ardour is repulsed.

Lesion begets lesion; the pawnbroker's whole life was determined by his cold rejection by the world when he was young and loving. He had wanted to react to everyone with all the generosity of his young heart – but they had all turned him down. That was why he had become a pawnbroker, and assumed a particular structure for life: 'What I had to cope with was a straitlaced, uncompromising attitude, ignorance of life, the cheap convictions of youth, the utter blindness of "a noble soul", and, above all the pawn shop. Good God, the pawnshop! Oh, how awful is truth in the world.'[37] This wretched man is so remote from the healthy stream of human communication that he can only talk to himself. His discourse has become ingrown. 'Insensibility. Oh nature! People are alone in the world. That's what is so dreadful. . . . Everything is dead. Dead men are everywhere. There are only people in the world, and all around them is silence – that's what the earth is.'[38]

In sharp contrast is the second story *The Dream of the Ridiculous Man*[39] which introduces the Myth of the Golden Age. The Ridiculous Man, who has himself been contemplating suicide, dreams a dream in which he dies, is buried, rises from the grave, and travels across interstellar space to a planet which is the identical twin of earth. The inhabitants are men, and they are in a state of unfallen innocence. Theirs is the analogue of the Garden of Eden. These people are beautiful and wise, but, strange to relate, the Ridiculous Man ends by corrupting them: 'I only know that the cause of the Fall was I. Like a horrible trichina, like the germ of the plague infecting whole kingdoms, so did I infect with myself all that happy earth that knew no sin before me.' Their first sin was not Adam's but one that was of more particular interest to Dostoevsky. We soon learn that the sin they became infected with was the primary sickness of universal harmony: 'They learnt to tell lies, and they grew to appreciate the beauty of a lie.' Again, the disease of discourse. And from it all other evils flowed: first voluptuousness, then jealousy – finally cruelty. Lying led to consciousness, and consciousness to great wickedness. Very soon they had conjured up for themselves all the blessings and curses of modern European man, and rejected their former values. The Ridiculous Man asks them to punish him for ruining them, but they only laugh at him and tell him he is a madman. They even show him how benificent he was to have shown them the light.

Rampant lying and obstinate silence are the opposite

twisted extremes of discourse. To tamper with the *natural* word is to introduce falsehood. Even the mildest and most innocent consciousness is already a distortion. No choice is left to any man, for his discourse has already been tampered with during his earliest years. Dostoevsky laid special stress on the innocence and inviolability of children which was to be defended and maintained at all costs. With age the discrepancy grows and in adults it is endemic. The only possible remedy is Beauty, the aesthetic sense, which alone can heal and make whole. We belong already to other people's worlds and words, and find ourselves enmeshed in several layers of reality and truth at the same time. In the words of Bonhoeffer:

> In our endeavour to express the real we, we do not encounter this as a consistent whole, but in a condition of disruption and inner contradiction which has need of reconciliation and healing. We find ourselves simultaneously embedded in several different orders of the real, and our words, which strive towards the reconciliation and healing of the real, are nevertheless repeatedly drawn into the prevalent disunion and conflict.[40]

Ethical relativity is both the blessing and the scourge of modern fragmented life. To avoid evil to others becomes virtually impossible, yet, to compensate for this, the resultant increase in personal Dread opens immense vistas of human possibilities; 'the greater the dread, the greater the man.'

NOTES AND REFERENCES

AN INTRODUCTION

1 Carr, E. H., *Dostoevsky* (*1821–1881*), London, 1931.
2 Bakhtin, M. M., *Problema tvorchestva Dostoyevskogo*, Leningrad, 1929.
3 Engel'gardt, B., *Ideologicheskiy roman Dostoyevskogo*, in Dolinin (A. S.) *Dostoyevskiy: Stat'i i materialy* ('Dostoevsky: Articles and Source Materials'), Vol. II, Moscow and Leningrad, 1925, pp. 71–108.
4 These include: Chizh, V. F.: *Dostoyevskiy kak psikhopatolog* ('Dostoevsky as Psychopathologist'), Moscow, 1885, and later Amenitskiy, D. A.: *Psikhiatricheskiy Analiz Stavrogina* ('A Psychiatric Analysis of Stavrogin'), *Sovremennaya Psikhiatriya*, Petrograd, 1915; and Dr. Delous: *Voprosy psikhoterapii v proizvedeniyakh Dostoyevskogo* ('Questions of psychotherapy in the works of Dostoevsky'), *Sovremennaya Psikhonevrologiya*, No. 5, 1925.
5 Bem, A. L. (Boehm, Alfred L.), *O Dostoevskom* ('On Dostoevsky'), Prague, Vol. I, 1929; Vol. II, 1933; Vol. III, 1936.

CHAPTER I

1 Woolf, Virginia, *The Common Reader*, London, 1925, p. 172.
2 Ibid., p. 177.
3 The English nearest equivalent of the more natural 'Tolstoyevshchina'.
4 Quoted from a letter to John Addington Symonds; Stevenson, R. L., Letters, Vol. II, pp. 23–24.
5 Lombroso, C., *The Man of Genius*, London, 1891.
6 Quoted in Helen Muchnic, *Dostoevsky's English Reputation*, pp. 44 and 57.
7 Unsigned article, *The Academy*, V, 63, p. 685.
8 Gissing, George, *Charles Dickens: A Critical Study*, London, 1898.
9 Murry, J. Middleton, *Between two worlds*, London, 1935.
10 Murry, J. Middleton, *Fyodor Dostoevsky: A Critical Study*, London, 1916.
11 Murry tells us that after reading a translation of various Egyptian manuscripts he became haunted with the repeated phrase 'The Boat of a Million Years'. 'Suddenly each faint impression united in my brain and I saw the boat. I was cold

with horror; it was as though my very spirit had frozen. I dared not move; I dared not look out of the window, for I knew that all that lay outside would be old and cold and gray' (p. 213).

On p. 36 of his book on Dostoevsky (see Note 12) there is an account of a visit to Regent's Park Zoo (The 'Zoological Gardens'). He stopped by a cage of vultures, perched up aloft, with bones and bits of flesh lying on the floor of the cage. 'Suddenly I looked up and saw the birds motionless, looking out with blind and lidded eyes. . . .' He murmured as in a dream: 'Obscene, obscene'. The word had taken on a new sense for him, a profounder meaning: 'The eternal and absolute obscenity.' 'There is in this a grotesqueness and obscenity which can freeze the mind which broods upon it with a palsy of horror, which reaches its climax in the sudden vision of the timeless world made apparent in that which is time.'

12 A remark of Prince Vyazemsky quoted in Volkonsky (Prince S.) *Pictures of Russian History and Russian Literature*, London, 1898, p. 248.

13 Op. cit., London, 1927, pp. 172–174.

14 James, Henry, *The Letters of Henry James*, Letter of Henry James to Hugh Walpole, May 29, 1912, Vol. 2, London and N.Y., 1920, p. 237.

15 Galsworthy, J., *Letters from John Galsworthy 1900–1932* (ed. Garnett), London and N.Y., 1934, p. 217. Letter to Edward Garnett, April 15, 1914.

16 Conrad, Joseph, *Letters from Joseph Conrad 1895–1924* (ed. Garnett), Indianapolis, 1925, pp. 240–241. Letter to Edward Garnett, May 27, 1912.

17 Lawrence, D. H., 'Letters to Koteliansky', *Encounter*, Vol. I, Dec. 1953.

18 Shestov, L., *All Things are Possible* (trans. S. S. Koteliansky), London, 1920, pp. 7–8.

19 Lawrence, D. H., 'Letters to Koteliansky', *Encounter*, Vol. I, Dec. 1953, p. 29.

20 Lawrence, D. H., *Selected Literary Criticism*, London, 1955, pp. 229–232. Letter to J. M. Murry and Katherine Mansfield, 17 Feb. 1916.

21 Lawrence, D. H., 'Letters to Koteliansky', *Encounter*, Vol. I, Dec. 1953, p. 30.

22 Lawrence, D. H., *Selected Literary Criticism*, p. 232. Letter to J. M. Murry, 28 August, 1916.

23 Lawrence, D. H., *Selected Literary Criticism*, 'Herman Melville's "Typee" and "Omoo" ', p. 374.

24 Lawrence, D. H., *Pansies*, Brooklyn, 1929 (Private Edn.), 'The Fate of the Younger Generation.'

25 Ibid., pp. 164–165. 'Now It's Happened.'

26 Lawrence, D. H., *Selected Literary Criticism*, 'Maestro Don Gesualdo', p. 276.

27 Ibid., p. 242. Letter to Catherine Carswell, 2 Dec. 1916.

28 Neuschäffer, W., *Dostojewskijs Einfluss auf den englischen Roman*, Heidelberg, 1935.

29 Carr, E. H., *Dostoevsky*, London, 1931.

30 Muchnic, Helen, *Dostoevsky's English Reputation*, p. 176.

CHAPTER II

1 Herzen, A., *Byloye i Dumy, Polnoye Sobraniye Sochineniy*, 22 vols. (edited by Lemke). Petrograd/1919–25. Vol. XIII, p. 599.

2 Ibid., p. 599.

3 Carr, E. H., *The Romantic Exiles*, London, 1949, p. 49.

4 Akhsharumov, D. D., *Priznaniya* (MSS. found amongst Debu I's papers) (*Delo*, 55, St. Petersburg (12), pp. 51–52).

5 Leykina, V., *Petrashevtsy*, Moscow, 1923, p. 9.

6 Zotov, V. R., *Petersburg v 40-kh godakh* (*Istoricheskiy Vestnik*, 40, St. Petersburg, 1889, pp. 536–537, 539–545).

7 Carr, E. H., *Dostoevsky*, London, 1931, pp. 52–53.

8 Veselevsky, K., *Vospominaniya o nekotorykh litseyskikh tovarish-chakh* (*Russkaya Starina*, 9, St. Petersburg, 1900, pp. 449–456).

9 Herzen, A., *Polnoye Sobraniye Sochineniy*, edited by Lemke, 22 vols. Petrograd/1919–25. Vol. VI, p. 504.

10 Bakunin, M. A., *Pis'ma M. A. Bakunina k A. I. Gertsenu i N. P. Ogaryovu*, edited by Dragomanov, Geneva, 1896, pp. 41–42. (Letter of 7 November, 1860, from Irkutsk.)

11 Shchegolev, P. V., *Petrashevtsy*, 3 vols. Moscow/Leningrad, 1928. Vol. 3, p. 201.

12 Leykina, V., *Petrashevtsy*, Moscow, 1923, pp. 27–30.

13 Dolinin, A., *Dostoevsky sredi Petrashevtsev*, edited by Bronch-Bruyevich, Moscow/Leningrad, 1936, pp. 529–530.

14 Leykina, V., *Petrashevtsy*, Moscow, 1923, p. 31.

15 Carr, E. H., *Dostoevsky*, London, 1931, p. 55.

16 Shchegolev, P. V., *Petrashevtsy*, 3 vols. Moscow/Leningrad, 1928. Vol. 3, p. 202.

17 Miller, O. F., *Materialy dlya zhizneopisaniya Dostoyevskogo*, St. Petersburg, 1883, pp. 85–95.

18 Almansky, P., *Aleksey Slobodin*, St. Petersburg, 1873, pp. 355–356.

19 Strakhov, N. N., *Biografiya*, St. Petersburg, 1883, pp. 105–107.
20 Shchegolev, P. V., *Petrashevtsy*, 3 vols. Moscow/Leningrad, 1928. Vol. 3, pp. 23–24.
21 (Letter to Katkov, 8 October 1870, n.s.), quoted in Mochulsky, K.: *Dostoevsky* (Russian edition), Paris, 1947, p. 335.
22 *Nechayev i Nechayevtsy*. Edited by B. P. Koz'min, Moscow/Leningrad, 1931, p. II.
23 Ibid., pp. 114–140.
24 Yanovsky, S., *Vospominaniya o Dostoyevskom* (*Russkiy Vestnik*, 4, Moscow, 1886, pp. 809–819).
25 Bakunin, M. A., *Pis'ma M. A. Bakunina k A. I. Gertsenu i N. P. Ogaryovu*, edited Dragomanov, Geneva, 1896, pp. 41–47.
26 Semevsky, V., *M. V. Butashevich-Petrashevsky* (*Golos Minuvshego*, 8, Moscow, 1913, pp. 71–77).
27 Leykina, V., *Petrashevtsy*, Moscow, 1923, pp. 47–49.
28 Ibid., p. 48.
29 Semevsky, V., *M. V. Butashevich-Petrashevsky* (*Golos Minuvshego*, 8, Moscow, 1913, p. 73).
30 Ibid., p. 77.
31 Op. cit., W. H. Auden and C. Isherwood, London, 1938, pp. 116–118.

CHAPTER IV

1 Weil, Simone, *The Need for Roots*, trans. A. F. Wills, London, 1952, p. 41.
2 Eliade, Mircea, *Myths, Dreams and Mysteries*, trans. Mairet, London, 1960, p. 164.
3 Granet, M., *Études sociologiques sur la Chine*, Paris, 1953, pp. 197–198.
4 McLuhan, M., *Understanding Media*, London, 1964.
5 This group became known as the 'Young Editors' and wrote for the journal *Moskvityanin* ('The Muscovite'). They were, so to say, schismatic.
6 The Russian word is usually *pochvennichestvo*, which might most aptly be translated as 'autochthonism'; the alternative *pochvennost'* does occur, and this would be better rendered as 'autochthony'; although neither of the Russian nouns contains an explicit equivalent of the Greek *auto*.
7 *Vremya* (*Time*) first appeared in January 1861, and it was to be published monthly. In practice the broader aspects of editorship fell to Dostoevsky, whilst his brother Mikhail concerned himself with the business side and with the routine aspects of editorial work. Police surveillance was especially close at this time owing to the fact that Dostoevsky had only recently been officially released from exile.

8 Strakhov gives a description of one young man called Dolgo-mostyev: 'All his thoughts were in shreds . . . but amidst all his ravings there was nevertheless a leading idea . . . this idea expressed the new tendency of the *pochvenniks*', in N. N. Strakhov, *Vospominaniya o Dostoyevskom* (*Recollections of Dostoevsky*), published in F. M. Dostoevsky, *Sobraniye Sochineniy* (*Collected Works*), St. Petersburg, 1883, Vol. I, pp. 205–206.

9 Grigoriev, Apollon A., *Osnovaniya Organicheskoy Kritiki* (*Foundations of Organic Criticism*), published in *Sobraniye Sochineniy A. A. Grigor'yeva* (*The Collected Works of A. A. Grigoriev*), edited by V. F. Savodnikov, Moscow, 1915, No. 2, p. 114.

10 Ibid., p. 71.

11 Grigoriev, Apollon A., *Russkaya Literatura v Seredine XIX veka* (*Russian Literature in the Middle of the 19th Century*), published in *Sobraniye Sochineniy A. A. Grigor'yeva* (*The Collected Works of A. A. Grigoriev*), edited by V. F. Savodnikov, Moscow, 1915, No. 9, p. 41.

12 *tsvet real'nogo. Osnovaniya Organicheskoy Kritiki* (see Note 9 above), p. 81.

13 N. A. Dobrolyubov (1836–61). Follower of the radical Chernyshevsky, former student of a theological seminary, Dobrolyubov identified literature with social service, and demanded from writers a conscientious effort at reforming society. For him art was an output of energy, and at its best ideological. He died of tuberculosis at the age of twenty-five, after having attracted a large following and a sensational reputation.

14 Strakhov, N. N., *Vospominaniya ob Apollone Aleksandroviche Grigor'yeve* (*Recollections of Apollon Alexandrovich Grigoriev*), published in *Vospominaniya* (*Recollections*), edited by Ivanov-Razumnik, Moscow-Leningrad, 1930, p. 445.

15 Dostoevsky, Fyodor M., *Primechaniya* (*Comments*), published in *Vospominaniya* (*Recollections*), edited by Ivanov-Razumnik, Moscow-Leningrad, 1930, p. 526.

16 Grigoriev, Apollon A., *Sobraniye Sochineniy A. A. Grigor'yeva* (*The Collected Works of A. A. Grigoriev*), edited by V. F. Savodnikov, Moscow, 1915, p. vi.

17 Grigoriev, Apollon A., *Osnovaniya Organicheskoy Kritiki* (see Note 9 above, p. 123.

18 Ibid., p. 128.

19 Dolinin, A. S., *F. M. Dostoevsky i N. N. Strakhov* (*F. M. Dostoevsky and N. N. Strakhov*), published in Piksanov, N. K., *Shestidesyatyye Gody* (*The 'Sixties*), Moscow-Leningrad, 1940, pp. 238–254.

20 Ibid., p. 240.

21 Strakhov, N. N., *O vechnykh Istinakh* (*On Eternal Truths*), pp. 54–55.

22 Dostoevsky, Fyodor, M., *A Gentle Creature and Other Stories*, trans. D. Magarshack, London, 1950, pp. 121–122.

23 Antonovich, M., *O Pochve* (*On the Soil*), 'Sovremennik', 1861, Vol. 90, St. Petersburg, pp. 171 ff.

24 Motchoulski, C., *Dostoïevski, l'homme et l'œuvre*, Paris, 1963, pp. 183–184 (French translation of 1947 Russian edition).

25 Letter to A. N. Maykov from Semipalatinsk, 18 Jan. 1856 (first publ. in 1883 posthumously) in Dostoevsky, Fyodor M., *Pis'ma* (*Letters*), edited by A. S. Dolinin, Moscow and Leningrad, Vol. I, 1928, p. 163.

26 In a series of articles published in *Vremya* (*Time*) in 1861, and published in Dostoevsky, Fyodor M., *Sobraniye Sochineniy* (*Collected Works*), St. Petersburg, 1906, p. 86.

27 Gessen, S. I., *Bor'ba Utopii i Avtonomii Dobra v Mirovozrenii F. M. Dostoevskogo i Vl. Solov'yova* (*The Struggle between Utopia and the Autonomy of the Good in the outlook of Dostoevsky and Vladimir Soloviev*), in *Sovremennyya Zapiski*, 1931, XLV, p. 290.

28 Rozanov, V. V., *Religiya i Kul'tura* (*Religion and Culture*) (1899), published in *Izbrannoye* (*Selections*), edited by Ivask, Y. P., New York, 1956, p. 63.

29 Dostoevsky, Fyodor M., *Dnevnik Pisatelya za 1873, 1876, 1877, 1880* (*The Diary of a Writer for the years 1873, 1876, 1877 and 1880*), Paris, 1951, Vol. II, p. 59.

30 Ibid., p. 59.

31 Ibid., Vol. III ('Confessions of a Slavophile') (July–August).

32 Ibid., p. 11.

33 The speech was delivered six months before his death, on the occasion of the solemn inauguration of a monument to Pushkin in Moscow. The date for the unveiling was 26 May 1880, and both Dostoevsky and Turgenev were present. (This latter fact, and also that they were rivals – or rather Dostoevsky at one time regarded Turgenev as a renegade – should be taken into account in assessing the Pushkin Speech.)

34 Dostoevsky, Fyodor M., *Dnevnik Pisatelya* (etc.) (*The Diary of a Writer*, etc.), Paris, 1951, Vol. III, p. 525.

35 It is sometimes forgotten that this novel was published some two years before the first outbreak of populist terrorist activities.

36 Berdyaev, Nikolai, *Dostoevsky*, trans. Attwater, New York, 1962, p. 165.

37 Ibid., p. 166.

38 Ibid., p. 180.

39 Ibid., p. 183.
40 Ibid., p. 185.
41 Rozanov, V. V., *Apokalipsicheskaya Sekta* (*An Apocalyptic Sect*), St. Petersburg, 1914, p. 10.
42 The reform began before Peter the Great (hence 'Petrine') with the revision of the liturgy in the seventeenth century, followed by reforms of church ritual. This was the cause of the Old Believers' schism. The Old Believers clung to the earlier forms. Peter the Great completed the process by taking control of the schools, the arts and sciences out of ecclesiastical hands.
43 Rozanov, V. V., *Apokalipsicheskaya Sekta* (*An Apocalyptic Sect*), St. Petersburg, 1914, p. 36.
44 Ibid., p. 12.
45 Rozanov, V. V., *Uyedinyonnoye* ('*Solitaria*'), published in *Izbrannoye* (*Selections*), ed. Ivask, Y. P., New York, 1956, p. 213.
46 Ibid., p. 213.
47 Ivanov, Vyacheslav, *Freedom and the Tragic Life*, trans. Cameron, London, 1952, p. 45.
48 Ibid., p. 62.

CHAPTER V

1 To A. P. Suslova, Wiesbaden, 12/24 August, 1865.
2 Spent in Wiesbaden.
3 To V. D. Constant, Paris, 20 Aug/1 Sept., 1863.
4 To M. M. Dostoevsky, Turin, 8/20 Sept. 1863.
5 1867.
6 Dostoyevskaya, A. G., Vospominaniya, Moscow-Leningrad, 1925, p. 103.
7 *The Idiot, The Devils, The Raw Youth* and *The Brothers Karamazov*.
8 'I know from his former visits to the tables that after exciting sensations such as these, after indulging his craving for gambling, Fyodor would return home calm and soothed. Then, realising the futility of his hopes of winning, he would sit down to his novel with renewed vigour, and in a couple of months he would make good his losses.'
9 Diary, May 15, 1867.
10 Dostoevsky's niece, Sonya.
11 Diary, June 9, 1867.
12 June 21.
13 Diary, June 25.
14 Ibid., June 27.
15 Ibid., July 6.
16 Ibid., July 18.

17 Ibid., July 22.
18 Ibid., July 23.
19 Ibid., July 29.
20 Ibid., July 30.
21 Ibid., August 1.
22 Ibid., August 5.
23 Dostoevskaya, A. G., *Reminiscences*.

CHAPTER VI

1 Sakulin, P. N., and Bel'chikov, N. F., (ed.) *Iz arkhiva F. M. Dostoevskogo Idiot: Neizdannyye Materialy (From the Dostoevsky Archives, The Idiot, Unpublished Material)*, Moscow-Leningrad, 1931, pp. 11–95.
2 Ibid., p. 14.
3 Ibid., p. 16.
4 Ibid., p. 20.
5 Ibid., p. 27.
6 Ibid., p. 55.
7 Dostoevsky, F. M., *Pis'ma (Letters)*, ed. Dolinin, A. S., Moscow-Leningrad, 1928. Vol. II, pp. 59–60.
8 Ibid., pp. 71–72 (letter to S. A. Ivanova; Jan. 1/13, 1868).
9 Sakulin and Bel'chikov (see note 1), p. 129 and 133.
10 Bem, A. L., *Snotvorchestvo (Dreamcreation)*, *Pravoslaviye i Kul'tura (Russian Orthodoxy and Culture)*, Berlin, 1923, pp. 181–196.
11 Carr, E. H., 'Was Dostoevsky an epileptic?', *Slavonic Review, 9*, 1930–31, pp. 424–431.
12 Strakhov, N. N., *Biografiya*, St. Petersburg, 1883, p. 213.
13 Mochulsky, K., *Dostoevsky: Zhizn' i Tvorchestvo (Dostoevsky: Life and Work)*, Paris, 1947, p. 305.
14 Hughlings Jackson, J., *Selected Writings*, Vol. I. *Also* Rows, R. G., and Bond, W. E., *Epilepsy, a functional mental illness*, London, 1926.
15 Whitty, C. W. M., 'Photic and self-induced epilepsy', *Lancet, 4*, June 1960, pp. 1207–1208.
16 Freud, Sigmund, *Dostoevsky and Parricide*, New York, 1947, pp. 87–109.
17 Mochulsky, K., p. 280.

CHAPTER VII

1 Dostoevsky, F. M., *Polnoye Sobraniye Sochineniy (Complete Works)*, 14 Vols., Moscow, 1904–6.
2 Komarovich, V. L., *Neizdannaya glava romana 'Besy' F. M.*

Dostoyevskogo (*An unpublished chapter of Dostoevsky's novel The Devils*), *Byloye* (*The Past*), Petrograd, *18* (1922), p. 219.

3 Ibid., p. 220.

4 Dostoevsky, F. M., *Pis'ma*, (*Letters*) ed. Dolinin, A. S., Vol. II, Moscow-Leningrad, 1930, Vol. II, p. 288 (letter to M. N. Katkov: Dresden, Oct. 8/20, 1870).

5 See N. Gorodetsky's *Saint Tikhon Zadonsky*, London, 1951.

6 Grossman, L., (ed.), *Zhitiye Velikogo Greshnika* (*The Life of a Great Sinner*), in *Tvorchestvo Dostoyevskogo* (*Dostoevsky's Work*), Odessa, 1921, pp. 7–11 (actually p. 71 in the rough drafts).

7 Komarovich, V. L., *Neizdannaya glava romana 'Besy'* (*An un-published chapter of The Devils*), p. 131.

8 *Ispoved' Stavrogina* (*Stavrogin's Confession*) in *Dokumenty po istoriyi russkoy literatury i obshchestvennosti* (*Documents on the history of Russian literature and social thought*), Vol. I, Moscow, 1922.

9 *Ispoved' Stavrogina* (*Stavrogin's Confession*), *Byloye* (*The Past*), *18*, Leningrad, 1923, pp. 227–252.

10 Op. cit., *Byloye* (*The Past*), *18*, Leningrad, 1923, pp. 219–226.

11 Ibid., p. 222.

12 Motchoulski, C., *Dostoïevski, l'homme et l'œuvre*, (trans welter) Paris, 1963, p. 383.

13 Komarovich, V. L., *Neizdannaya glava romana 'Besy'*, pp. 224–226.

14 In Dostoevsky, F. M., *Polnoye Sobraniye Sochineniy* (*Complete Works*), ed. Tomashevsky and Khalabayev, Moscow-Leningrad, Vol. 13, 1926–30.

15 S. S. Koteliansky and Virginia Woolf appear to have been using the draft from which the 'Moscow version' was compiled. Theirs is very close to the Russian published version of the latter.

16 The previous chapter ends:

Stavrogin went up the steps without answering.

'Stavrogin,' Verkhovensky called after him, 'I give you a day . . . two, then . . . three, then; more than three I can't – and then you're to answer.'

In place of 'A visit to Tikhon' which would have been the next chapter 'A Raid at Stepan Trofimovich's' is substituted.

17 In Chapter X of *The Devils* there occurs the following passage:

'. . . An hour before Stepan Trofimovich and I came out into the street, a crowd of people, the hands from the Shpigulin factory, seventy or more in number, had been marching through the town, and had been an object of curiosity to many spectators. They walked intentionally in good order and almost in silence. Afterwards it was asserted that seventy had been elected out of the whole number of factory hands, amounting to about nine hundred, to go to the governor and try to get from him . . . a just settlement of their grievances against the manager who, in closing the factory and dismissing the workmen, had cheated them in an impudent way . . .'

This passage occurs in the very next chapter to the substituted one, further evidence that immediately after the rejection by Katkov of 'A visit to Tikhon', Dostoevsky abandoned the idea of including it in later editions.

18 The dignitary at the head of this monastic community. The suggestion is that the Father Archimandrite, in the eyes of the monks, was a person of much greater importance than this obscure retired bishop, and hence a far more interesting subject of conversation. Also he was known to have been critical of Tikhon's slack mode of living.

19 This occurs in the final section of Part 2, Chapter 1. The dialogue runs as follows:

'Listen. Go to Tikhon.'

'To whom?'

'To Tikhon, who was once a bishop. He lives retired now, on account of illness, here in the town, in the Our Lady Spaso-Yefimev Monastery.'

'What do you mean?'

'Nothing. People go and see him. You go. What is it to you? What is it to you?'

'It's the first time I've heard of him, and . . . I've never seen anything of that sort of people. Thank you, I will go.'. . .

In the novel there is no sign of Tikhon, only his gross caricature, Semyon Yakovlevich (Part 2, Chapter V).

20 The similarities to Zosima's reputation in *The Brothers Karamazov* are striking. Compare the following extract:

. . . There were, no doubt, up to the end of his life, among the monks some who hated and envied him, but they were few in number and they were silent, though among them were some of great dignity in the monastery, one, for instance, of the older monks distinguished for his strict keeping of fasts and vows of silence. . . .

21 See my essay (XI) *Stylistics and Personality* for the significance of this description of Tikhon's cell.

22 It is worth observing that a number of Dostoevsky's characters experience 'negative delusions'; that is, they either unconsciously forget or deny having been in a particular situation on

a particular occasion, or having had a particular idea. Raskolnikov, Myshkin, Velchaninov, and later Ivan Karamazov all exhibit this kind of 'negative delusion'.

23 This refers to the occasion earlier in the novel when Shatov struck Stavrogin a hefty blow on the face. Instead of retaliating, Stavrogin resisted the impulse and withdrew his hands from Shatov's shoulders. (Part I, Chapter V (8).)

24 Refers to the equally 'scandalous' duel with Gaganov (Part 2, Chapter III (2).)

25 This is an adumbration of the famous scene in *The Brothers Karamazov* when Ivan Karamazov is tormented by what he believes (but yet refuses to believe) to be an apparition of the Devil.

26 Translation taken from the Revised Standard Version (1952): Revelation 3: 14, 15.

27 Reminiscent of the theme of Baudelaire's poem 'Anywhere out of the world' (title borrowed from Poe): 'This life is a hospital, in which the sick are all obsessed with the desire for a change of bed. . . .'

28 This paragraph and the one previous are lacking in the 'Moscow version'.

29 At this point other versions differ sharply from the 'Petersburg version' used in the present translation. The Koteliansky and Woolf translation runs as follows:

'When all was over, she was confused. I did not try to reassure her and no longer fondled her. She looked at me, smiling timidly. Her face suddenly appeared to me stupid. The confusion rapidly with each minute took an increasing hold over her. At last she covered her face with her hands and stood in the corner with her face to the wall motionless. I was afraid that she might be frightened again, as she had been just before, and silently I left the house.

'I think that all that happened must have seemed to her, in the end, infinitely horrible, a deadly horror. Notwithstanding the Russian swear words and all sorts of queer conversations that she must have heard from her very cradle, I am completely convinced that she did not yet know anything. For indeed it appeared to her in the end that she had committed an immense crime, and was guilty of a mortal sin. "She had killed God." That night I had the row in the bar which I mentioned in passing. But I woke up in my rooms in the morning; Lebiadkin took me home. My first thought when I awoke was whether she had told or not. . . .' [From this point the 'Petersburg version' recontinues.]

30 The dialogue section just past is missing in other versions.

Readers may judge for themselves whether this version is the more effective (compare with extract in note 36 which it replaces).

31 In Part 2, Chapter 1 (6) of *The Devils* there occurs the passage: 'Within a day or two I intend to make a public announcement of our marriage (to Marya Lebyadkina) here in the town.' 'Is that possible?' Shatov whispered, almost with horror. 'I don't quite understand you. There's no sort of difficulty about it, witnesses to the marriage are here. Everything took place in Petersburg, perfectly legally and smoothly, and if it has not been known till now, it is simply because the witnesses Kirillov, Pyotr Verkhovensky and Lebyadkin (whom I have now the pleasure of claiming as a brother-in-law) promised to hold their tongues. . . .'

It seems highly unlikely that Dostoevsky would have allowed this passage to stand if he had intended to include his unpublished chapters at some later time.

32 In 1870 Dostoevsky wrote to his niece Sonya as follows: 'I have a terrific and almost irresistible desire to travel in the East before returning to Russia, that is to say, to Constantinople, Athens, the Archipelago, Syria, Jerusalem and Mt. Athos.'

33 This incident which took place in Germany and the dream of the picture of Acis and Galatea are reproduced almost word for word in Versilov's 'confession' to his illegitimate son Arkady (*The Raw Youth*, Part 3, Chapter VII).

34 Could this be yet another reference to the duel? If so, Dostoevsky is repeating himself.

35 There is no mention of this incident in other versions.

36 An allusion to the fact that Stavrogin had become a citizen of the Swiss Canton of Uri.

37 A quotation from Luke 17:1.

38 In other versions it is Tikhon who tells Stavrogin this.

39 Tikhon is suddenly out of his depths. His 'style' is inept when it comes to dealing with the world. His moving and often 'liturgically' expressed sentiments rapidly deteriorate, into cant almost, a deterioration which corresponds to a shift in *content*. This is deliberate on Dostoevsky's part, and executed with great art. Dostoevsky seems to be indicating that worldliness is morally and aesthetically wrong at the same time.

40 The ending in the Koteliansky and Woolf translation is as follows:

Stavrogin shuddered with anger and almost with fear. 'You cursed psychologist!' he suddenly cut him short in fury and, without looking round, left the cell.

CHAPTER VIII

1 Mochulsky, K., *Vladimir Soloviev*, Paris, 1951, p. 126.
2 D'Herbigny, M., *Vladimir Soloviev, a Russian Newman* (trans. Buchanan), London, 1918, p. 31.
3 Dostoyevskaya, A. G., *Vospominaniya (Reminiscences)*, Moscow-Leningrad, 1925, p. 181.
4 Dostoevsky, F. M., *Letters to his wife* (trans. Hill and Mudie), London, p. 244.
5 Ibid., p. 246.
6 Ibid., p. 247.
7 Mochulsky, K., *Vladimir Soloviev*, p. 107.
8 Ibid., p. 80.
9 D'Herbigny, M., *Vladimir Soloviev, a Russian Newman*, p. 86.
10 Mochulsky, K., *Vladimir Soloviev*, p. 80.
11 Gershenzon, M., ed., *Sochineniya i Pis'ma P. Ya. Chaadaeva (Chaadaev's publications and correspondence)*, Moscow, 1913, p. 292.
12 Soloviev, V. S., *Sobraniye Sochineniy (Collected Works)*, ed. Soloviev, S. M., and Radlov, E. L., St. Petersburg, 1901, Vol. I, pp. 227–235.
13 Ibid., p. 171.
14 Ibid., pp. 173–174.
15 Ibid., p. 175.
16 Ibid., p. 177.
17 Ibid., p. 287.
18 Ibid., Vol. III, p. 17.
19 Op. cit., *Critique of Abstract Principles*.
20 Soloviev, V. S., *Sobraniye Sochineniy*, Vol. III, p. 18.
21 Dostoevsky, F. M., *Brat'ya Karamazovy*, Paris, 1933–34, Vol. I, p. 85.
22 Ibid., p. 87.
23 Mochulsky, K., *Vladimir Soloviev*, p. 125.
24 Dostoevsky, F. M., *Dnevnik Pisatelya za 1875, 1876, 1877, 1880 (Diary of a Writer, etc.)*, Paris, 1951, Vol. III, pp. 10–11.
25 Ibid., pp. 525–526.
26 Soloviev, V. S., *Sobraniye Sochineniy (Collected Works)*, Vol. III, p. 174.
27 Ibid., pp. 174–175.
28 For instance see Stremooukhoff, D., *Vladimir Soloviev et son œuvre messianique*, Strasbourg, 1935, p. 64.
29 Mochulsky, K., *Dostoevsky: Zhizn' i Tvorchestvo (Dostoevsky: Life and Work)*, Paris, 1947, pp. 329–330.
30 Soloviev, V. S., *Sobraniye Sochineniy*, Vol. III, p. 177.
31 Ibid., pp. 171–172.

32 Ibid., p. 181.
33 Ibid., Vol. II, p. 339.
34 Ibid., Vol. III, p. 122.
35 Ibid., p. 170.

CHAPTER IX

1 Kierkegaard, S., *Philosophical Fragments* (trans. Hong), Princeton, 1962, p. 65.
2 Ibid., p. 66.
3 Kierkegaard, S., *Kierkegaard's Attack upon 'Christendom' 1854–1855.* (trans. Lowrie), London, 1946.
4 Kierkegaard, S., *The Concept of Dread*, p. 110.
5 Ibid., p. 122.
6 Ibid., p. 139.
7 Kierkegaard, S., *The Journals of Kierkegaard, 1834–1884* (trans. Dru), London, 1958, p. 250.
8 Berdyaev, N., *Freedom and the Spirit* (trans. Clarke), London, 1935, p. 163.

CHAPTER X

1 Op. cit. (trans. Hayward & Harari), London, 1958, p. 74.
2 Peterson, N. P., *Pis'mo k izdatelyu Russkogo Arkhiva* (*Letter to the publisher of the Russian Archives*), *Russkiy Arkhiv* (*Russian Archives*), 6, Moscow, 1904, pp. 300–301.
3 Ibid., p. 301.
4 Berdyaev, N., *Slavery and Freedom* (translated by R. M. French), London, 1943, p. 252.
5 Berdyaev, N., *Tri Yubileya: L. Tolstoy, G. Ibsen, N. F. Fyodorov* (*Put'*, II, 1928, pp. 88–94).
6 Bartenev, S., *Dva razgovora o voskreshenii Myortvykh* (*Two conversations about the resurrection of the dead*), *Russkiy Arkhiv* (*Russian Archives*), 1, Moscow, 1909, p. 122.
7 N. F. Fyodorov, *Filosofiya Obshego Dela*, Moscow, 1906, Vol. I, p. 442.
8 Ibid., p. 330.
9 Ibid., p. 318.
10 Ibid., p. 315.
11 Ibid., p. 139.
12 Ibid., pp. 8–9.
13 Ibid., p. 148.
14 Ibid., p. 193.
15 *Russkiy Arkhiv*, Moscow, 1904 (3), pp. 402–403.

16 Dostoevsky, F. M., *Pis'ma (Letters)*, *Polnoye Sobraniye Sochineniy (Complete Works)*, St. Petersburg, 1883, Vol. I (letter of 1868).

17 Mochulsky, K., *Dostoevsky: Zhizn' i Tvorchestvo (Dostoevsky: Life and Work)*, Paris, 1947, p. 337.

18 Dostoevsky, F. M., *Dnevnik Pisatelya (Diary of a Writer)*, Paris, 1951, Vol. 2, pp. 15–16.

19 Dostoevsky, F. M., *Dnevnik Pisatelya*, Paris, 1951, Vol. 3, p. 153.

20 Dostoevsky, F. M., *Materialy i Issledovaniya (Source Materials and Research)* (edited by A. S. Dolinin), Leningrad, 1935, pp. 89–90.

21 Ibid., p. 96.

22 Dostoevsky, F. M., *Dnevnik Pisatelya*, Paris, 1951, Vol. 3, p. 237.

23 Mochulsky, K., *Dostoevsky: Zhizn' i Tvorchestvo*, Paris, 1947, p. 468.

24 Berdyaev, N., *Mirosozertsaniye Dostoyevskogo (Dostoevsky's World-outlook)*, Prague, 1923, pp. 213–215.

25 Dostoevsky, F. M., *Materialy i Issledovaniya* (edited by Dolinin, A. S.), Leningrad, 1935, p. 150.

26 Fyodorov, N. F., *Filosofiya Obshchego Dela*, Moscow, 1906, Vol. I, p. 429.

27 Ibid., p. 430.

28 Dostoevsky, F. M., *Materialy i Issledovaniya* (edited by Dolinin, A. S.), Leningrad, 1935, p. 157.

29 Mochulsky, K., *Dostoevsky: Zhizn' i Tvorchestvo*, Paris, 1947, p. 471.

30 Dostoevsky, F. M., *Materialy i Issledovaniya* (edited by Dolinin, A. S.), Leningrad, 1935, p. 85.

31 Ivanov, V. I., *Freedom and the Tragic Life* (translated by Cameron), London, 1952, p. 160.

32 Fyodorov, N. F., *Filosofiya Obshchego Dela*, Moscow, 1906, Vol. I, p. 53.

33 Dostoevsky, F. M., *Materialy i Issledovaniya* (edited by Dolinin, A. S.), Leningrad, 1935, p. 84.

34 Dostoevsky, F. M., *Dnevnik Pisatelya*, Paris, 1951, Vol. 3, p. 223.

CHAPTER XI

1 Bakhtin, M. M., *Problemy tvorchestva Dostoevskogo (Problems raised by the work of Dostoevsky)*, Leningrad, 1929, p. 19.

2 Ibid., p. 43.

3 Ibid., p. 85.

4 Ibid., p. 191.

5 Heidegger, Martin, *Being and Time* (trans. McIntyre and Ramsey), London, 1962, pp. 56–8.

6 Bakhtin, M. M., op. cit., p. 188.

7 Ibid., p. 52.

8 Ibid., p. 51.

9 Grossman, Leonid, *Poetika Dostoevskogo* (*Dostoevsky's Style*), Moscow, 1925, p. 12.

10 Bakhtin, M. M., op. cit., p. 99.

11 Askol'dov, S., *Religiozno-eticheskoye znacheniye Dostoevskogo* (*The Religious and Ethical Significance of Dostoevsky*), in Dolinin, A. S. (ed.), *Stat'i i Materialy*, St. Petersburg, 1922, Vol. I, p. 4.

12 Ibid., pp. 212–213.

13 Bakhtin, M. M., op. cit., p. 155.

14 Ibid., p. 165.

15 Grossman, Leonid, *Poetika Dostoevskogo* (*Dostoevsky's Style*), p. 175.

16 Bakhtin, M. M., op. cit., pp. 46–47.

17 McLuhan, Marshall, *Understanding Media*, London, 1964, passim.

18 Taken from the version published in *Byloye* (*The Past*), 18, Petrograd, 1922, p. 232.

19 Dostoevsky, F. M., *The Devils* (trans. Garnett), London, 1931, Vol. I, Part II, Chap. V (2).

20 Grossman, Leonid, *Poetika Dostoevskogo* (*Dostoevsky's Style*), p. 144.

21 Dostoevsky, F. M., *Ispoved' Stavrogina* (*Stavrogin's Confession*), pp. 237–8.

22 Grossman, Leonid, *Poetika Dostoevskogo* (*Dostoevsky's Style*), p. 162.

23 Bakhtin, M. M., op. cit., pp. 144–147.

24 Bonhoeffer, Dietrich, *Ethics* (trans. Horton Smith), London, 1955, pp. 104–5.

25 Camus, Albert, *The Rebel* (trans. Bower), London, 1953, p. 12.

26 Ibid., p. 12.

27 Kafka, Franz, *The Trial* (trans. Willa and Edwin Muir), London, 1953, pp. 242–243.

28 Bonhoeffer, Dietrich, op. cit., pp. 327–328.

29 Ibid., pp. 327–328.

30 Ibid., pp. 327–328.

31 Kierkegaard, Søren, *The Concept of Dread* (trans. Lowrie), London, 1944, p. 65.

32 Ibid., p. 55.

33 Ibid., p. 139.

34 Ibid., p. 139.
35 Published in the *Diary of a Writer* for 1867, occupying the entire November number. The Russian title of the story is *Krotkaya*.
36 Dostoevsky, F. M., *The Gentle Creature*, etc. (trans. Magarshack), London, 1950, pp. 221–222.
37 Ibid., pp. 225–226.
38 Ibid., p. 251.
39 Published in the *Diary of a Writer* for 1877, in the April number.
40 Bonhoeffer, Dietrich, op. cit., p. 332.

INDEX

This index is of names of authors and personalities only. References to Dostoevsky's works are given under Dostoevsky, Fyodor.